MW00616549

1295

FRANCIS DE SALES
SAGE AND SAINT

ANDRÉ RAVIER, S.J.

Francis de Sales Sage and Saint

TRANSLATED BY
JOSEPH D. BOWLER
Oblate of St. Francis de Sales

Revised Edition

IGNATIUS PRESS   SAN FRANCISCO

Title of the French original:
Un Sage et un Saint: François de Sales
©1985 Nouvelle Cité, Paris

© 1988 Ignatius Press, San Francisco
ISBN 0-89870-193-7
Library of Congress catalogue number 87-83532
Printed in the United States of America

CONTENTS

CONTENTS

CONTENTS

CONTENTS

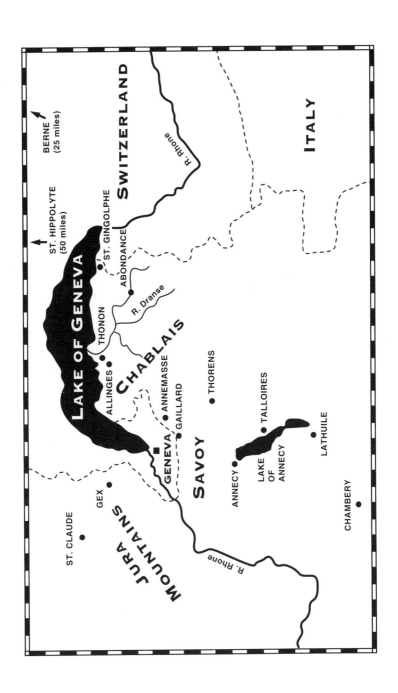

A doctor of both civil and canon law, a priest and bishop of a diocese torn by Calvin's schism and ravaged by Genevans; a diplomat, a pastor, a director of souls, and a spiritual writer of Savoy and France . . . how does one encompass in a brief biography a personality of such diverse aspects? Francis de Sales lived during an era that marked a turning point in history: the former European Catholicism versus the recent fragmentation of Protestantism, the Renaissance versus classicism, the Church of the Middle Ages versus the Church of the Council of Trent. . . . What a welter of events and adventures in his lifetime! In order to avoid getting lost in this morass, there is only one solution: strike out boldly for the heights, and take the "path of the crests". And so, dear readers, we shall do just that, if it is agreeable to you.

The path of the crests . . . Up high we command a view of the countryside. Things seem orderly and proportioned; we cease noticing details. "But", you will tell me, "it is you who have selected this itinerary, and especially the beautiful sites where we are to pause. How do I know that they are good?" Why should I deny it? I can allow myself a certain arbitrariness. My excuse is my long familiarity with the life and works of Saint Francis. This is verified by the list of sources, which includes many of my own writings about him.

The path of the crests . . . You are free to wander off, sometimes, if you want to. You can go down into the valleys for a while to observe things at close range or to explore some fact in detail with the aid of more learned writings, and you can mull over a particular letter among Francis' incomparable correspondence or a special chapter from the books that he has left us. But then, knowing the complete man that Francis de Sales was, you will better appreciate, perhaps, his anecdotes or counsels. And if you are sometimes astonished to see me take the course opposed to that of better-known authors on some chronological point (notably about what concerns the student days of the young Francis in Paris or in Padua), understand that I have done this in light of the most recently discovered documents. Of course, I may also be mistaken . . . like my predecessors.

The path of the crests . . . If I employ this image, it is because Francis de Sales liked to compare his existence — our existence — to a "rough and slippery" road. Let's not be afraid if we are warned that "this road leads us to the foot of the Cross". The guide is reliable, and he "lends us his hand . . . to walk more safely" (Pl., 185).

A final word: perhaps you will think I am too enthusiastic about my hero! Indeed, to reach today's readers, is it not presumed that we find in the saints certain defects, even faults? I have carefully scrutinized the life of Saint Francis. I have listened with a critical ear to the reproaches that were made against him, even during his lifetime: a rather enervating sentimentality, angry outbursts, ability pushed to the point of duplicity (yes, they go so far!), good humor that is cloying to our taste . . . and I don't know what else! And each time, I have had to drop my arms and bow my head in defeat — like those students in Padua who were jealous of his virtue and attacked him with naked swords one night, and whom Francis quickly routed.

"I AM IN EVERY WAY A SAVOYARD, BOTH BY BIRTH AND BY OBLIGATION"
1567–1578

Birth and Ancestry

On Thursday, August 21, 1567, in the master bedroom of the Château de Sales, a little boy was born: he was the first child of Monsieur and Madame de Boisy. He came into the world two months prematurely, and he appeared to be "so delicate and in danger of dying" that he was immediately baptized *in extremis* and bedded down in cotton-wool!

Let us lose no time getting disentangled from all these proper names.

At Sales, very close to the Château de Thorens, lived two brothers who got along so marvelously that they were able to live together. Louis, the elder, bore the title of Sales; he had three sons: Aimé, Louis (who became a priest and the great missionary companion of our Francis), and Gaspard. The younger brother's name was Francis, and prior to his marriage he bore the title of another of the family estates, Nouvelles.

Francis de Nouvelles was married in 1566, at the age of forty-three, to his charming cousin, Frances de Sionnaz, who was only fourteen years old. Frances' mother, Damoiselle Bonaventure de Chevron-Villette, the widow of Melchior de Sionnaz, had given the castle, land, and title of Boisy to her daughter as a dowry on the condition that Francis de Nouvelles would bear the name. However, their children, among whom was our Saint Francis, would be called de

Sales, at least until the day when Monsieur de Boisy would give them one of his estates.

Baptism in the Church in Thorens

"It was remarkable that in this dangerous birth the young mother did not lose her life." In order to feed the baby they had to have recourse to a strong village woman from Thorens. Her name was Pétremande Lombard. Her nursing care was efficacious: the newborn Francis gained enough strength to be solemnly christened on August 28, 1567, in the Church of Saint Maurice in Thorens. Later, having become bishop and prince of Geneva, Francis would choose for his consecration this humble church where he had been christened. "It was the feast of Saint Augustine, for whom he bore an incomparable love." The godfather was François de la Fléchère, the godmother was the maternal grandmother, Damoiselle Bonaventure de Chevron-Villette, and both gave their Christian names to their godchild: he was named François-Bonaventure de Sales. On that August 28 there was great rejoicing at the castle: "numerous nobles and others" had wished to attend the ceremony, and they were offered a sumptuous feast. The poor were not forgotten: "From daybreak until night fell there was general almsgiving."

The child remained frail, and his health caused some anxiety. The godmother-grandmother (a "forceful woman", we are told) obtained permission to bring him to the Château de Monthoux, where he would breathe the good air of Salève perfumed by fir trees. The cure succeeded. When the child was weaned at Sales in November 1569 — two years after his birth, according to the custom of the time — he was a gracious and lively boy who delighted the entire household.

From 1569 to 1573, Did the Boisy Family Settle at Brens?

This question would be of minimal importance were it not that Brens was located at the foot of the Voiron, in the Chablais — the same Chablais that, later on, would be for Francis de Sales his "mission territory" par excellence and that he would win back from Calvinism.

One thing is certain: in 1568 M. de Boisy purchased the Château de Brens from the Baron Amédée de Villette, and he took possession of it on February 14, 1569. But was it he or his elder brother Louis who moved into it? The historians dispute this because, at this time, the two brothers had just "established a partnership". In any case, when Marie de Luxembourg, according to her right, purchased the Thorens estate in 1572, and because the de Sales brothers had to separate, it was Louis who moved into Brens, with Francis remaining at Boisy. But the two families were together at Brens for the summer months.

Sales, Brens . . . what does it matter? It was still beautiful Savoy with its contrasting landscapes. Francis flourished amid its splendors: snow and sun, high peaks and low valleys, forests and wild flowers, cattle, birds, wild beasts, and, of course, its lakes. There was only one blight for his child's gaze, above all when he went to the Chablais: the ruins that remained after the alternate occupations by the troops of the duke of Savoy and of the Genevans and the Bernese. Imaginative as he was, the child Francis remembered these sights, and with the help of his devout mother, he yearned to know God.

The Education of a Future Lord of Sales

For six years Francis remained the only son of M. and Mme de Boisy.[1] Did he not risk appearing to be and even becoming a "little prince" in the family household? All the more so, since he radiated an irresistible natural charm. "I always knew him as a remarkably gracious child, beautiful, affable, gentle, and familiar. . . . He was so wise and so full of kind words that everyone loved him." This was Pétremande Lombard's deposition at the process for canonization—proper for a wet nurse, of course. But the biographers agree that early in the life of little Francis a kind of golden legend was spun around him.

Too golden. It is certain that he was extremely affectionate. How could he have been otherwise? His exquisite, very pious mother—a

---

[1] There were, however, thirteen children. Five died in infancy. Nine years separated Francis (1567) and his brother Gallois (1576). Within this long interval we must (it would seem) place several of the dead infants.

bit melancholy and even anxious—watched over him, and she was not twenty years old. "He was always dressed very properly; she preferred him in page-boy costume rather than in play clothes."

These dainty touches were hardly bearable to M. de Boisy, who saw in his eldest son the hope of his race. De Boisy had remarked the child's lively intelligence and his thirst for knowledge: he would be able to pursue serious studies that would open to him the highest offices in the duchy. But it was indispensable that the man of law, if he became that one day, should also be a gentleman who would conduct himself nobly in war, know how to wield the sword and handle the dagger skillfully. He, François de Boisy, had personally shone at the court of the Valois, and not only by his culture and his sense of business but also by his courage. He hoped that the heir to his name would imitate him, and even surpass him. Already his dream was taking shape!

M. de Boisy therefore imposed on Francis an education that reinforced his body and his character: "wholesome food, sleeping alone in the dark"; games in the open air with his cousins Aimé, Louis, and Gaspard; with the sons of his friends in the vicinity; and sometimes with the boys in the parish. Little Francis learned to ride a horse and to handle the hunting arms.

M. and Mme de Boisy were in total agreement regarding certain goals, including first of all the education of their son. Calvinism was not only ravaging the Chablais and the Gex territory; it was infiltrating everywhere. But M. de Boisy wished to be totally faithful to the Roman Church and to the duke of Savoy, his sovereign, and he found in Mme de Boisy a resolute ally. Together they cautioned their son against any weakening of his faith. They inculcated in him a lively sense of fidelity. Before him they practiced their religion strictly, but without ostentation. They participated in parish life, and they treated their servants and the poor with a just and great charity.

Again, in unison, they formed the conscience of the child: reason, frankness, and courage are the virtues that "honor man", and even more the Christian. If Francis questions his father and mother, they reply "truthfully". If he steals a carpenter's tool, they give him a spanking, and this before all the domestics in the château, being careful to "soften" the chastisement because the guilty party had admitted his theft. If, tempted by gluttony, the boy enters the forbidden kitchen, and the cook maliciously drops an oven-hot cake in his palm, his mother takes care of him, but since Francis does not denounce the imprudent cook, no one questions his courageous silence. And so it goes, day after day.

In confidence—much later on—Francis permits us to estimate to what point he benefited from this education. He was told, and told repeatedly, that a young lord must never be afraid; but Francis, as a boy, was afraid of the dark. He believed that there were "certain spirits" lurking in the shadows. Writing to a nun in 1619, he told her: "When I was young I was afflicted with this fantasy, and, in order to rid myself of it, I forced myself, little by little, to go alone—my heart armed with confidence in God—into places where my imagination threatened me with fear. Finally, I fortified myself so well that the darkness and the solitude of night delighted me." It is true that in 1619 he discovered in this darkness "the complete presence of God, which is most gratifying in this solitude".

Let us not conclude too hastily that Francis was a kind of adult from his childhood. Everything inclines us to believe that he passed through those phases of maturation that today's educators describe for us. "Be what you are", he will repeat tirelessly later on to Philothea and Theotimus, "but desire to be as best you can what you are." As a child he wished to be a child, but a child who—already, by a courageous struggle—wished "to be as best he could what he was", or at least to become it. One day his father found him in a reflective and pensive mood: "Well, Francis, what are you thinking about?" The boy replied: "I am thinking about God and of being an upright man." That was precisely what his father had recommended several days earlier. Francis had taken the advice very well!

A child of this stamp is a far cry from having a sentimental piety, is he not?

1573–1575: The Schoolboy at La Roche-sur-Foron

The chronology of Francis' studies could not be more confused than it is. After a new examination of documents we are inclined to the following conclusion; it is similar to what Father Lajeunie adopted, except for the order of the studies at Paris.

In October of 1573, after "the grape-gathering vacation", Francis entered the celebrated Collège de La Roche, where the young nobles and bourgeois were educated, but also the sons of farmers and of artisans who proved themselves capable of the studies and whose parents hoped that they would climb up a rung of the social ladder. Francis was six years old! Yet this was not unusual for the time. At this age, called tender, certain sons of the nobility were pages in some courts, and the children of common people worked on farms or in shops.

Francis, moreover, was not alone but was with his three cousins Aimé, Louis, and Gaspard. A "prudent and learned" tutor accompanied them, and they were not to be boarding students at the college but would live in the home of Dumas, the schoolmaster. A trusted servant of the Boisy family would be especially preoccupied with young Francis. M. and Mme de Boisy had numerous friends at La Roche. And besides, La Roche was only three leagues from Thorens. M. de Boisy, who had some property in this small town, would frequently come there to check on his business, and when it was the time for certain holidays, he would fetch Francis back to the Château de Sales. We must not be astonished if, at the moment of departure—according to the first biographers—Mme de Boisy did not weep, and if Francis was "completely overjoyed".

We do not know very much about Francis' stay in La Roche-sur-Foron. Three qualities, however, are repeated in the testimonies: "docility", "facility in learning", "piety". Let us, rather, remember this astonishing souvenir recollected by Mother de Chaugy: "When he was withdrawn from the Collège de La Roche, most of the school accompanied him, and they wept, saying that this was the blessing of their town that was being taken away from them." A child eight years old! And he had only been in this town three years. It is not certain whether or not M. de Boisy appreciated this precocious canonization of his son.

This was in 1575.

1575–1576: Francis at the Chappuisien Collège in Annecy

It is said that politics might have motivated Francis' change in schools. The hypothesis is plausible. Around 1574 the duke of Nemours, who had the county of Geneva as an endowment, planned to reconquer Geneva without informing the duke of Savoy, his sovereign. In this conflict between the two dukes, M. de Boisy opted for the duke of Savoy. Was the duke of Nemours going to take revenge on the castles of Thorens and of Sales? M. de Boisy took refuge at Brens with his family.

But another simpler explanation is proposed. M. Louis de Sales, the father of Aimé, Louis, and Gaspard, could have judged that it was time to bring Aimé to the Collège d'Annecy (founded by Eustace Chappuis in 1549, hence the name of the Collège Chappuisien), which was attended by the sons of great nobility and high magistrature. The courses, in particular the teaching of French, were also flourishing more than at La Roche. Louis and Gaspard followed their brother. Francis, younger than his three cousins, could not remain alone at La Roche.

However it may have been, here is our nine-year-old scholar at the college in Annecy. He acquits himself easily in these French authors, whom his teachers take pride in cultivating. They tell us that "he likes to dispatch his sentences". Francis composes, according to the methods of the time, some "collections of choice expressions and some of the most beautiful sentences". They assure us that "he declaimed charmingly", that he had "a bearing that was open, noble, and majestic, a body that was well built, a face that was attractive, and a voice that was very good". In short, Francis was the perfect disciple. But the student Francis also knows how to look farther than just at his books: Annecy, with its castle, its lakes, its churches, and its sumptuous mansions, enchants him. And when he reaches Brens (or returns there) with his cousins, this little knight opens his eyes wide at the scenery, because he is as avid to see as to know.

These precocious successes could have turned his head! But no, he preserves all his spontaneous and simple piety. Besides, he is such a good comrade, to the extent of offering himself to the teachers to take the punishment of the guilty boys. Was he beaten one day in place of his cousin Gaspard, a regular client of the school's "disciplinarian"? Certain biographers affirm it. But Francis declared at least twice that "he had never been whipped" while at the college. Perhaps he did not count his substitutions?

Two Great Events in Francis' Religious Life

Was it in 1575 or in 1577 that Francis received the sacrament of confirmation, which preceded by several hours his First Communion? The historians differ. The date 1575 seems most probable to us.

Communion and confirmation took place during the Ember Days of Advent, in the Church of Saint Dominic, very near the college. Judging from their fruits, Francis took these two sacraments very seriously: thereafter, he received Holy Communion at least once a month; he enrolled in the Confraternity of the Rosary; he finally decided to read, during vacation, the *Lives of the Saints.* One reliable tradition traces for us the picture of this little "scholar" reading at home with "his hostess" several pages of a saint's biography. It is as legendary as it is edifying. The boy had a predilection for the *fioretti* of his patron saint, Francis the *Poverello.*

Thus three uneventful years passed. The life of a bright little scholar, studious and joyous, is not game for a biographer. It seems that between 1575 and 1578 the attraction Francis experienced for the mystery of God from his earliest years had matured and become a veritable vocation. Perhaps his conversations with his favorite cousin, Louis, who was thinking about becoming a priest, had something to do with it. Whatever it was, Francis asked his father's permission to be tonsured. M. de Boisy was startled: to receive "tonsure" meant to "belong to the Church", and he was nourishing more ambitious projects for his eldest son, although at the time he had three other sons. Everything was regulated in the mind of this gentleman, who was as authoritarian as he was foresighted: it would be Gallois, the second son, who would enter the Church; Louis would serve in the army. Jean François? His father would see that he would get him settled in the world.

But Francis would be his father's "heir", charged with making the family name and fortune more illustrious and more enhanced. Francis resisted. His father yielded: after all, "tonsure" did not engage the future. In spite of the decrees of the Council of Trent it could, on occasion, give access to copious ecclesiastical benefices. Fortified by paternal authorization, Francis thus presented himself for the examination by Monsignor Justiniani, whom he delighted with his answers. The authorization was immediately granted, and Francis was tonsured on September 20, 1578, at Clermont-en-Genevois by his father's friend Gallois Regard, bishop of Bagnoréa. When the bishop declared that he was giving Francis "the Lord for the part and portion of his heritage", he experienced "an indescribable joy" . . . but nonetheless, when he saw his beautiful blond curls (which reached his shoulders) fall under the scissors, he could not hold back "a little sigh of regret". The precious sigh!

The blond hair would grow back, but Francis' commitment will persist. Years later he will confide to Mother Angélique Arnauld: "From my twelfth year I had resolved so firmly to belong to the Church that I would not have changed my mind for a kingdom." To one of his Philotheas he said: "From the time I had the grace to know a little the fruit of the Cross, that sentiment entered my soul; it has never left it." Grace . . . the Cross . . . two solid pillars for a vocation. The Holy Spirit takes no account of ages.

Francis de Sales Leaves the Chappuisien Collège for Paris

The biographers discuss the date: Did the departure take place in 1578, 1580, or even 1582? It seems likely that the first historian of Francis, Charles-Auguste de Sales, is right: he indicates 1578 as the year. The age is not an objection: at eleven or twelve years and even before, the sons of the nobility often took their first days at the courts of some princes.

As to the choice of the college where Francis would study, we have known about that a bit longer. At first his father wanted him to go to the College of Navarre, which was frequented by the elite of the Parisian nobility. But Francis had "heard it said that the students were not given to piety there as much as those at the college of the Jesuit

Fathers (the college called 'Clermont'),[2] whose renown and esteem had filled his ears". He had no other reason, except that in his heart he preferred the College of Clermont to the College of Navarre. But how could he win M. de Boisy over to his decision? Francis, already a fine diplomat, had recourse to his mother. She succeeded so well that when our student of eleven years arrived at Paris "under the guidance and care of Jean Déage", it was at the Collège de Clermont that he was to present himself.

The three cousins Aimé, Louis, and Gaspard arrived at Paris at the same time as Francis, but it seems that Louis de Sales had them registered at the Collège de Navarre. In any case, the four boys would share the same lodging. The severe Déage would watch over them, while personally studying theology at the Sorbonne because he aspired to the title of doctor.

The little group left Savoy around September 25. They took the route through Lyons, Bourges, and Orléans. Francis was enchanted, because he was crossing beyond the boundaries of his natal duchy for the first time. Nonetheless, already, how many sad spectacles would mark the religious sensitivity of the child? At Lyons he saw the church of Fourvière devastated; at Bourges, the façade deprived of its saints and martyrs, the Virgin, whom he would have loved to venerate— she was called Notre Dame de Sales—was no longer there.... The Huguenots had burned her just as they had burnt the Cathedral of the Holy Cross in Orléans. The Saint Bartholomew Massacre was only six years past, yet the combat between Catholics and Huguenots had hardly ceased creating ruins. The boy, astonished, stared ... and his gaze would become even more profound in the course of the years to come. This social and political sundering of two religious factions, both of which claimed the authority of the gospel, would be for him an insupportable scandal: to resolve it would be his concern until the end of his life!

Finally, Paris could be seen silhouetted on the horizon. From the heights of Bagneux, our travelers saw the city girdled with its high walls and seemingly cut in two by the Seine River: on one side "the City", and on the other "the Latin Quarter", where fifty-four schools

---

[2] Today, the Lycée Louis-le-Grand.

and thousands of students were packed together. The little party entered the city through the Gate of Saint James, the gate of the pilgrims from Compostella. They skirted the domain of the Jacobins, and they took lodgings at the Hotel of the White Rose, not far from the College of Clermont.[3] If we can believe one of his first biographers, almost immediately after his arrival, Francis removed his gentleman's sword and ran to the Collège de Clermont nearby "to introduce himself to the Jesuit Fathers".

---

[3] The "White Rose" was situated a little toward what is today the rue Saint-Jacques. Later, after 1580, they found lodgings near Saint Geneviève.

THE HUMANISTIC AND MYSTICAL
STUDENT AT PARIS AND PADUA
1578–1591

1. PARIS: 1578–1588

Francis' Scholarly Progress

The stages of Francis' education are certain: the *Ratio Studiorum* with the Society of Jesus and the regulations of the University of Paris are our sources. But their chronology is, we admit, conjectural. We are only certain of when they ended: summer of 1588. If we accept the testimony of Charles-Auguste de Sales—"Francis continued the study of the humanities at Paris"—here is how we can reconstruct the order of his studies.

From October 1578 until August 1581, he took three classes of the cycle of "grammar".

From October 1581 until August 1584, he pursued courses in the humanities and rhetoric. (This rhetoric could be increased for students who desired to improve their knowledge of Greek.) At the conclusion of these courses, Francis obtained the "baccalaureate".

From October 1584 until January 1, 1588, he took the "arts course" (which was also called "philosophy", although it included instruction in mathematics, cosmography, natural history, music, and the like).

Starting from January 1, 1588, Francis prepared for and passed his "license", then the "master of arts", which he would need to enter the school of law.

At the Jesuits' School

Francis quickly impressed his teachers and his fellow students with his intelligence and his zeal for study, as well as his docility and courtesy. His professors were highly qualified: the still-young Society of Jesus staffed its college in Paris with an elite faculty because, in the Latin Quarter, scholarly institutions were numerous and competition was intense. In the school of these humanists, Francis was introduced to those authors of antiquity whom he would later love to cite: Cicero, Virgil, Pliny the Elder, Epictetus, Plato, and so on. Also, even though the courses were given in Latin, he perfected himself in the "French language", whose naturalness and musicality appealed to him; Ronsard was honored at the Clermont college, at least among the young.

Concerning Francis' religious life until about 1583 (at which time he was studying rhetoric), no very noteworthy souvenir has come down to us, but the child who had chosen the Collège de Clermont "because in the other schools they did not pay much attention to piety" would certainly enter with fervor the religious prescriptions of the *Ratio Studiorum:* daily Mass, confession and Communion at least once a month. He voluntarily visited, on the way to and from school, one or other of the numerous churches that he passed. He had his favorites: the Dominican Church of Saint-Étienne-des-Grès, in which he would venerate "the Black Virgin of Paris", a statue of "Notre Dame de Bonne Délivrance", carved from a block of limestone and "painted by an inexperienced and naïve brush". He would confide to her his secret desire to become a priest.

In 1583, Francis sought admission to the Sodality of the Blessed Virgin, and his request was granted "with alacrity". His comrades even elected him, eventually, "assistant", and then "prefect". He was nicknamed "the angel of the college", alluding to the famous surname of Saint Thomas Aquinas. Francis was radiant: the famous Jesuit Étienne Binet, who was his classmate, would one day acknowledge that he owed "his vocation to the example and the discretion of Francis".

"On the High Seas of the World"

Studious, pious . . . let us not make a porcelain image of Francis. To begin with, the young Parisians, his comrades, were not all saints, and they were not always discussing studies and devotions!

Then again, M. de Boisy insisted that the future Seigneur de Sales must frequent the court and make himself known to all the powerful and influential friends, whom he himself knew when he served at the palace of Luxembourg. Francis did not shirk these obligations. He was to be seen at the home of his cousin, Charles de Chaumont, Seigneur de Charmoisy. He had access to the homes of Philippe-Emmanuel de Lorraine, Duc de Mercour, governor of Brittany, whose sister was the Queen of France. There he heard talk of the League; of King Henry III and his "minions"; of the political and amorous intrigues of those great lords and beautiful ladies; of Henry of Navarre, that Huguenot who would ascend the throne of France should the king happen to die. . . . Our gentle Savoyard was indeed well launched "upon the high seas of the world"!

Besides, Francis was at an age . . . fifteen . . . twenty . . . when crises would jolt him just as they did anyone else. He was aware that he was welcome wherever he went and that the young ladies found him a handsome and desirable cavalier. He excelled in the "arts of the nobility": horsemanship, fencing, dancing. And his heart was not made of marble. His sensitivity was aroused quickly and keenly. Let us not falsify this adolescent. Let us leave him the honor of his combat.

Because he does struggle, he prays; he mortifies himself. . . . And with what energy, it seems. He has obtained from his spiritual director permission sometimes to wear a hair shirt under his elegant doublet.

"I Wish to See . . . Sacred Theology"

Under the violence of this combat, a crisis was unleashed within Francis, in December of 1586, a crisis that would last six weeks; it would not be terminated until January of 1587. In order best to understand it, we must go back to the Sunday of Quinquagesima,

1584. On that day, the Carnival season in Paris was in full swing. In the Latin Quarter the students were cavorting. Francis remained in his room. He was sad and melancholy. The Reverend Déage, to distract him, suggested that he go outside and mix with the revelers. Francis refused, and—recalling from the Gospel that he had heard at Mass that morning—he cried out with the blind man on the road: "Lord, grant that I may see." "And what do you want to see?" Déage asked. "I wish to see sacred theology! It alone will teach me what God desires to show to my soul." Déage had the prudence not to oppose this desire. The next year Francis would enroll in the arts course. Apart from his university status, M. Déage himself would provide the young philosopher an initiation into theology by communicating to him his own most interesting courses. Two acts of prudence had to be observed: to say nothing to M. de Boisy, who would undoubtedly take it very badly, and to assure a strict fidelity to the arts courses at the Collège de Clermont, so that the Jesuit teachers need not become ruffled.

And so we see Francis engaged in an inhuman work rhythm. He philosophizes so well that at the end of his studies he will be declared "perfect in philosophy" and "one of the top students at the university". But as soon as the courses at Clermont are ended, Francis joins Déage at the Sorbonne. He catches "on the wing" a course or a portion of a course. "Upon returning home, having a little leisure, he used to copy his tutor's notebooks" (one of his comrades affirms). He is so avid for theology that he sometimes neglects his meals! Unfortunately, Francis' theology notes are lost; only a few pages from them remain,[1] but they inform us as to the subject of the course he was attending: predestination and grace.

The crisis of 1586–87 reveals to us a Francis who believes himself predestined to damnation by the infallible judgment of God. "He fell", Jane de Chantal tells us, "into a great temptation and an extreme anguish of mind. It seemed to him absolutely that he was damned and that there was no salvation for him."

What happened then?

---

[1] There are two manuscripts, one of which is preserved in the rectory of Saint Sulpice, Paris, and it bears the date 1586 several times, starting in the middle. The other is at the Grand Seminaire de Grenoble, and it bears the date 1586 twice.

The Crisis

It seems—because we must advance with prudence in these analyses—
that this crisis stemmed from a violent conflict between the spiritual
uplift that had been released in Francis upon reading the commentary
by the prestigious Génébrard, and the doubts about his eternal salvation that took root in his mind from the doctrine of Saint Augustine
and of Saint Thomas regarding predestination as presented by the
doctors at the Sorbonne.

In the autumn of 1584, Francis heard the lectures of the Benedictine
Gilbert Génébrard at the royal college. These were lessons of a
rigorous scholarship, but which gave to the *Cantique* a boldly mystical interpretation: the "loves of the Sulamite and of her shepherd"
were presented as symbolic of the relationship between God and the
human heart, between Christ and the Church. This was a revelation
for Francis. From that time, he was no longer able to conceive of
the spiritual life except as a love story, the most beautiful of love
stories.

But what does he now hear them teaching at the Sorbonne? The
assertions of Luther and Calvin concerning predestination agitate the
world of theologians. "We call predestination", Calvin had declared
since 1560, "the eternal counsel of God, by which he determined
what he wished to do with every man. Because he did not create all in
similar condition, but orders some to eternal life, others to eternal
damnation." To support their thesis, Luther and Calvin leaned on the
authority of Saint Augustine and of Saint Thomas. Francis avidly
waits for his teachers at the Sorbonne to refute this claim of the
Protestant teachers and to furnish a less depressing interpretation
of the two great doctors of the Church. He is disappointed. The
thought of Augustine and of Aquinas plunges him into a dolorous
perplexity: "I, Francis, am I among the number of those whom God
has ordered to eternal life?" And this perplexity very quickly turns to
the conviction that he is, on the contrary, numbered among those
whom "God has ordered to eternal damnation". Then he draws from
the Psalms some anguished appeals: "Save me, O my God, because
the waters have engulfed my soul." He transcribes them; he repeats
them unceasingly, day and night.

What is being played in this drama, let us carefully note, is the love of God, which he has already experienced and of which he will be forever deprived. "I, miserable as I am," he writes in his notes,

> should I then be deprived of the grace of him who has made me taste so suavely of his gentleness, and who has shown himself so lovable to me? O love, O charity, O beauty in whom I have placed all my affections. Ah! I shall never more enjoy these delights . . . and you will no longer flood me with the torrents of your pleasure. . . . O Virgin, pleasing among the daughters of Jerusalem, shall I never see you then in the realm of your Son? . . . And shall I never be made a sharer in this tremendous benefice of redemption? . . . And my sweet Jesus, did he not die for me as well as for the others? . . . Ah! Whatever it is to be, Lord, at least let me love you in this life if I am unable to love you in eternity.

These tragic confidences of Francis date from 1586. In December of that year, the tension reached an almost unbearable degree, even physically. He could endure no more. There seemed to be no way out of this spiritual drama, when one day in January 1587, while returning alone from the university, he entered, as customary, the Dominican Church of Saint-Étienne-des-Grès. "It was the day when it pleased Divine Providence to deliver him", according to the words of Mother de Chantal. Thanks to the confidences of Francis himself, we can follow the stages of this remarkable deliverance, even if the accounts diverge on a few details.

Once inside the church, Francis went "directly" to the chapel of the Black Virgin. He then made an act of heroic abandonment: "Whatever you have decided, Lord, in the eternal decree of your predestination, and of your retribution, you whose judgments are an immense abyss . . . , I shall love you, Lord, in this life at least, if it is not granted me to love you in the eternal life. . . . If, because my merits demand it, I must be cursed among the accursed who will not see your most sweet face, grant me, at least, not to be among those who will curse your holy name." Then Francis took a tablet hanging from the railing in the chapel. It proposed to the visitor the text of the *Memorare*. Francis recited it "through to the end". The temptation vanished. "At

that same moment," Mother de Chantal reports, "he found himself
perfectly and entirely cured, and it seemed to him that his sickness fell
at his feet like the scales of a leper."[2]

The Mystical Character of This Crisis

Writers have given diverse interpretations of this crisis: the student's
overwork, a basic anxiety in his temperament, the influence of a
passionate theological milieu, and the like. It is incontestable that
there is, in each of these explanations, a portion of truth. Nonetheless,
we perceive that, even while reinforcing one another, they do not
capture the essence of the problem. As to the tempest that buffeted
Francis, they seized the whirlpool, not the "eye". With Francis himself,
we are forced to recognize here a "temptation", an intervention,
permitted by God, by the "angel of Satan". This temptation bears a
name in the psychology of mystics: it is the temptation to despair, and
those who have passed through it confess that this trial is a veritable
"hell's fire".

In what spiritual state was Francis in fact? Three sentiments, which
are excluded in ordinary states, coexisted in his soul: a passionate love,
exalting God, Jesus, and the Virgin Mary; the conviction of being
among the number of the condemned; a desperate call upon the
divine mercy. Let us note well that it was not a question of a "night of
the soul" in the manner of Saint John of the Cross. On the contrary,
Francis' faith in this combat is revealed as being very lively and total:
it is because he believed in the happiness of heaven and in the
torments of hell, because he felt them even in the very fibers of his
being, that the drama was so violent. It is difficult, finally, not to
notice a mysterious correlation between this crisis and the apostolic
destiny to which God was going to call Francis. The symbiosis, the
conciliation (*concordantia*) of divine grace and human liberty would
be at the base of these great struggles, the most intense and the most
urgent: Protestantism, political-religious unity of the state, paganizing

[2] Concerning the problem of the connection between divine grace and human
liberty, see below, page 159.

humanism, the deviations of spiritual direction, and so on. To confront these combats, he would have need of a lucid, solid doctrine. This doctrine would be efficacious only because it would not only be conceived by his mind but born of a tragic experience.

And so Francis, at twenty years of age, has known the trial through which God permits the greatest souls to pass, under one form or another: the "temptation to despair". Francis emerges from it — he too more pure, more strong, more "loving of God".

Francis Leaves Paris

Because "it seemed to him that his illness fell at his feet like the scales of a leper", was Francis completely cured of his "strange torment"? His writings from the time of Padua will prove the contrary. It is because Saint Augustine and Saint Thomas remain his masters in his thinking. At least his health was sufficiently restored and his mind was free enough to bring his philosophical studies to their term. We can scarcely notice that his life was made more withdrawn from contact with the world around him. The conversion of Joyeuse, the favorite courtier of Henry III (in September of 1587), and his joining the Capuchins thrilled Francis.

In the spring of 1588 Francis completed his arts courses. He then successfully passed the examination for the licenciate and the master of arts, like all his comrades, at either Notre Dame de Paris or the Church of Saint Geneviève. The time had come for him to commence the study of law. But his father had decided that he would do so at the University of Padua. Why this change? Perhaps the political-religious situation, the gravity of which had just been demonstrated in the "Day of the Barricades" (May 1588), had something to do with it. Or again, perhaps M. de Boisy judged that it was time for his eldest son to immerse himself again in the Savoyard milieu, and that this brilliant student should get to know the great families of the duchy. To all these motivations it is possible to add another, in itself undeniable. Paris, at that time, did not possess a school of law, but only "doctoral schools", which did not assure even the complete cycle for the doctorate and whose buildings were dilapidated:[3] the students who were aspiring for the doctorate in law were obliged to achieve it at Bourges.

And so Francis left Paris, not without regret, to study at the celebrated University of Padua. "Four young French gentlemen did him the honor of accompanying him as far as Lyons, and they did not part company without tears, so great was the love that each bore him." M. de Boisy had sent a gentleman "with horses" to Lyons to escort Francis home.

Francis found his family at Brens. The Bernese and the Genevans were ravaging the region of the Château de Sales. At Brens "the whole household was waiting for him with joy". His mother embraced him "with all her former tenderness". His father "received him with unparalleled pleasure upon seeing him so accomplished". Francis became acquainted—or reacquainted—with his brothers and sister: Gallois was twelve years old, Louis was eleven, Jean François was ten, Gasparde's age is unknown, Bernard was five, and Melchior was three. "They took him around to visit their relatives and friends, and he won hearts everywhere."

Around mid-November Francis took the route to Padua.[4] He brought along his brother Gallois, who was to study at the college in the city. The Reverend Déage, who was supposed to complete his theological formation, would be their guardian.

2. PADUA: 1588–1591

The City and Its University

Padua, in the state of Venice, was a very pleasant city, where one breathed freely the air and the art of the Italian Renaissance. Its

---

[3] It is not until April 1679 that a decree stipulates four lessons in the morning and obliges these "schools" to look for a less wretched location (cf. M. S. Charlety and Jean Bomerot, *L'Universite de Paris du Moyen Age à nos jours,* Larousse, p. 77).

[4] Francis' name is inscribed in the *Registre des exemptions,* dated December 25, 1588, with this notation: *"Sabaudus Gallus"* (French Savoyard).

university attracted students from all over Europe. Its law faculty was then at its zenith, with Pancirolo and Menocchio. Its medical faculty was scarcely less celebrated, ever since, in 1540, Antonio Vesseli had introduced the experimental method there. But this influx of students (reputedly around twenty thousand) also made of Padua a city of pleasure, even though the cult of Saint Anthony remained very lively there: *"Il Santo"* watched over the city!

As is customary, pleasure entailed violence. At night, the street belonged to the students; it was wiser to stay at home once night fell and to barricade oneself inside until daybreak. Swords and daggers leaped from scabbards in the dark.

Father Possevin

One of Francis' first concerns upon arriving at Padua was to find a spiritual director. He selected—probably out of loyalty to his teachers at Clermont—a Jesuit, Father Anthony Possevin. Possevin was about fifty years old at this time. A writer, an orator, a theologian, he had acquired, in the course of his thorny pontifical mission in Sweden, Denmark, Russia, Poland, and France, a great experience of the world and man. He had been at Padua only a year, but already his reputation as a spiritual director was attracting toward him the Christian elite of the city and of the university.

Francis opened his soul to Possevin, not omitting the crisis in Paris. Possevin encouraged him to continue "to think about things of God, and to study theology"; he confirmed Francis in his vocation. "Your spirit", he told Francis, "is not for the business of the bar, and your eyes are not made for its dust." Then began long exchanges between the guide and the disciple, of which one and the other—as was proper—kept the secret, but of which we perceive the effects through Francis' conduct and his notes. Francis soon had himself enrolled in the Congregation of Our Lady established at the college. He regulated, with Father Possevin, the rhythm of his spiritual life: prayer, daily Mass, monthly confession and Communion, penances. He put in focus his relationship with his friends and comrades, in minute detail.

Francis, moreover, did not confine himself to the college circle. He liked to go pray at the Church of *Il Santo* or at the Barnabites' church and, most certainly, at the chapel in the convent of the Conventuels, where he gladly listened to the sermons of the Franciscan Philippe Gesualdi.

Law Studies

Possevin told him: "Work seriously at law. That is the present will of God for you." Francis gave himself generously to these studies, even to the most arid sections of his program. The three manuscript notebooks from his law notes that have come down to us are testimony to that. Again he does not forbid here and there a humorous comment: "We are treating here at length about *military* discipline. . . . I do not think it worthwhile to *perspire* over these questions, considering that in this time we have enough to *transpire.*" He even amuses himself one day by creating an anagram from his name: *Foi sans descaler.*

Theology Studies

He agreed with M. Déage that he would continue in theology, still without his father's knowledge! He found the study of theology more to his taste than the study of law. It does not seem that he had at this time followed regular courses of theology but rather a personal program, organized, no doubt, by Gesualdi and Possevin, and that he reviewed in more depth what he had learned at Paris. Above all, he read the texts of the great masters: Augustine, Jerome, Bernard, John Chrysostom, Cyprian (whose style enchanted him). His master for reference and of preference remained Saint Thomas Aquinas. He kept the *Summa* within arm's reach, and he had recourse to it "for understanding some other books". He kept six notebooks of his lectures, so voluminous that the notaries of the process of canonization gave up transcribing them. Fortunately, enough pages from them remain to enable us to know how Francis had concentrated his work on the problem of predestination.

The grace of Saint-Étienne-des-Grès had cured the anguish of his heart, not the agitation of his spirit. He searched and leaned still more toward a way of seeing things more favorable to human liberty, and "more worthy of God's grace and mercy"; however, he was ready to affirm that, if the Church should one day come to a decision in a different meaning, he would immediately concur. But here is the drama: his "opinion" was no longer at all compatible with the position of Saint Augustine and Saint Thomas. He had to make a decisive choice, and this choice tore him apart.

In 1591 the deed was done: Francis separated from Augustine and Thomas—but solely on the point of predestination. For the rest of theology they remained his "luminaries", and it is "prostrate at their feet" that he finally drafts his "protestation", which is one of the jewels of all spiritual literature.

> Prostrate at the feet of Saints Augustine and Thomas, I am ready to ignore everything in order to know him who is the wisdom of the Father, *Christ crucified.* In fact, although I do not doubt that the things that I have written are true, because I see nothing that can form a solid doubt about their truth, nonetheless, because I do not see everything, and because so profound a mystery is too brilliant to be able to be confronted by my little owl eyes, if, subsequently, the contrary should appear—which, I think, will never happen—even more, if I knew myself to be damned (let that not happen, Lord Jesus!) by this will that the Thomists place in God so that God may demonstrate his justice, struck by stupor and raising my eyes toward the Supreme Judge, I would willingly say with the Psalmist: *"Will not my soul be submissive to God?"* Amen, "Father, because it thus appears good to you; *may your will be done!"* And I would say this so many times in the bitterness of my heart until God—changing my life and its sentence—answered me: *"Have confidence, my son, I do not wish the death of the sinner, but rather that he be converted and live."*

And Francis accumulates the biblical texts, above all the evangelical texts that affirm the will of God to save all men. He then continues:

> And because you have willed to glorify my name, even in suffering, if there was need of it (even in that, this glorification and exaltation of my name, which is not *condemner* but *Savior,* is little), *I shall establish you over many* so that you may laud me in the eternal beatitude in which the glory of my name bursts forth. *By myself I*

have sworn: because you have done this, that is to say, because you have prepared your heart to obey my justice, and *because you have not spared* yourself, acquiescing to my will, even as far as to *gehenna* for my sake, *I shall bless you with an eternal benediction* and *you will enter into the glory of your Lord.*

Then I shall no longer have to answer any differently than formerly: "Amen, Father, because it appears good to you thus, *my heart is ready, O God,* to suffer because of you. My heart is ready for glory because of your name, Jesus.... Amen, *Jesus, Marie.*"

"Precious relic, less palpitating, less passionate than Pascal's amulet", Henri Bremond writes concerning the *Protestation,* "but of far superior wealth of doctrine" (Br, I, 71).

The quarrel between the Thomists[5] and those whom they already call Molinists (from the name of the Jesuit Molina, whose *Concordia liberi arbitrii cum gratia donis* appeared in 1588) will endure until August 1607. But in 1605 this quarrel *De Auxiliis* passed through a particularly acute phase. The most celebrated Dominican and Jesuit theologians crossed swords recklessly (to say the least!). In 1606 Pope Paul V, undoubtedly on the advice of Bishop Anastasius Germonio, would consult Francis de Sales, by then bishop of Geneva, concerning this thorny question. Francis' response is lost, but we know the tenor of it through the *Treatise on the Love of God.* It is that of Molina.

If we believe Charles-Auguste de Sales, Francis' response in 1606 to Bishop Germonio would have emphasized that "the dispute about this question was extremely dangerous and had in its extremities certain heresies.... Starting from there, there were many other things over which the Church groaned and that ought to be dealt with rather than the clarification of this question, which would not bring any benefit to the Christian republic, and which could cause it much harm.... And as for these subtle minds of the Dominicans and Jesuits, they could always reach sufficient agreement."

[5] In his beautiful biography of Saint Francis de Sales, Father Lajeunie demonstrates how the position rejected by Francis de Sales is not that of Saint Thomas himself but of his interpreters, "as a result of a dreadful misconception" committed by Henri de Gand (1220–95). Cf. L, I, 153.

Francis' Student Life at Padua

As dedicated as he was to his law studies and to resolving an intellectual problem that excited the theologians at that time—and one that concerned him personally—Francis led his student life simply and courteously. He had drawn up for himself some regulations for "conversations and encounters". He practiced them with ease. He diffused around himself an atmosphere of sterling worth, and he established some beautiful and solid friendships among his Paduan comrades.

Since 1589, he carried on his person, and reread each month in its entirety, a little book that had recently appeared in Venice: the *Spiritual Combat* of the Theatine Lorenzo Scupoli. Francis received his copy from the hand of the author himself, and he had even recopied on the end pages the spiritual regulations that he had worked out with Father Possevin. Later, having become a bishop, he would love to reread some passages from it, and we may easily find the inspiration from it in several of his writings, especially in the *Treatise on the Love of God.*

Let us be very careful not to create a sweet, angelic image of our student. Francis, contrary to the legend, was a fighter in his spirituality, and he had to prove it on many occasions.

Was he prone to anger? His biographers discuss it. It is certain that his first reactions were quick: when insulted, "he changed color and his face became florid", they tell us. So what! That does not make him a choleric person.

What is beyond doubt is that he possessed a noble courage and reacted swiftly and well in danger. Three Savoyard students, debauched and quarrelsome, learned this at their own expense. Exasperated by the perfection of their compatriot, they concocted a trick to dishonor him: they ambushed him one day, at dusk, and assailed him, rapiers in hand. Such a devout fellow could only be a coward! But Francis drew his sword and parried with so much skill that he sent the rogues packing. It is reported that one of them lost the seat of his britches as well as his dignity!

On another occasion these rascals plotted an assault of another kind. They brought Francis to a courtesan's home on the pretext that she was the wife of a very famous legal expert. The legal expert failed to appear, and the three students contrived to leave Francis alone with the woman. As soon as he became aware of the trap, Francis gave the prostitute a severe scolding, spat in her face, and left. He also experienced, however, a more delicate adventure. A princess (the real thing this time) who was traveling through Padua perceived him praying in church and fell madly in love with him. But how could she manage to have Francis visit her? She was rich, and she obtained the complicity of a "friend" of Francis. But the audacious mediator had hardly time to insinuate his message: he was shown to the door with a tongue-lashing worthy of a prison guard! These adventures were circulated around the city and, without seeking it, Francis earned himself a reputation of being a "perfect gentleman, handsome but unfeeling".

These anecdotes are not only concerned with students' pranks. Francis' courage had the opportunity to manifest itself in a more noble way. Toward the end of the year 1590, he was stricken with a severe fever, accompanied "by a troublesome dysentery". On January 15, 1591, the doctors judged Francis lost, and Déage was delegated to inform him of his approaching death. Francis received the news "with courage and joy". Déage ventured to ask him: "Where do you wish to be buried? What funeral arrangements do you want carried out?" "I see I have only a spiritual testament to make: that I give back my soul to God. As for my body, when I am dead, give it, I pray you, to the medical students so that—having been of no use to the world during my life—it may be useful for something after my death. . . . I would consider myself fortunate if by this means I could prevent one of the quarrels and killings that the students engage in when they need the corpses of criminals for dissection." A gesture of charity and humility, certainly, but we must see in it also one of the characteristic traits of Francis: he was keenly interested in the natural sciences and most especially in the knowledge of the human body, which appeared to him as the marvel of creation. The anatomical research of the physicians of Padua intrigued him. Once he completed his "brief testament", Francis asked for the sacraments, made his confession to Father Possevin, received holy Viaticum and extreme unction . . . after which he was seen to improve considerably. He recovered his health and gallantly resumed "his studies and his spiritual exercises". Now, more than ever, he wanted to belong to the Church, but he confided his secret to no one, unless to Possevin.

The Doctorate in Law: September 5, 1591

Francis "was in his twenty-fourth year, and the time that he had allotted for the study of law had run out, when he received the command from his father to become a doctor".

In the days that followed the feast of the Assumption, the promoters of the school of law summoned Francis de Sales and made him take a rigorous examination. He came out of it well, "with all the favorable votes". The prior of the law faculty was thus able to admit him to the solemnities of state and confer on him the honors of the doctorate.

The great legal consultant Guido Pancirolo, "a man equally perfect in virtue and knowledge, and whose spirit seemed more angelic than human", became strongly attached to Francis. He wished to personally preside over the oral examination, for which he assembled no less than forty-eight doctors to interrogate the candidate.

The session opened with an examination in civil law and another in pontifical law. Francis brilliantly satisfied the questions of the jury and responded "very solidly" to the objections posed by his adversary. The applause was general. "Those who judged him more devout than learned were astonished that he was as learned as he was devout."

Guido Pancirolo then stood up to give the usual discourse. Francis knew that his modesty would have to submit to a trial: it was customary! But the fact surpassed his apprehensions. "One cannot love virtue", Pancirolo said, "without loving you: humane, charitable, compassionate even to leaving your body for the public good when you were at the portals of the tomb . . . You have preserved your purity in the midst of a voluptuous city, like the fountain of Arethusa, which mixes its waters at the sea without contracting its bitterness." And the remainder continued in the same vein. We can imagine the face of our hero! The prior then announced the results of the examination: "We make and create Francis de Sales *doctor in one and the other laws.*"

Francis stood up in turn and replied in a discourse that custom dictated should be pompous and redundant. The best and most moving passage was undoubtedly when he recalled his indebtedness to his father and to the schools at La Roche, Annecy, and Paris. A tremor of emotion passed over the audience when Francis evoked Paris, at that time besieged by Henry IV: "This school of Paris, illustrious Mother of Letters, is desolate from the terrors of war, and at first glance (may God spare her this misfortune!) is threatened with becoming a desert. It was there that I first applied myself to the humanities, then to all the branches of philosophy, with even more facility and fruit because the roofs of Paris and her walls, so to speak, *seem to philosophize* — so much is that city given to philosophy and theology." Then he eulogized Padua and its eminent masters who had formed him in law, and most of all Guido Pancirolo: "Prince of Jurisprudence, your light and your glory". Francis then received the insignia of the doctorate: the books of canon and civil law, the gold ring, and the doctor's cap. And Pancirolo gave him "the kiss of peace with the doctoral benediction".

The next day it was M. Déage's turn to be received as a doctor of theology, after nine years of studies! So the regulation demanded.

Francis then made his farewell visits to his friends. He felt especially compelled to express to the Jesuit Fathers of the college, where Father Possevin resided, all that he owed to his thirteen-year-long association with them.

Portrait of a Young Doctor

Before Francis leaves Padua, let us see where we stand. He had revealed in the course of his studies some remarkable gifts of intelligence, of judgment, of energy, and of courage—even physical—and a conscientiousness in the accomplishment of his duties which his teachers and classmates recognized. Despite all that he radiated an incontestable charm: he was a young lord, and M. de Boisy had many reasons for envisioning for the future of his eldest son the highest magistratures of the state. But it is above all on the spiritual plane that Francis astonishes us: *Was* he "perfect"? His contemporaries vie with one another in saying so. Let us leave them the responsibility for their eulogies.

What is certain is that Francis was exceptionally equipped to confront the fundamental problem of his time—and undoubtedly of all time: the connection between divine action and man's freedom. He avowed that he had grappled with this problem "from his youth". He had made its primordial importance—as had his contemporaries as well—the center of his research. He had lived it personally and, with the grace of God, he had dominated it. He could immerse himself again in religious quarrels, in political imbroglios, in discussions with the humanists, in brief, in the obscure and laborious genesis of a new world. None of that disconcerted him. He was sure of himself because he was sure of God.

And he was only twenty-four years old! But more than ever he sensed that God had called him to "belong to the Church". And, in fact, he would be the man of God in his time . . . and beyond his time!

The Return to Savoy

Historians are not in agreement as to the dates and the itinerary of this return from Padua to Savoy—about the activities of Francis, the Reverend Déage, and Gallois from October 2 until February 24. It seems likely that they are lacking several documents that would be indispensable for seeing clearly into this problem. Let us, therefore, consider several indications of this that Francis himself gives us (E.A., XXII, 91): in a text written "in a leisure moment, November 20, 1591". Everyone is free to fill in the blank spaces, depending on his sources or his imagination.

On October 8, 1591, the trio embarked for Venice at nightfall. "On the eighteenth day of the same month, the feast of Saint Luke, after a not at all dangerous voyage (which was God's blessing) we landed at Ancona at daybreak. On the same day we entered Loretto." (Francis, at the time of his serious illness in Padua, had vowed to make a pilgrimage to Loretto if he were cured.) On October 19 our three pilgrims went to confession and Communion: "We poured out our prayers to God and his Mother in the very room where they had dwelt." (It was then that—while Francis was praying after Mass—his face became "extraordinarily flushed and radiant"; he burst into tears and "was scarcely able to leave there". [It is M. Déage, a witness of the ecstasy, who relates it.]) The next day our travelers heard Mass and then took the route to Rome. But bandits infested the country and "were devastating the entire beach of Ancona, principally the roads leading to Rome. We returned, in spite of ourselves, to the place from which we had come." At Ancona they again boarded their boat and set sail for Venice: "This crossing was much more difficult." On November 5, toward evening, "after having paid the owner of the boat", they finally disembarked before the columns of the piazza of Saint Mark. "With our chagrin at having renounced our pilgrimage to Rome—which we regretted above all else—we mixed the joy of setting foot on *terra firma.*"

What did Francis do between mid-November 1591 and the end of February 1592? Tradition and Mother de Chantal maintain that he took the trip to Rome, but M. Déage's wallet was very nearly empty, and the price of horses and guides largely exceeded their funds. So? It is also certain that at this time Francis was reviewing "the course that he had begun in order to survey all the law titles", and this demanded tranquility and recollection. It is also known that on January 21, 1592, he received his "letters patent" from the Congregation while at Padua, and that Father Possevin visited him there. This delay at Padua thus seems to have been a stopover foreseen in the plan for the trip, whether the pilgrimage to Rome took place or not. If it did not occur, then the delay was quite simply prolonged and the studious Francis took advantage of the time to complete some work left unfinished. Let us admit that we are confronted with a gap in the story—nothing serious, fortunately.

In February 1592, Francis, Déage, and Gallois arrived at the Château de La Thuille, to the south of Lake Annecy, where M. de Boisy was "impatiently awaiting his dear son". He had retired there with his family because the region of Brens was too dangerous. The Chablais was devastated in turn by the Bernese and the Genevans and by the ducal troops. They were right in the middle of the "war of the castles"; each of the armies was burning and destroying these fortified dwellings, which could serve as support spots for the adversary!

3

A PRIESTHOOD DEARLY ACQUIRED
February 1592–December 1593

Family Welcome

"It is difficult to express the joy that Francis' father and mother experienced upon his arrival home. The two of them could not get enough of looking at him after the pleasure of first seeing him." This joy, however, was not without some sorrow: Mme de Boisy was suffering from a serious loss of vision, which rendered her incapable of guiding herself without the support of a friendly arm.

La Thuille was a modest dwelling, but its views of the lake and the mountains made it pleasant. At least they could honorably receive their friends there, and these friends returned the courtesy. Many were invited to La Thuille to celebrate Francis' return. "All the neighbors", we are told, "hurried to visit him, because they had never seen anyone more courteous or less conceited than he, and his parents seemed to be rejuvenated by his presence." Francis lent himself good-naturedly to these receptions, but he would have preferred — after so long an absence — to enjoy some sweet repose among his family.

Francis' Great Perplexity

Francis secretly suffered a great dilemma. He never had any doubts about his vocation "to belong to the Church", and he was less doubtful than ever. But how was he going to tell his father, who had placed such high hopes in him? Besides, M. de Boisy was seventy years old. If he were to die, who, if not Francis, would maintain the house? Who would advise and sustain Mme de Boisy? Gallois was only sixteen years old, and anyway M. de Boisy had destined him for the Church. Gallois himself had already acquired a canonry of Saint Peter at Geneva, and he did not seem, moreover, to have the qualifications to be the head of a family. Louis was fifteen, and M. de Boisy had decided that he would become a Knight of Malta. All this little world had yet to mature.

With an eye to the future, M. de Boisy had bought an estate for Francis, who was to assume the title and the property upon his arrival at La Thuille: henceforth Francis would be called Seigneur de Villaroget. His father had assembled, tome by tome, a rich library of law books for him. The prudent gentleman also nourished other great projects for his son.

How could Francis tell his father that all these dreams were in vain? Above all, at what moment, and on what terms? What would his father's reactions be? Francis would keep his secret until it seemed to him that "God's hour" had come. He remained waiting, but the "hour of God" seemed to recede rather than approach.

First, there was the episode of the betrothal. According to the custom of the times, M. de Boisy himself selected a spouse for his son. Her name was Françoise Suchet, the only child and sole heiress of Jean Suchet, "Seigneur de Vergy", counselor to the duke of Savoy and principal judge of the Chablais. Françoise, his daughter, was an adolescent of fourteen, "truly noble of blood and virtue" and, even more, ravishingly beautiful. The two young people were formally introduced at the Château de Sallanches, the home of a mutual friend. Francis "was as polite and as courteous as he could be", but only that! Françoise, accustomed to being fawned upon, was disappointed. M. de Boisy was furious. During the whole return trip he sternly rebuked his son, who listened to him, his head uncovered. M. de Boisy did not consider himself beaten. He mobilized his closest friends, the Seigneur de Chevron-Villette, the Seigneur Perrucard de Ballon, the Seigneur Sénateur Favre, and several others, to persuade the insensitive, handsome young man that this marriage was an exceptional opportunity for him. "They wasted their efforts." Jean Suchet and his beautiful daughter had the courtesy to take into account Francis' reserve and the "coldness" of the first meeting. The project was renewed. But, Father de la Rivière tells us, "Providence put into order the necessary things and allowed certain defects to arise that would break up—little by little—these marriage negotiations."

The rupture took place at the beginning of summer. It was simply because he wished "to belong totally to God, with undivided heart", that Francis had caused his father's plan to miscarry, because—as he confided to his friend Albert de Genève-Lullin—"his heart might have yielded had not his desire to give himself to the service of the Church and had not his love of chastity, which he had vowed, been stronger".

Francis understood that he had to rule out quickly any other project for marriage and to confide the secret of his vocation to two or three friends, who might be able to help him first to inform his father and then get him to reflect. He opened his heart to an excellent priest, Aimé Bouvard, delegated vicar to the parish of Thorens, who had gained the confidence of M. and Mme de Boisy to the extent that they had invited him to follow them to La Thuille. He also alerted his cousin Louis de Sales, four years his elder, with whom he had shared at Paris the desire to belong to the Church. But, on October 14, 1592, Messire François Empereur, the provost of the Geneva chapter, died. The most honored post in the diocese, after that of bishop, was open. Francis' confidant had the inspiration of persuading Bishop Claude de Granier secretly to request Rome—unknown to Francis— that he be designated to succeed the dead provost. They had to act quickly, because candidates for the honorable charge of provost were not lacking.

While these matters were being expedited, M. de Boisy ordered Francis to have himself registered in his capacity of lawyer at the bar of Chambéry. M. de Boisy's great dream! "My house", he said, "is richer in coats of arms than in revenues; you must cooperate". He had no doubt that his son, the young doctor of law, would have a brilliant career. At this particular time, the profession of lawyer—and even of senator—was not incompatible with the priesthood. Even after his ordination, Francis would intervene in several civil cases, at least until July 1597. He therefore "promptly" obeyed his father's wish and had himself called to the bar on November 24, 1592. All took place to the great satisfaction of the examiners, to the extent that Aimé Bouvard says that they were talking "about having him made a judge" already. Francis took the customary oath and paid the "two golden ecus". They were hasty because the duke—struggling with the Huguenots—had just called the Savoyard nobility to arms. Nonetheless, Senator Antoine Favre (known as the "ornament of the red robe") assisted at the ceremony, and from that day he desired to establish "a fraternal friendship" with this son of his friend de Boisy. That friendship would endure until the death of Francis in 1622!

What Happened in the Sionnaz Woods on That Return Trip?

There was an incident on the way that Francis saw as a sign of his vocation. There are, however, two extant accounts of the incident.

The first report—repeated by many biographers—comes from Father de la Rivière and dates from 1624. After his trip to Chambéry, Francis was returning to La Thuille by way of the Sionnaz Woods, accompanied by Father Déage. Suddenly his horse stumbled and fell. His cavalier's sword came out of its scabbard; the scabbard became detached from the belt in such a way that the sword and the scabbard formed a cross. Francis climbed onto his saddle again. Shortly afterward, there was another fall and a new cross on the ground. And a third time. Apart from the fact that this anecdote as told scarcely does honor to Francis' equestrian ability, it has the drawback of requiring a kind of miracle.

The second version is that of Michel Favre, and it dates from the process of canonization. It has the advantage of making no appeal to the marvelous and of being restrained and nuanced: "While the Blessed Francis was returning home, after he had been registered a lawyer, his horse threw him, and his sword, coming out of its scabbard, was found to have its point turned against him, from which he took the decision that it was so much better to believe that God wished him in his service and to hope that he would give him the means." Michel Favre's source is good: it was Louis de Sales, Francis' trusted cousin, who recounted this anecdote to him.

Whichever version we choose, it is certain that this incident moved

Francis to the extent that, on the spot, he spoke confidentially to Father Déage about his vocation.[1]

Our two cavaliers continued on their way, plunged into a great perplexity, "and both of them, amid their reflections, found themselves close to Thuille sooner than they thought".

And Francis continued to remain silent.

Francis Refuses the Title of Senator

Several weeks after he had been admitted to the bar at Chambéry, another "glory" surprised him. Baron d'Hermance brought him from Turin certain "letters patent" naming him a senator. A senator at twenty-four years of age, at a time when no one could aspire to this dignity until he was at least thirty! And the duke was graciously bestowing these "letters patent" without Francis ever having solicited them. How had such a favor come to him? It was Antoine Favre who had obtained it for Francis, with support from three influential friends. M. de Boisy was bursting with joy, but was soon plunged into disbelief. Francis refused this unhoped-for opportunity. His friends insisted, but Francis remained obdurate. All of them wondered what could be the motive for this strange refusal. The imbroglio was becoming unbearable.

The Roman transactions for the provostship were going smoothly, under the aegis of Canon François Deronis, who "had some great contacts at Rome". On March 7, 1593, the bulls were signed, and they arrived at Annecy on May 7. For Francis, who, we repeat, was unaware of these arrangements, this nomination was an evident sign from God: the hour had come for him to inform his father of his vocation and to obtain his consent.

"Father, May It Please You to Permit Me to Enter the Church"

Francis felt that his mother's support in this proceeding would be of great help to him. He made her *au courant* of the situation. Mme

---

[1] To study theology, in the sixteenth century, did not signify—any more than in our time—that one had decided to become a priest.

de Boisy wept but "promised to appease M. de Boisy with all her power".

The interview between father and son took place on May 9, 1593. Francis declared that he wished to ask for only one thing, "and, if it pleases you to grant it to me, I shall never again ask you for anything. . . . May it please you to permit me to enter the Church." Louis de Sales and François Deronis were present, with the bulls for the provostship in their hands, that sign that God confirmed Francis' desire. The old gentleman struggled. He brought up the argument that so tormented Francis' secret heart: "I was hoping that you would be the staff of my old age. . . . You have brothers whom you ought to serve as a father, when I am gone, as I go dying from one day to another." But Francis had reflected on this a long time: "Father, I will serve you until my last breath. I promise every kind of service to my brothers." And to declare that his decision to belong to the Church dated "from his early boyhood", had he not asked to be tonsured by the bishop of Bagnoréa? Mme de Boisy courageously supported her son's request. M. de Boisy grew silent; he wept, and finally said to Francis: "Do then, by God's command, what you say he inspires you to do." And he added—with the generosity of his faith: "I give you my blessing in his Name." He then shut himself in his study.

We think especially about Francis during this decisive hour. But it would be unjust not to admire the strength of soul and the faith of M. de Boisy: this was for him the end of a long dream, of a marvelous hope, a broken place in his life. He could not, at this time, foresee with what splendor Francis would make his name and the house of Sales shine!

Francis de Sales "Takes the Habit of Saint Peter"

The "blessing" of M. de Boisy liberated Francis. He was happy—indeed, he was truly another man! He, perplexed, anxious, "melancholic", immediately made some decisions. He would no longer drag along his paths; he would become a "trailblazer".

From the day after his interview with his father, on May 10, 1593—it was a Sunday—he wore the cassock. The ceremony took place "early in the morning" in the church at La Thuille before the Blessed Sacrament. Messire Aimé Bouvard was so impressed by Francis' fervor that he told him: "Truly one would have thought that you were taking the habit of a Capuchin." "Ah, sir," Francis replied, "I am taking the habit of Saint Peter. It is only by dispensation that we are secularized exteriorly; the interior obligation remains in the bonds of the Prince of the Apostles." Then, inspired by Saint Paul, he added, "I have put on the armor, I have buckled on the baldric, and I am enrolled in the militia of Jesus Christ." Then he assisted at Mass and received Holy Communion.

The next day, May 11, he went down to Annecy to present the bulls to François de Chisse, especially delegated by Rome to confer on Francis "the provostship with its sinecure and benefice ... which did not exceed an annual value of twenty-four gold ducats." This conferring was accomplished apart from any official ceremony. Louis de Sales and Francis Deronis served as witnesses. Following this, Francis took the customary oaths.

On May 12 the new provost took public possession of his charge "by kissing the high altar with all the prescribed ceremonies". All Annecy had assembled to see the Seigneur de Villaroget in ecclesiastical habit.

The new provost then went to pay his respects to his bishop, Monseigneur Claude de Granier, and both of them decided that Francis would receive the four minor orders and the subdiaconate on the Saturday after Pentecost—within a month to the day.

On May 13, Francis achieved his first act as provost: he presided at the Office in his stall in the cathedral.

Francis rearranged his priorities according to his new state of life. He renounced his right, as eldest son, to his title of Lord of Villaroget: henceforth he would again be called Francis de Sales.

Francis the Provost "in Solitude" at the Château de Sales

It was at the Château de Sales, and not at that of La Thuille—too noisy and perhaps laden with too many memories—that Francis wished to withdraw to prepare for his first ordinations. He was accompanied by only his friend and confessor Aimé Bouvard. They arrived at Sales on May 18 and did not leave it until June 7. Time for reflection and prayer, during which—if we are to believe certain allusions made by Francis himself—he knew some interior trials. Was it his promotion to senator that troubled him? His friends had not given up the idea of making him accept this exceptional honor: after all, in the senate there was no lack of bishops and abbots, such as Messire Empereur, his predecessor. The only document that we possess concerning these "temptations" seems at first quite naïve and almost humiliating for Francis. Here are the facts such as they have been reported to us. On the first day of his retreat, May 19, Francis asked Aimé Bouvard to cut his hair, "which was blond and beautiful", and he felt such repugnance that there was released in him a wave of temptations against his vocation. "Alas, Father," he admitted to Messire Bouvard,

> for two days I have suffered great struggles against my vocation; the demon has forgotten no corner of my soul to prod me, and he has tempted me to the very ends of my hair, giving me a great aversion for this tonsure. The strength of Samson was in the ends of his hair, and I think that a part of my weakness was in the ends of mine because, since it has been cut off, I feel stronger in the service of God, and I have truly promised his Divine Majesty that I shall put off the old man entirely, so as to live totally with his grace, in newness of life with Jesus Christ.

The evening of May 19, he was still writing in his notes these words, which he "forgot to erase": "Francis, you must remember what God has done for you by his great mercy on the nineteenth day of May, in the year 1593, through the intercession of the great Saint Celestin, protector of your preparatory retreat for Holy Orders."

On May 26 the Reverend Bouvard surprised Francis in the chapel "drenched in tears". He was reading, in the *Ricordi* of Philip Neri, the story of one of Philip's companions who had "deserted". "Ah, Father Bouvard, my good friend, God places this example before my eyes that finding a little treasure is worth more than expecting a greater one that one has to go to find."

If we take these two brief confidences together, are we not inclined to see in his "temptations" a final assault of his great temptations at Paris and at Padua? He will admit to his friend Antoine Favre that at the approach of the priesthood he was "assailed by the greatest disquiet that he had ever experienced . . . because there is nothing more difficult or more perilous for man . . . how easy it is to sin and to sin gravely, and how difficult it is to fulfill worthily these sacred functions." In this struggle, Francis counts, however, on "the mercies of God". "Do not persuade yourself", he adds in the same letter, "that the sacred mysteries inspire in me a dread so great that it leaves me no place for hope and joy far superior to what my own merits might deserve." This letter is related to the protestation at Padua!

At the same time that he was preparing himself spiritually for ordination, Francis studied for the canonical examination that he was supposed to submit to "like the others", and he reedited, according to the customary rule, his first sermon (which he never gave), on the mystery of Pentecost.

Holy Orders

Wednesday, June 9, Francis received in the Cathedral of Annecy the four minor orders from Bishop de Granier; on the eleventh of June he was promoted to the sacred order of the subdiaconate. Bishop de Granier was delighted with this ordination, and, in his enthusiasm — exceeding other canonical regulations—he called upon Francis to preach on the feast of Corpus Christi (*la Fête-Dieu*). It was only a few days away. Happily, Providence intervened and accorded a respite to our novice preacher. It was on June 24, the feast of Saint John the Baptist, that Francis preached his first sermon. They tell us that "at the hour when the bell was announcing the sermon", Francis experienced the fright that often seizes apprentice orators. He was obliged to lie on a couch for a few moments. He regained his composure and preached, they tell us, "with great courage". He spoke about the Blessed Eucharist.

Soon this young subdeacon revealed himself to be singularly active. He punctually attended Office in the cathedral, visited the sick and the prisoners. Employing his knowledge of law, he reconciled; he talked with several Protestants whom his sermon on June 24 had already disturbed, in particular Antoine de Saint Michel, le Seigneur d'Avully. Summer was not over before he established a confraternity, the "Penitents of the Holy Cross", which would very quickly extend beyond Annecy as far as Chambéry. In short, he upset the good, cozy routine of the Catholics and involved them in all his activity. Some saw him as "shining like a beautiful sun"; others reproached him for undertaking too much!

Francis received the diaconate on September 18, in the Cathedral of Annecy, and the priesthood was conferred on him on December 18 by Bishop de Granier in the same church. The bishop, while he was imposing his hands on the head of "his chief son", could not restrain his tears. As for Francis himself, "enraptured by the thought of his high calling, he resembled a man in another world".

The very next day Francis went on retreat to prepare to celebrate his first Mass. In the course of this triduum he received, he said, "certain great lights". Finally, on December 21, the feast of Saint Thomas, he sang his first Mass; his relatives, his friend Favre, and a crowd of the faithful received Communion from his hand. "In this first sacrifice", he would confide to Mme de Chantal one day, "God took possession of my soul in an inexplicable manner." After the Office of Vespers, Charles-Auguste de Sales adds in a model of understatement: "Francis gave a very fervent homily on the subject of sacrifice." According to the custom of that time, this sermon was undoubtedly a "circumspect disclosure" concerning his vocation and his intimate feelings. Alas! It has not come down to us. Shortly after his ordination, Francis had the joy of baptizing Jeanne, the last-born of Mme de Boisy. He was her elder by twenty-six years.

The "Installation" of the Provost of Geneva

Now that he was a priest, Francis de Sales was able to be "installed" as provost of the Geneva chapter. The ceremonies took place several days after Christmas, and the bishop was eager to preside. On this occasion Francis delivered one of his most important speeches, a veritable "keynote address", by which all his activity as provost, then as prelate, would be inspired. The theme? "We must regain Geneva."

The tone? It is a call to arms—to spiritual arms, to be sure!—the proof of which is that he dared call the "venerable canons" his "valiant comrades in arms".

In order to gain a fuller appreciation of the excitement this speech provoked—a speech in which Francis suddenly revealed his clear-sighted, daring leadership, . . . as well as the breadth of his apostolic vision, we must consider carefully the Geneva Chapter's situation in Annecy at the end of the sixteenth century. The Geneva chapter was then—like the prince-bishop himself—exiled in Annecy; in short, deprived of their cathedral and of their possessions. They yearned to return to Geneva, which would finally be liberated from the Calvinist usurper. "We must regain Geneva"—these fiery words fell upon an audience ready to be inflamed. Their eyes were fixed upon the orator, who spoke while standing in front of his choir stall.

But these canons were not "venerable" because of the privilege of age. They represented, in fact, the elite of the clergy, a lively force in the diocese, who formed the bishop's council. Their chapter even constituted a power nearly equal to that of the bishop. Ever since, during the Genevan troubles, Bishop Pierre de la Baume had fled his lands, the Pope had placed the chapter under his immediate jurisdiction. The provost's "veneration" for his canons was not academic!

It was in light of these nostalgic longings that Francis, daringly, launched his call to battle. "What shall we do then, canons of Geneva?" There was no ambiguity in the provost's project: "We must bring down the walls of Geneva with *charity;* we must invade Geneva with *charity;* we must recover Geneva with *charity.* . . . I do not propose to you iron or that powder whose odor and stench recall the infernal furnace. . . . Let your camp be the camp of God. . . . It is by hunger and thirst, endured not by our adversaries but by ourselves, that we must repulse the enemy." Francis posed the question: "Do you want an easy method for carrying out an assault on the city?" The orator took his answer from Sacred Scripture: Holophernes, attacking Bethulia, cut off the aqueduct and made them guard all the wells that quenched the city's thirst. Thus they must do for Geneva: "It is an aqueduct that nourishes and enlivens, so to speak, the entire race of heretics. These are the examples of perverse priests, their actions, their words—in short, the iniquity of all—but, above all, of the ecclesiastics. It is because of us that the name of God is blasphemed every day among the nations." The canons need not search anywhere else than in their own chapter for these guilty ecclesiastics! "In a word—for we must terminate this discourse—we must live according to the Christian rule, in such a way that we are canons, that is to say, regulars (living by the Rule), and children of God not only in name but also in fact." This was the very reform promulgated by the Council of Trent. Such would be the apostolic strategy of Francis de Sales throughout his life.

A Priest of the Country

And since he knew that it was vain to preach reform of life if one did not first reform himself, Francis—from the time of his official installation— began to strive to show to all the true visage of the priest of Jesus Christ. He was assiduous in participating in the Office of the chapter. He catechized and he preached; he heard confessions; and he visited the poor, the sick, and the imprisoned. He performed and acquitted himself zealously in all the duties of his charge. "From that time on, they regarded him as a man of God", Mother de Chantal affirms. A significant trait was his dedication to the confessional. Bishop de Granier had named him the "penitentiary" of the diocese, which meant he had given to him the most extensive powers of absolving. Francis "had a confessional built for hearing penitents' confessions in the cathedral church very close to the door on the gospel side. There he would remain sometimes from dawn to almost noon, surrounded by a great number of the faithful of both sexes, and without any discrimination."

He was also pleased to render assistance—provost that he was—to the other priests, whenever they were overburdened or prevented by illness. He refused, moreover, any money for this ministry, even though his revenues were very meager, since the provostship had been despoiled of all its benefices by the Genevan Calvinists. He found, on the contrary, the means to give alms and to "assist, on the sly, the embarrassed poor". He solaced, consoled, reconciled. He was consulted more and more about questions of law—civil or canonical—and of theology.

The source of this activity, of this tireless charity of Francis de Sales, was the Mass. He did not say it every day until after his episcopal consecration, but he already celebrated it "often". It is the fervor, not the frequency, that is important. But his eucharistic fervor impressed and always would impress those who attended his Masses. Testimonies abound as to the profundity of his recollection. "This Divine Sacrament", Mother de Chantal declared, "was his true life and his strength, and in this action he seemed to be a man wholly transformed into God." Later it frequently happened at Mass that he was so seized by devotion that he stopped. André de Sauzea, who knew him closely, is precise in his remembrance: "Whenever I served his Mass, I noticed that after the Consecration I saw him stopped and carried away with sighs in a kind of rapture, and when that lasted a while, I would point my finger to the next part of the Mass, and then he would continue, and that happened almost regularly."

So much zeal, so much dedication to the service of God and of souls astonished—and even disturbed a little—M. de Boisy. "One day", Francis himself tells us, "my father took me aside and told me: 'Provost, you are preaching too often. Even on work days I hear the bell for the sermon, and they tell me: "It is the provost, the provost!" ... In my day, it was not like that. Sermons were much more rare, but what sermons they were!... Now you are making this exercise so common that people take them for granted, and they no longer have the same esteem for you!' "

This was only an affectionate tirade on the part of M. de Boisy. But the provost's apostolic fervor and zeal did not fail to provoke some annoyance, even some jealousy, among certain clerics. Some even tried to arouse the bishop against him. They whispered that Francis, bit by bit, was supplanting him in the diocese. Then the calumny began to thicken: they claimed that this dear provost "spoke badly of the bishop in his absence; that he 'rather freely' expressed his opinions about some of the bishop's dealings, and all the while in words that conveyed innuendo". This time Bishop de Granier did get upset: he revealed (to the provost) "the rather bad feeling in his soul by the change in his countenance". Francis took note of this but kept silent.

"He continued to proceed at the same pace in his occupations in the confessional, the pulpit, the visits to the sick", and in his duties as provost.

He did this so well that Bishop de Granier, "weary of so long a suspicion, led his innocent son along a path in his garden and unburdened his heart once and for all". Light broke through, and friendship was renewed between the bishop and the provost. Bishop de Granier thought about punishing the "knaves" and the "calumniators"; Francis knelt at his feet to obtain their pardon.

Decidedly, something was stirring in the diocese, and even outside it. Antoine Favre—whom Francis calls in his correspondence *"Frater suavissime, amantissime, dulcissime"*—founded at Chambéry a Confraternity of Penitents in imitation of the one at Annecy. On Tuesday of Pentecost 1594 they met at Aix, where a relic of the Holy Cross was kept. Their friendship was going to grow closer each day. This was most opportune, because Francis was soon going to undertake a dangerous mission in which Favre would be his staunchest supporter.

4

MISSIONARY AT THE RISK OF HIS LIFE
1594–1598

At this time, an event of considerable importance occurred in the life of Francis de Sales. This provost of the Genevan canons, who seemed committed to a life of certain crises, but without risk, was about to become for four years an itinerant, needy, poor, constantly threatened missionary who at certain critical times would not have recovered his "breath" or courage except for the examples of Saint Francis Xavier or the recent English martyrs. He personally would have to be the first to lead the attack to which he had challenged the canons of his chapter—if not against Geneva, at least against the ministers of Geneva. At the order of the duke of Savoy, Bishop de Granier would send him to "reconquer" the Chablais to the Catholic religion. In the lifetime of Francis de Sales there is probably no period when he appears greater. Let those who see in him only a gentle pastor watching over tender sheep and lambs in the midst of meadow flowers accompany him in his missionary combat. They will discover in him the warrior about whom Saint Paul tells us, who "has put on the armor of faith and of love; and for a helmet, hope of salvation".

The Chablais

The Chablais is that territory—about thirty miles long, fifteen miles wide—that borders Lake Leman on the north and the mountains of Faucigny to the south. Thonon, on the banks of the lake, plays the role of a little capital.

In 1594 Charles-Emmanuel, the duke of Savoy, had just won back the Chablais, which before the vicissitudes of the Reform constituted a part of his domain, but under the jurisdiction of the prince-bishop of Geneva. The religious situation had deteriorated gravely since the arrival of Calvinism in Geneva. Of the some twenty-five thousand souls who inhabited the area, only about a hundred Catholics remained. All the others passed—either by choice or by force—into Protestantism. "One part of this diocese of Geneva (the Chablais)", Francis wrote to the nuncio Bishop J. C. Riccardi, on February 19, 1596, "was invaded by the Bernese sixty years ago and remained heretic, but—with the passage of time—this territory, by force of arms, would again come under the domination of His Highness, and was joined to his former patrimony."

"A good number of inhabitants, more touched by the blasts from arquebuses than by the sermons that were given them by order of the bishop, returned to the Faith and were restored to the bosom of Holy Mother Church, but afterward these areas—having been infested by the incursions of the Genevans and the French—fell again into their mire." The years when Francis was a missionary in the Chablais would be years of political uncertainty, and as a consequence—for such was the misfortune of the time—of religious insecurity. These circumstances conferred on the mission to the Chablais a frankly evangelical character: it was in poverty, dangers, contradictions, calumnies, and insults that Francis would open up the spiritual reconquest of the Chablais.

Bishop de Granier's Choice

How then was Francis chosen for this harsh and perilous ministry? The duke, from the end of 1589, had begged Bishop de Granier to reestablish some pastors in the approximately fifty former parishes in the Chablais. This was done. But a year later, in February 1591, the fifty priests had been expelled anew by the Calvinists. This was established proof that the method employed was no good! It would be better to send there—at least as a start—two or three priests only, who would work "apostolically", bravely canvass the territory, and who might be received here and chased there, but who would also be priests with great learning, capable of answering the attacks of the Calvinist pastors and of enlightening the people. "This great prelate (Bishop de Granier)"—Charles-Auguste candidly recounts—"therefore looked around on all sides for those who might be capable of resowing the seed of the word of God in these lands. Almost all went into hiding, because of the terror that the danger cast into their hearts. From the first Bishop de Granier had virtually fixed his glance on his son, the lord-provost de Sales, but because of certain considerations— which he himself suggested—he did not dare propose it to him." The bishop then had the idea of convoking his clergy in an assembly and of requesting volunteers. No one breathed a word. The bishop then turned his gaze upon the provost. Francis stood up: "My Lord," he said, "if you judge me capable, ask; I am ready."

In fact, the mission that Bishop Claude de Granier entrusted to him was not only that of a "physician capable of curing so great an infirmity", as the nuncio Riccardi wrote on February 19, 1596, "but more like that of an "explorer or a precursor, in order to examine the means to be taken so as to provide the country with remedies and physicians". It was not a question of simply restoring fifty ousted pastors. The Church in the Chablais would have to be rebuilt— stone by stone. And that was precisely how Francis would carry out his mission. When we follow his existence during these four years, we quickly discover there a shrewd, perspicacious strategy, which carried his effort to the salients of the Protestant occupation, in order that the work, this time, would be solid. Far from rendering his mission less perilous, however, this strategy would cost him labors, contra-dictions, hatred, even setbacks—at least temporarily—harder than those that he would have known by walking through hamlets and villages as a simple missionary.

Francis Leaves for the Chablais

As soon as he had received Bishop de Granier's "command", Francis prepared all that he would need for this apostolic expedition. "He made sure of the prayerful support of the canons of his chapter, and of those of the good priests and religious of the diocese"; he selected several books: the Bible, the *Controversies* of Bellarmine, and "a few others". His "dear cousin", Canon Louis de Sales, would accompany him. Louis "was a man of a very bright and very gentle spirit, who had already given strong evidence of his theological acumen and his ability to preach the word of God".

The two missionaries left Annecy on September 9, 1594. Their route took them past Sales, where M. and Mme de Boisy were living. Francis decided to stop there in order to "receive their instructions, but, to be sure, the Seigneur de Sales instructed him to do nothing other than to stay, saying that he was going to put himself in danger of being killed", or—even worse for a gentleman—of failing and being "the laughingstock of the world". Francis remained respectfully firm, but it was a firmness that was totally apostolic: "Father, God will provide. It is he who helps the strong; we only need to have courage.... And supposing we were being sent to the Indies or to England? ... This is a laborious task, it is true, and there is no denying it, but why are we wearing these cassocks if we do not want the responsibility?" The old gentleman remained obstinate.

The two missionaries spent two days at Sales in order to prepare themselves by prayer and penance for their apostolic labor. The evening of the second day, September 13, Francis bade his mother good-bye; his father did not wish to see him!

On Wednesday, September 14, the feast of the Exaltation of the Holy Cross, Francis and Louis set out. They carried their light luggage on their shoulders because M. de Boisy had forbidden anyone to accompany them, and he did not give them a sou for their journey. As far as the bridge of Boringe they were quite familiar with the countryside of their youth, but once within the Chablais, what desolation! The Genevans had passed through there, and they had destroyed and sacked the churches, burned the crosses and the castles ... even the Château de Brens was devastated.

Soon they reached Saint-Cergues and found themselves in the sumptuous plain of the Chablais; they hastened toward the fortress of Allinges "situated on a round mountain", so as to present themselves first to the lord-governor, Baron d'Hermance, a great friend of M. de Boisy. They arrived there at dusk: the baron welcomed them warmly.

Then Francis handed him his credentials: the letter from the duke and the one from the bishop. From that moment the two missionaries felt at home at Allinges. Each evening they would return to the fortress, because their lives would not be safe in any other lodging.

Baron d'Hermance still cautioned the missionaries to exercise great prudence with regard to the Protestant ministers. They must not rekindle quarrels that were hardly extinguished. From the high battlements of the fortress, Francis contemplated and reflected. Below, to the north, on the shores of the magnificent lake, Thonon, the capital, counted no more than a handful of Catholics. On the other shore one could discern Lausanne. And further on, behind a promontory, Geneva crouched, invisible but omnipresent in all this Savoyard countryside. Geneva, which was ready at the slightest favorable opportunity to invade the country once again, or at least to carry out a raid. Mass was no longer celebrated in this ravaged country. Francis and Louis would only be able to say it in the little Romanesque chapel of the castle, with its windows as narrow as slits. The Chablais was truly "missionary territory".

Strategy

Francis, in the light of the instructions that Baron d'Hermance had furnished him, put his apostolic strategy into action. He would have to carry out his first effort at Thonon, the administrative, intellectual, and religious capital of the Chablais. But neither Thonon nor its environs would be safe for Catholic priests. Each evening our missionaries would have to take shelter in the fortress at Allinges. Ten miles in the morning, ten miles in the evening, and this via some roads that would not be very easy in the late autumn, much less during the winter. So what? Their relations with the populace would be even more difficult! And then, in these comings and goings, Francis and Louis would encounter—not without risk of insults, blows, and even death—the rustic people from the country . . . for whom a papist priest was a "sorcerer" or even a "devil".

At Thonon, Francis could count on the support of the wise magistrate Claude d'Orlier and of the comptroller Claude Marin, or on the benevolence of Antoine de Saint-Michel, Seigneur d'Avully, who was the brother-in-law of Baron d'Hermance, and who—although he was president of the consistory—was in search of the truth. The town's mayor, Pierre Fornier (or Fournier), would not be hostile to Francis. He would be "correct", which was already a lot in this atmosphere of antipapist tension. Francis, on the other hand, collided with the hostility of the two pastors, and above all of Pastor Louis Viret. Thonon was totally Calvinist; there were scarcely seven or eight families that remained Catholic. The two churches in the town, Saint Hippolytus and Saint Augustine, were turned over to the Protestant cult; however, the Catholics had the right to preach at Saint Hippolytus since the withdrawal of the Bernese.

It was agreed upon by Claude Marin and the missionaries that on Sunday, September 18, Francis would preach his first sermon at Saint Hippolytus, immediately after the Protestant service, and he would continue to do so every Sunday. There was an uproar in the city. This audacious papist would have to be driven out!

Saturday, September 17, Francis therefore presented himself to Pierre Fournier, gave him the letters from the duke, and informed him of his project for the next day. M. Fournier bowed.

On Sunday, after the Protestant minister finished preaching, Francis gave his sermon. The audience was sparse; there were a few Catholics present and they were trembling a little, but there were also some curious Calvinists. Francis spoke about the authority of the Church: "Saint Paul," he said, "who had seen Christ, preached, nonetheless, only with the permission of the apostles." Luther and Calvin were not mentioned, but the allusion was clear.

When all was said and done, things seemed at first to have turned out well. The governor and several Catholics decided that a few peasants from the outskirts and the townspeople from Évian could come to hear the missionary on the following Sundays.

Then the Protestants reacted. On Sunday, October 2, "the leaders of Thonon, having assembled their council," Francis wrote, "swore . . . that neither they nor the people would ever listen to Catholic preaching. . . . This took place, I was told, the day before yesterday, at the city hall, and several had already passed this resolution at the assembly that they called their consistory. . . . They would assuredly like to make us lose hope of bringing our affairs to a good end, and, as they were leaving, they urged us to withdraw." They had indeed underestimated Francis de Sales. "It will not be so: because as long as we are permitted by the truces and by the will of the princes—ecclesiastical and secular—we are absolutely resolved to work at this task unrelentingly, so as not to leave a stone unturned, *to entreat, and to reconvert with all the patience and the knowledge that God will give us.*" And here he had already formulated a bolder project. "We must reestablish the celebration of the Holy Sacrifice as soon as possible, so that the *enemy of man* may see that by his artifices he has given us *courage* instead of *discouragement.*"

And Francis added these few words, which say much about the mixture, in these affairs, of politics and of religion: "But in this, great prudence must be exercised in the anticipation of this situation in order to know whether the temporary peace that we are enjoying will endure." The fear of a return of the Bernese and the Genevans would paralyze anyone who might want to be converted!

Everything conspired during this winter (1594–95) to discourage Francis and Louis de Sales: the rigor of a season that was particularly severe; the relentlessness of the Protestant ministers, which proved to be very influential over the people. They hurled "a thousand jibes and mockeries" at him, as one of his biographers said; they called him "hypocrite, idolater, false prophet"; they accused him of magic and sorcery; they "set up ambushes" for him. It was bruited about that they had the right—even the duty, perhaps—to put him to death, since he was violating public order!

In these threats Francis perceived a presage of approaching harvests: "It is now that we must have courage, cousin," he said to Louis de Sales, "and provided we are not afraid, we shall see that we shall have a good yield." But the greatest danger came from Annecy itself, where some were trying to force the bishop to recall the two missionaries. "I hope", Antoine Favre wrote to Francis in a letter dated October 31, "that my messengers will no longer have to carry my letters to you in the solitude where you are living, but in this city where soon—I foresee—you will remember not only the vow of a very concerned father, but also the orders of a very loving bishop.

Because, between them—in my presence—there has been much question of recalling you and of giving you a successor." This successor was already designated: a Capuchin, Father Chérubin de Maurienne. And the recall was, in fact, decided. Fortunately they consulted Baron d'Hermance, who judged the provost's departure impossible. The bishop immediately took advantage of this to revoke his decision. M. de Boisy remained obstinate.

Francis and Louis, nonetheless, continued their missionary labors. Francis decided to preach Advent (1594) at Thonon, but in what conditions? "God makes me undertake a task worthy of the sovereignty of his law. I am beginning today to preach the Advent sermons to four or five persons; all the others maliciously ignore what Advent means." Since he could not reach the others by word, he got to them by those spiritual means to which he had made allusion in his provost's speech: "Prayer, alms, and fasting are the three strands that comprise the rope broken with difficulty by the enemy; with the help of divine grace we are going to bind the adversary with that rope." And so he went from Allinges to Thonon, from Thonon to Allinges, through the snow, "in foul weather", and whenever he had some time, he strolled through the hamlets and villages. He preached to and confessed some Catholics who had been deprived of all the sacraments for a long time.

These walks were not taken without risk. Peril from the snow and the cold: one evening Francis and Louis had to abandon hope of getting back to Allinges. They knocked in vain at all the doors in the village; they finally huddled together in the rear of a public oven. Peril from wild animals: one night Francis, returning alone, found himself suddenly assailed by a pack of wolves. He only had time to climb a tree, and for fear of falling off he tied himself to a branch with his belt. Peril from men paid to put him to death: let no one suspect that the historians have unduly exaggerated this danger! We possess an incontestable document that must be cited to take the measure of the events and of Francis' courage. M. de Boisy finally came around to sending a young servant, George Rolland, to Francis and Louis. But one evening, toward the end of February 1595, Francis, accompanied by Rolland and two other persons, was going up to Allinges when two men leaped from behind a bush, swords in hand. Francis walked right up to them, stared them steadily in the face, and spoke to them calmly. The two assailants, stupefied, begged his pardon: they had nothing against him, they protested, but they had been paid to kill him. The incident would have ended there if Rolland, panicking, had not leaped upon a horse the next day and rushed to give "a very ample account" of this adventure at the Château de Sales.

M. de Boisy summoned his son home, and here is Francis' response (mid-March 1595): "My very honored Father, if Rolland were your son—even though he is only a valet—he would not have had the cowardice to recoil from so little a shock as this that he experienced, and he would not have described it as a great battle. No one can doubt the bad will of our adversaries, but you are mistaken when you doubt our courage. . . . I beg you, therefore, Father, not to attribute my perseverance to disobedience, and to regard me always as your most respectful son." It is safe to assume that M. de Boisy was more proud than furious upon reading this letter.

Things reached the point where the Baron d'Hermance proposed that Francis should fortify himself with an armed escort, which Francis, horrified, refused. The baron therefore had Francis trailed secretly, and at a distance, by several soldiers. In fact Francis had other weapons for self-defense: his calm, his contempt for death, his humility, his "dignity", his unfailing charity, and his gift of friendship that accompanied him all his life. And finally everyone—at least secretly—"began to like him".

As for Francis, arousing sympathy was only an approach: it was *faith* in the apostolic succession that had to be restored. Faith, certainly, he explained in his sermons at Saint Hippolytus; however, the congregation was very small, because the interdict launched by the consistory had neatly blocked the movement of curiosity that he had initiated.

The Controversies

In the beginning of 1595 Francis made an important decision: he wrote—article by article—a collection of *Meditations* (which he also called a *Memorial*), and he posted them in the public places, or he slid copies under doors. This earned for him today the title "patron of journalists"!

In truth what Francis wanted to establish with the people of Thonon was a large-scale dialogue, inasmuch as the Boisy family enjoyed good relations, even friendship, with several distinguished citizens of Thonon. A fig for those discussions and quarrels where people insult or mock each other! The stakes were too high, let them study together seriously, beginning with the same texts of the Bible that are the foundations of the apostolic Roman Church.

The "Epistle to the Gentlemen of Thonon", which would preface the book later, indicated the aim and set the tone: "I have put here some of the principal reasons for the Catholic Faith. . . . But I am recommending them to you and presenting them with a good heart, hoping that the occasions that deter you from listening to me will not prevent you from reading what is written. I assure you, as for the rest, that you will never read anything written by a man more desirous for your spiritual service than I."

The Controversies —such is the definitive title that Francis would give to his book when he organized these "meditations" with a view to publishing them—are thus not a systematic treatise of theology concerning the Church, although we find in them, curiously enough, certain answers to our most modern problems. Glycera did not scatter her flowers here, and certain authors are reminded—perusing certain pages—of Pascal's *Provinciales.* Francis, however, was writing "without leisure or time to breathe", amid his missionary labors, and he was virtually without books, except for his Bible and several works that he found in the libraries of his Catholic friends. It is believed that he did not complete this book until the end of January 1597!

Francis Settles in Thonon

Around mid-February 1595, Francis informed Antoine Favre of a new, important decision: "I am going to Thonon for the remainder of Lent. That is what seems best to me." Best? For the Chablais, certainly: his presence would give them courage and hope. As for the Calvinists who might want to consult him secretly? Yes, again. But for himself and his own safety? He found lodging at the home of an elderly Catholic lady, his relative, Mme de Fong, who owned a modest little house a short distance from the city. But it would be impossible—the agreement between the duke and the Genevans precluded it—to celebrate Mass in Thonon. So what? Each morning, in all kinds of weather, Francis would cross the Dranse River and go as far as the little chapel in Marin, located in Valasian territory, at that time Catholic. "I have finally settled in Thonon", Francis wrote to Favre on March 7, 1595. And he recovered in a flash the tone of the sermon he had given as provost: "Let the enemy be ready for a lance vibrating with the tension of being delayed. Having been attacked from the distant heights of my citadel (Allinges), he has scorned just terms, so I shall deliver the final assault."

Francis was not deluding himself. Citing Saint Paul, he wrote to Bishop de Granier at the beginning of April 1595: "We are marching, but in the manner of an invalid who—after having left his bed—finds that he has lost the use of his feet, and, in his frail health, no longer knows whether he is healthy or sick." Writing to Father Possevin, his former spiritual director, his trust made him even more frank; he was aware that, thanks to his family relations, he could hold the post alone, but that his effort could scarcely be productive.

I have some relatives here and some other persons who respect me for certain particular reasons that I cannot mention, and this is what keeps me totally committed to the work. I would already be very annoyed with myself if there was not the hope that I am doing my best. Beyond that I am well aware that "the miller is not wasting his time when he pounds on his millstone." Besides, it would be a great waste for another to expend his energy here for nothing when he could produce more fruit elsewhere, whereas I am hardly good enough to preach to bare walls, which is what I am presently doing in this town.

First Yield

Finally, a first success came to reward Francis' perseverance. On April 11, 1595, he wrote to Favre, "At last, a few ears of grain are beginning to sprout from this great harvest." Numbered among these ears was Pierre Poncet, "a very erudite legal expert", "the most esteemed lawyer in the entire district", and "right-thinking" (E.A., XI, 124 and 142). What obstacles for the neophyte! "It was easy to detach him from the Calvinist sect . . . but it was more difficult to help him return to the fold of the Church." "Fear of losing his possessions, the censure of his friends, uncertainty about the duration of the treaties . . . all united to impede his conversion." Elsewhere rumor was circulating that the Lord d'Avully had been frequenting the company of Francis de Sales for some time. Was he also going to be converted?

Interruption at Thorens and Annecy

After Easter the provost returned to Annecy, where there was to be a synod. There was much talk about the mission in the Chablais, because the political and financial imbroglio was critical. Duke Charles Emmanuel had taken sides with the League, and the conversion of Henry IV put him in an awkward position. He had many cares other than that of sustaining the missionaries in the Chablais. And the Knights of Saint Maurice-et-Lazare, who were withholding the benefices of the former pastors, were hardly disposed to relinquish them. Moreover, M. de Boisy was persisting in his opposition and refused any subsidy to Francis. It was only the little gifts that Mme de Boisy had sent secretly to her son that enabled him one day to reorganize the Church in the Chablais.

Francis could only trust in God.

Francis divided this time of delay between Annecy and Sales. He obtained at this meeting the benefice of the parish at Cornier, which his brother Gallois—now wanting to be married—had just given up. He approved the marriage of his sister Gasparde to Melchior de Cornillon, which M. de Boisy opposed. At Annecy Francis preached several times during Pentecost season.

On the feast of Corpus Christi (*la Fête-Dieu*), Saturday, May 25, God favored Francis with extraordinary graces. "At three o'clock in the morning, as he was meditating profoundly on the most blessed and most august sacrament of the Eucharist," Charles-Auguste de Sales and Father de la Rivière related shortly afterward, "he felt himself enraptured by so great an abundance of light and joy in the Holy Spirit . . . that his heart began to race from too many delights, and he was finally forced to throw himself on the floor while exclaiming: 'Lord, hold back the floods of your grace; withdraw from me because I can no longer withstand the greatness of your sweetness, for which I am compelled to prostrate myself.'"

Return to the Chablais

Francis set out for the Chablais the beginning of June 1595. At Thonon he again found his faithful little flock, violently persecuted by the Calvinists who, during his absence, and in spite of the presence of Louis de Sales, had renewed their attacks.

Again he courageously went back to work. It seems that he had, at this time, toiled a lot over his *Controversies*. The letter that he wrote to Peter Canisius, on July 21, 1595, shows us what care he brought to his work. He admits that he had come to grips with some theological difficulties that the Calvinists had brought up, that he could not solve them "even with the help of Bellarmine's works" and the several books that he had at his disposal. Having realized that he was separated from Canisius, "so to speak, only by Lake Leman", he suggested writing to him from time to time in order to submit to him certain questions "concerning theological matters and the difficulties that they present, so as to receive your instructions also by letter". Francis took the arguments of the Huguenots seriously. Were these leaflets printed at that time? The Visitandines affirm it; Dom Mackey denies it. In any case, "each week a new leaflet was distributed to each of the houses in Thonon, and to those in the countryside".

Lassitude and Bursts of Hope

July 1595 was not occupied only with theology. "I have spent the whole month either in peregrinations or in indispensable errands", he wrote to Favre from Annecy on August 2. Was this fatigue? Excess of work? Under the always courageous attitude a lassitude is apparent. "The harvesting of Thonon is a yoke that surpasses my strength, but I have resolved to abandon it only with your agreement, by your order. I continue, nevertheless, to prepare—by all kinds of devices and industry—some new workers for this project, and to find for them some means of subsistence. I perceive no end, no outlet among these infinite ruses of the enemy of the human race." And this precious confidence: "I have been tormented, and I still am, my brother, by seeing—among so many disasters that try our souls—that there scarcely remains a moment to cultivate the devotion of which we have such a pressing need. We must, however—counting on the mercy of our Lord—raise our hearts to better hopes. . . . I am returning tomorrow to my Sparta."

In fact, at Sparta-Thonon things became somewhat improved. The letter that Francis wrote on September 18, 1595, to Antoine Favre is a masterpiece that—by itself—could reveal for us the missionary ardor, faith, and heart of him who wrote it:

> Here at last, my brother, let a larger and more beautiful gate be open to us in order to let in this harvest of Christians, because there was need of it yesterday when M. d'Avully and the syndics of the town—as they are called—came openly to my preaching because they had heard it said that I was supposed to speak about the most august sacrament of the altar. They had so great a desire to hear me explain the belief of Catholics and the proofs touching this mystery that—not having dared to come publicly, for fear of appearing to forget the law that they had imposed on themselves—they listened to me from a certain location where they could not be seen; nevertheless, the weakness of my voice presented no obstacle to them.

For Francis, this was the success of his apostolic strategy: "The people of Thonon have resolved, by common agreement, to present us, in writing, their confession of faith in those points where it differs from ours, so that we may be able to discuss them in particular, either in friendly talks or in writing." These particular discussions with the "principal citizens" of the Chablais had always seemed to Francis to be the masterpiece of his apostolic action. "Assuredly, we are on the right track." His faith in "the force of the word of God" was total. "As us, having great courage by the grace of God, we are awaiting with eagerness and joy this struggle, which gives good hope."

We possess only a summary of this sermon of September 17; however, anyone who would like to know the apostolic heart of Francis need only reread his *exordium,* which is almost entirely preserved in writing. "If anyone would like to question me about his doubts, whether in writing or otherwise, he will oblige me to him infinitely, and I shall take it as a singular favor, and I shall try to explain it to his total satisfaction with all charity and respect."

This same day, September 17, 1595, Pope Clement VIII finally granted King Henry IV pontifical absolution. The news spread through Savoy as it did in France. From the first days of October Francis rejoiced in a letter to Antoine Favre: "I understand . . . that the Holy Father has very recently sent the happy message to Henry: 'Greetings and apostolic benediction to the King of France'. If it is so, *may joy reign through the power of the Lord!"*

The event would, in fact, have some considerable influence on the apostolate of Francis in the Chablais. The people of these territories would now be less hesitant to compromise themselves, and Duke Charles-Emmanuel himself, no longer having to worry about collusion between France and the Genevans, would be able to devote more attention to the internal affairs of the duchy. In fact, at the end of 1595, he inquired of M. d'Avully as to what the missionary might need. Francis asked him for some funds to support some pastors and some missionaries, and above all officially to confirm the reestablishment of the Catholic liturgy. He would wait a long time for the answer.

By the end of 1595, Francis' activity appears to have been prodigious. He preached, he catechized, he visited the sick, and if they were Catholic he brought them the Eucharist. A great part of his time was spent in talks with some Calvinists who came for discussions with him; among these were Antoine d'Avully, the lawyer, and Claude de Prez. He began to draw up—regarding the juridic code, which Antoine Favre had prepared (the celebrated *Codex Fabrianus*)—an explanation of the principal heresies against which the legislator would have to guard: ardent pages that are among the most vigorous written by Francis; they would be included in Favre's book under the first title *"De Summa Trinitate et Fide Catholica"*. The better to confound the "heretics", Francis plunged into the study of the *Institutes of the Christian Religion* by Calvin, but not without having sought permission from Rome, humbly, like a simple cleric. All this in the perspective that no jurist of the time would call into question: "One faith, one law, one King". It was only little by little that Francis would arrive at harmonizing in himself the jurist and the apostle of Jesus Christ.

On February 19, 1595, Francis wrote to the nuncio Riccardi: "We are presently—thanks to this news of a proximate peace—on the eve of harvesting what we have sown up till now."

Peace, however, would take time to be established. But Francis was right. The time of the labors and the seed sowing, and the time of the missionary heroism, were practically fulfilled; the time of garnering was approaching.

It was important for us to slow down in order to consider this time of seed sowing. Never will Francis appear to us more purely the apostle in the manner of Paul or of Francis Xavier. He was alone, or virtually alone. Even when his cousin Canon Louis de Sales was in the Chablais, it was Francis who took upon his shoulders the heaviest burden of the mission. He was poor and deprived of resources. He was without human assistance; undoubtedly Baron d'Hermance watched over him discreetly, but Francis refused to preach the Gospel in the shadow of pikes and halberds. As for the duke, after having demanded that the mission be inaugurated, he kept silent, he granted the missionary no official letter, and he consigned to him no subsidy, whereas the Protestants in the Chablais felt strong because of all the power and money they received from Geneva.

Slowly, patiently, Francis worked: his hope was in God. He prayed, fasted, mortified himself. His daily Mass, celebrated at what a price we know, was his great source of courage. He treated with respect and charity those Protestants who kept away from him, who sometimes insulted him or assailed him, and above all he took them seriously. For them he studied, wrote; preached because it was the Gospel, the Scriptures, and the Church that he had to present in all their purity so as to make them accessible. By speech, undoubtedly, but especially by his entire life and entire faith, the priest had to reveal to his separated brothers the spirit and the heart of Jesus Christ.

Francis himself, in these perilous years, employed the most significant gesture of all this heroic apostolate: when accused of using magic and sorcery, or when threatened with death, he would break into a laugh, and—making a large sign of the Cross—he would say: "Here are all my signs and charms."

1596–1597: The Time of the Great Confrontations

Things were decidedly progressing at Thonon. The hostility of the people against the provost dwindled. Thonon got accustomed to his presence. A current of frank curiosity, and even of sympathy, passed through the town. Francis felt it, and, with the sense of the opportunist that characterized him, he hit upon a little stroke of daring. One market day he lectured a crowd of all classes: bourgeoisie, peasants, merchants . . . and they listened to him for two solid hours!

This was entirely too much. The town officials went to find their minister, Louis Viret, to persuade him to defy—once and for all, and publicly—"the papist priest". To defy Francis—Viret, who was scarcely trained in literature or theology and who, in addition, was timid, had little stomach for such a debate.

But Louis Viret could not dodge it. He suddenly summoned his confreres in the province, and, with them, several ministers from the district of Vaud. Together they organized a plan of attack in the presence of M. d'Avully, who was still president of the consistory. They decided that the debate with Francis would take place at the city hall, in a solemn and public meeting. Francis accepted the challenge.

On the specified day, and in the specified place, "the entire town of Thonon assembled out of curiosity". Francis was there. But none of the ministers appeared. Suddenly Pastor Viret came alone. He declared that he and his colleagues from the Chablais and from Vaud were ready for combat, but "that they did not deem it appropriate to begin a thing of such great importance without the express consent and permission of His Highness".

That did not hold! That same day, Francis went up to Allinges and obtained authorization from Baron de Lambert, successor to Baron d'Hermance. But Viret and his colleagues invented other pretexts to escape.

The shock to the crowd was considerable. "Many conversions found their stirrings here." And Francis profited from it by multiplying sermons, instructions, and catechizing. Winter, however, was rough in this beginning of 1596, and the missionary's errands did not pass without adventure. Every morning he had to cross over the Dranse River in order to say Mass, but the bridge was broken; a simple plank served as the deck between two piles, and this plank was then coated with ice. And so "he got down on his hands and knees on this plank, and crawling on hands and feet and knees he pushed himself across by sliding". The governor, informed of the situation, was so deeply moved that he had them refurbish the chapel of an ancient convent on the banks of the Dranse, at the foot of the cliff that overlooks the town. From that time on the provost would say Mass there.

The Abjuration of Antoine de Saint-Michel, Seigneur d'Avully

The recantation of Pastor Viret was destined to have a consequence of the highest importance for the mission of the Chablais: Antoine de Saint-Michel, the Lord d'Avully and president of the consistory, would finally take the decisive step of conversion. On February 19, 1596, in the church at Thonon, he confessed the Catholic Faith, and on August 26 he would make his abjuration in the presence of the nuncio from Turin.

We must carefully take the measure of this gentleman. Son of a Genevan family, this lord, "one of the most valiant in war", was at the same time one of the most learned and most headstrong Calvinists. A sermon by Francis at Annecy had initiated in him a desire for religious research. But how slow and prudent his progress was! His private conversations with Francis went on for more than a year. "Almost every day, in order to escape intruders, the provost and the baron would go out to the countryside with only two servants, whom they made wait at a distance while they disputed sometimes for the space of two or three hours." Loyally, Avully finally submitted his views to the ministers from Geneva and besought them to "answer him seriously and solidly". He got no response.

There was a great uproar in Geneva when news of this conversion reached there. One of the ministers, Antoine de la Faye, who was already regarded as the heir presumptive to Theodore de Bèze, lost no time announcing that he would go in person to Thonon and confront Baron d'Avully. This promise calmed the panic of the Thononais. Francis accepted the challenge, but la Faye delayed his visit. The baron grew impatient. Were the people going to suspect Francis of putting some obstacle in the way of this encounter? From the height of the pulpit he announced his decision: since Geneva did not come to Thonon, Thonon would go to Geneva. He then left in the company of Lord d'Avully, Poncet, Ducrest, Fourier, his cousin Louis, Rolland, and "several others from Thonon whom he had taken as witnesses", and they went "directly to the home of Minister de la Faye".

M. de la Faye could not escape. With great courtesy Francis allowed him the control of the dispute. Where did it take place? Some locate it in the public square at Molard, but not one Geneva chronicler speaks of it. Others say it was carried out in the very house of the minister. M. de la Faye's tactic was skillful; he successively raised questions about the Real Presence, Purgatory, the invocation of the saints . . . On the first point, Francis pressed the minister "so strongly" that the latter "became enraged, and he broke off the dispute by this tactic".

Avully came away from Geneva "confirmed" in his Catholic faith.

The Silences and Promises of the Duke of Savoy

When Duke Charles-Emmanuel learned of the daring enterprise of the provost, and of his success, he again considered elevating Francis to the rank of senator. There was indeed a question of this, although—in spite of his promises—the duke had still not granted to the missionary official authorization to reestablish the Catholic liturgy in Thonon, nor had he allocated money to place pastors in parishes or for maintaining more missionaries. How staggering is this letter that Francis wrote to the nuncio in September 1596:

> It is that that makes me still more desirous of going to Turin in person in order to obtain a declaration of His Highness' good pleasure. . . . If he is agreeable and promptly gives some orders, I shall return safe and certain of soon seeing the ripening of a happy harvest of several thousand souls. If, on the contrary, he does not give them, I shall request your blessing and permission to abandon this enterprise to others more capable than I. It breaks my heart to find myself unable to satisfy entire parishes that yearn to be fed holy Catholic doctrine for lack of means to send them a sufficient number of preachers and pastors to do this. . . . I can no longer remain alone here to become the scapegoat of our enemies, who — seeing that no one any longer gives any order — scorn my ministry, for which, however, I must be zealous in every way.

It was true, to the duke's relief, that the conversion of Henry IV singularly realigned the political chessboard at that time.

But at this point Charles finally made up his mind to summon Francis to Turin. Autumn had already settled in the Alps, and that made traveling dangerous. So what? The opportunity was too rare not to go to plead the cause of the Chablais at Turin, where it could be won. Francis set out on horseback, accompanied by his faithful George Rolland. They crossed over the Grand Saint Bernard, not without peril, and arrived at Turin. The nuncio, Jules Riccardi, welcomed them warmly. The duke manifested a sincere "joy": he admired the results already obtained by the missionary "without coming to any personal harm". He seemed to grasp remarkably the needs of the Chablais. He promised Francis his official support in the form of letters patent and granted him at once — from the benefices of the Church retained by the Knights of Saint Maurice-et-Lazare — the stipend for the six pastors. The duke also asked Francis to present in a report, which he would send to the nuncio, a comprehensive survey of his projects: Thonon deserved "the support of the entire duchy", the traditional religion would be established there, and a school would be founded for the youth. Francis returned to Thonon by way of the Petit Saint Bernard and Annecy, with his heart full of hope. Alas! All those beautiful promises were slow in being realized, and the Huguenots laughed about it.

However, Christmas was drawing near, and the desire for conversion abounded. At the beginning of December, Francis counted eighty converts, "as many among children as among adults".

The Three Christmas Masses at Thonon

At this time Francis made up his mind to execute a stroke of great daring: he would celebrate the three Christmas Masses in the Church of Saint Hippolytus. This news caused a great hullabaloo in the town. In spite of the juridic quibbling of the syndics and the threats—even armed—of the Huguenots against the workmen who came to repair the ruined altar, Francis held firm. "By the nobility of his countenance and the mildness of his words", he made the angry yield. A wooden altar was erected—temporarily, the syndics hoped.

Francis, helped by his friends, decorated the church

as best he could, because he was limited by having to start from scratch with pictures, rugs, candles, and lamps, and at midnight of the Nativity of our Lord Jesus Christ, he celebrated the Holy Sacrifice of the Mass before his children, who were weeping with joy and tenderness. He gave all of them Holy Communion, and—at the conclusion of the Mass, standing before the center of the altar—he explained the story of this birth with such great emotion and love that he inflamed their hearts with his intense, glowing zeal and heavenly love for the Divine Infant, born for the redemption of men. Then he celebrated a second Mass at dawn, and the third Mass between nine and ten o'clock.

The duke was forced to take a clear position. On January 5, 1597, the letter arrived that Francis had been expecting for three years:

Dear beloved and faithful Reverend Father,
    In response to what you have written, we declare that we find it good that you have had an altar erected in the Church of Saint Hippolytus, as well as the other good works that you are going to undertake there for the glory of God and the extirpation of heresies.

We are displeased by the opposition that you have encountered, but
that nonetheless you have surmounted, as you have described for us.
For which reason you are to continue with discretion and prudence
whatever you deem suitable.

Another equally cordial letter from His Highness granted Francis
immunity from the calumnies and interference of the Protestant syndics.

1597: The Visits to Theodore de Bèze

Although the Knights of Saint Maurice caused many delays and
tried hard to avoid eventually handing over the promised money for
the reinstatement of the pastors, Francis continued his apostolic action
as best he could: in the year 1597, he reopened the parish at Allinges,
then that at Cervens. On February 4 Pierre Fournier, counselor and
former first syndic of Thonon, solemnly abjured Calvinism. Lent was
reestablished at Thonon, not neglecting—to the great amusement of
the Protestants—the ceremony of ashes. As Easter approached, Francis
was worn out by preaching, confessions, and other ministry. "These
brothers," he wrote to Nuncio Riccardi on April 23, 1597, "the new
Catholics, have exhausted me by their general confessions, but I have
experienced a tremendous consolation seeing them so pious."

So much so that in the beginning of April Francis was obliged to
take a few days' rest at Sales. "I have been compelled", he had written
to the nuncio on April 11, "to get away for a few days in order to
attend the synod, to put in order certain matters, and to prevent an
illness with which I have been threatened for a long time. But this
absence will be brief, and I shall return soon after to continue my
interrupted works with more ardor."

"To put in order certain matters": the expression is spontaneously
nebulous, because among these "certain matters" there was a singularly
delicate mission wherein the least mistake could have made everything miscarry. It was a question—neither more nor less—of meeting,
man to man, the "patriarch of Geneva", Theodore de Bèze, Calvin's
successor. What circumstances could have inspired Francis with such
an audacious project? Bèze was ending his life as a great theologian, a

renowned writer, faithful to the Reformation, surrounded by the veneration of the entire Church of Geneva. But the rumor was spreading that, without changing his convictions, his aversion for the Roman Faith had been blunted, and that a rapprochement with it—if not a complete accord—was possible. In a public letter to King Henry IV, had he not expressed his desire for unity? He said, "If one could only know how to purchase it", he would give a "thousand livres" for it. Pope Clement VIII had been informed of this change of heart and had asked Francis to attempt a reconciliation.

Already, during the winter of 1596–97, Francis had tried to meet Bèze privately, but he had failed. Bèze was always "accompanied". Finally, on April 3, Francis, attended by his cousin Louis de Sales, was able to have the private interview for which he had yearned. Concerning this encounter we have—in Francis' handwriting—only the report that he sent to Clement VIII, dated April 21. It is an official report, brief, sober, in which results are noted, without any description of the scene. We are able to reconstruct it starting with the accounts left us by Longueterre, Rivière's father, and especially Charles-August de Sales.

When Francis and Louis presented themselves in the very house in which Calvin had lived and died, Theodore de Bèze was alone in his reception room. The conversation between the grand old man of seventy-eight and the young provost began with the courtesy and amiability that befitted two "lords", each of whom esteemed the frankness, honesty, and learning of the other. Soon, all the ice broken, Bèze led Francis into his study.

The conversation then became more personal. Francis told Bèze the purpose of his visit: knowing his "reputation for doctrine", he came to him "to reveal his most secret thoughts", and—wanting to have his opinion on certain points of controversy—he wished to chat with him "with doublet unbuttoned".

Bèze reflected a few moments and finally said to Francis: "Sir, you oblige me by much courtesy, and you proceed with me as I have always wished others to do, because I esteem nothing so much as candor and sincerity. What is more, I shall try to satisfy your propositions, though limited by the smallness of my mind and the experience I have acquired over so many years."

"Sir," Francis then said, "can one achieve his salvation in the Roman Church?"

This question took Bèze by surprise. He remained silent for some time, his eyes fixed on a corner of the room. "Permit me to think about this a bit more profoundly." And, giving Francis a little book "to peruse", he passed into the next room, where Francis heard him pacing. The interval lasted a quarter of an hour.

"You have asked me", Bèze said, "if one can achieve his salvation in the Roman Church. Certainly, I answer you affirmatively; it is possible without any doubt, and no one can deny the truth that she is the Mother Church."

Francis went on: "Since that is so, why have you planted this Reform with so many sackings, ruins, conflagrations, rapes, murders, destructions of churches, and other innumerable evils?"

"I do not deny", Bèze replied, "that you are achieving your salvation in your religion. But there is this misfortune that you embroil souls in too many ceremonies and difficulties, because you say that good works are necessary for salvation, which, however, are merely decency."

"Indeed," Francis replied, "can you ignore the reason why our Lord, when instructing his apostles as to what he wished them to expect at the Last Judgment, makes no mention of sins committed but speaks only of how he will condemn them because they will not have performed good works: 'Go, you accursed, to eternal fire: because I was hungry and you did not give me anything to eat.' And the rest. If these were merely decency, as you say, would we be punished so rigorously for having neglected to do them?"

At this Bèze lost his self-control, and "let himself utter a few words unworthy of a philosopher".

"Sir," said Francis, "I have not come here to vex you, God forbid! I have come only to confer with you about a few points of controversy and to explain frankly and in good faith my small objections, and I was hoping to know your feelings about them. But since I see that you are upset, I pray you to excuse me. This will never happen again through my fault."

Bèze had the graciousness "to acknowledge that he had been to blame". "One is not always in control of one's first feelings", he confessed, and he attributed this "incivility" to his zeal for religion. He now very courteously "invited the provost to come often: M. de Sales would oblige him enormously by paying him another visit."

Before leaving Geneva, Francis was able to distribute to a handful of Catholics the consecrated hosts that he had brought from Annecy. Among these clandestine communicants was Anne-Jacqueline Coste, that servant at the "Inn of the French Ecu" who—fifteen years later—would put herself at the service of the three first Visitandines.

On June 23, 1597, a messenger arrived from Rome, bearing a new brief from Pope Clement VIII dated May 20. The Pope lauded Francis for his "dedication to the Catholic Faith and for his zeal for the salvation of souls". Then, referring to the Bèze affair, he added: "Although this affair—whose happy issue we desire so earnestly—may, as you write, be very difficult, nonetheless—because it is a work of God, whose glory we seek and on whose mercy and assistance we lean—we vigorously exhort you not to abandon what you have begun, but, on the contrary, pursue it in an urgent manner with the help of God."

But Francis had barely returned to Thonon, at the end of April, when he was urgently recalled to Annecy. "I received word that our Most Reverend Bishop was very ill and that—feeling himself in danger of death—he was extremely desirous of seeing me. I set out immediately." Francis had no illusion as to the reason for this summons. At the end of 1594, he already knew that Bishop de Granier was thinking of making him his coadjutor with right of succession (E.A., XI, 386), and Duke Charles-Emmanuel had willingly agreed to this proposal, at least from January 1596. But this project met with a refusal from Francis.

His desires were turned in a totally opposite direction: the parish at Petit Bornand was without a pastor, and Francis applied for the title and its benefices so as "to have something to live on according to my condition". In exchange he would "offer his resignation from the provostship, while requesting only the favor of retaining the title of canon in order that, coming here (to Annecy) I may have a place in our choir because the Divine Office is celebrated there with such dignity that it is one of my great consolations."

Around February 8, 1596, he had replied to the duke's secretary: "As to the coadjutorship, all reasons and my own experience forbid my desiring it, and the duty, honor, and zeal that I have for my Most Reverend Lord Bishop will always prevent me from thinking of the bishopric as long as God allows him to be my prelate, and, once God will have deprived me of him, my own incapacity will prevent me from thinking of it" (E.A., XI, 182–83).

Things, for the time being, would remain there. Bishop de Granier, although not fully recovered, survived his crisis, and Francis was forced to let them relegate the project to an indefinite future.

He therefore returned to the Chablais. He conducted himself there as a veritable missionary leader because he had just been accorded three assistants: two Capuchins (Father Esprit de Baume and Father Chérubin de Maurienne) and a Jesuit (Father Jean Saunier). To these religious were added the pastor of Annemasse, the Reverend Balthazar Maniglier, and the canon Louis de Sales. Francis did not forget his mission regarding Theodore de Bèze. On July 3 he returned to Geneva; this time he was accompanied by Antoine Favre, recently named president of the Genevan council, and by Serge Suchet and the faithful Rolland. The interview took place "very secretly"; it lasted three hours. Starting with Bèze's proposition at the time of the first interview, "The Roman Church is the Mother Church", Francis maintained that there could not exist *two* true Churches. Bèze replied that the Roman Church was only a part of the universal Church; even if one granted that she is the principal part, it remained to be proved that she "had ever been ordained by God as the perpetual and infallible rule of truth". One could separate oneself from the Roman Church without leaving—for all that—the Catholic Church. In the course of this exchange, Bèze uttered these words of humility and sincerity: "If I am not in the right path, I pray God every day that, in his mercy, he will please put me there." The atmosphere was cordial, and when his visitors withdrew, Bèze followed them to the antechamber and shook the provost's hand.

There was a third interview, the exact date of which we do not know. It was not a question of faith, but Francis came to assure Bèze, on behalf of the Pope, that a pension of four thousand gold ecus would be bestowed on him in the event that, being converted, his possessions were to be confiscated by Geneva. Such was the misfortune of the time. To change religion meant to doom oneself to lose position, livelihood, and sometimes even to break away from one's dearest relations. We have no knowledge of the scenario of this third interview. What is certain is that Francis strove to keep in contact with the celebrated theologian of Geneva. We know, in particular, that in 1603, Francis—by now bishop—dispatched his friend and official André de Sauzea (who testified to it) to visit Bèze. Bèze died in 1605.

The Forty Hours at Annemasse

While Francis, in this spring of 1597, was conducting these proceedings in the greatest secrecy, his missionaries, in particular, the ardent Father Chérubin de Maurienne—with Francis' approbation—were erecting a more spectacular plan of action. This began with a project for a public conference between the pastors of Geneva and the Catholic missionaries, a project that got overshadowed by other things month after month. Then our missionaries decided to celebrate the Forty Hours at Annemasse, across from Geneva, on September 8 and 9, 1597. The idea found a very favorable response among the Catholics and the new converts of the Chablais. Considerable crowds set out on the way, in long processions, following a cross carried aloft. For two days this was the "festival" at Annemasse, a festival above all religious, but the ceremonies, processions, sermons, and so forth were mixed with popular songs and music—even the detonations of arquebuses. The star attraction was the erection of a cross facing Geneva, on the site of a ruined Calvary.

The Calvinists were dismayed. They decreed that on September 14 there would be a day of public and general penance in Geneva, and the minister, Antoine de la Faye, rapidly composed a "Brief Treatise Concerning the Virtue of the Cross and the Manner of Honoring It". To which Francis de Sales would respond with his "Defense of the Standard of the Cross", which would not appear until 1600, that is to say, too late. The missionaries exulted; Francis rejoiced for this homage rendered to the Cross, but he hardly appreciated the somewhat aggressive, provocative attitude that was mixed in it. He said: "We ought to act as we would during Holy Week: to uncover one side of the cross, then the other—little by little—and finally the whole cross, while reverently singing: *'Ecce lignum Crucis, venite adoremus'*" (E.A., XI, 258–59). Certain persons had wished that he would sometimes let loose with some words "of vinegar". To this he replied: "I assure you that whenever I have made use of stinging replies, I have repented of it afterward. Men accomplish more by love and charity than by severity and rigor." To the collection of these "stinging replies", we can ascribe this epithet, which he fired at Calvin in the course of a public instruction: "That stinker!" Stupefied, his listeners immediately blessed themselves with a great sign of the Cross.

Francis Accepts the Coadjutorship of Geneva

But Francis had still not said a "good round yes" to the project of the coadjutorship. A little while after the splendid ceremonies at Annemasse, Bishop de Granier decided to undertake the supreme assault against Francis' humility. One day while the provost was at Sales, the bishop dispatched his first almoner, Pierre Critain, to him. The day after his arrival, under the pretext of reciting the Breviary together, Critain led Francis into the gallery of the château and attacked him head on. Francis resisted a long time. Finally, he proposed to the chaplain that they go celebrate their Masses in the village church: "You say your Mass first, and I shall serve you; I shall say the second. We shall invoke the grace of God, and we shall do what he will inspire us to do." From prayer, Francis emerged vanquished. "You will tell the bishop", he said to Critain on the way back, "that I have never desired to be bishop. . . . But since he wishes it, and since he commands it, I am ready to obey and to serve God in all things." The duke, very favorable to Francis' candidature, was informed of this acquiescence, and, on August 29, 1597, he communicated to Bishop de Granier the letters patent by which—according to the custom of the time and the place—he "besought" the Pope and the Sacred College of Cardinals that they be willing "to promote Messire François de Sales, either for coadjutorship or otherwise".

Francis returned to Thonon, but only to hand over the charge to his colleagues. Because Francis appreciated his apostolic zeal (if not the bellicose accents of his voice), he placed at the head of the group Father Cyprien Chérubin, who—in complete charge—would accomplish considerable work in the Chablais.

A Serious Illness Delays Francis' Trip to Rome

Around October 20 Francis left Thonon and returned to Annecy. He had to make, in the name of Bishop de Granier (still convalescent), the *ad limina* trip for the diocese and submit to the formalities of his nomination of coadjutor.

But suddenly in November, at Annecy, Francis "took to his bed with a persistent and violent fever. He was burning up with internal flames and was reduced to such a piteous state that the physicians did not know what remedy to apply to him."

By the beginning of January Francis had reached that point of weakness where they despaired of his life. His mother came down to Annecy and "she was deputed to bear him the news of death". The invalid "was astonished at first"; then he was seized by a great fear of God's judgments. He overcame this crisis by throwing himself upon the mercy of God. The canons of the cathedral "came in a body to bid him final farewell and to ask his blessing". Exhausted by their visit, Francis fell into a faint "for the space of an entire hour" so deep that they thought he was dead.

He was then suddenly seized by a terrifying temptation against the Real Presence of Jesus Christ in the Eucharist. The trial was violent, and Francis was only able to deliver himself "by the sole invocation of the name of Jesus, uttered from the depth of his soul". When again in control of himself, Francis found the solution that he had been unable to find at the height of the crisis, but the memory of this struggle remained poignant to him. He never volunteered to reveal the argument of this temptation, and as for his remembrance of it, "he always made the sign of the Cross, fearing that it might be a stumbling block for weak spirits".

Francis was cured, thanks, it appeared, to "a bouillon of drinkable gold". The canons who had wept so much now came to regale him with a concert of zithers and lyres. And upon learning that his provost was out of danger, Bishop de Granier "came on foot"! The provost's convalescence lasted four months more: "Now that—by the divine goodness—I am convalescing, I still feel such weakness, especially in my legs," he wrote on January 14, "that I do not know if I shall be able to make the trip to Rome before Easter, although I desire infinitely to be there for Holy Week."

The few letters that have come down to us from this year 1598 were written by Francis while at Sales. In April he told the nuncio: "Today I am going to Thonon, where I shall be needed for some time." This was because Father Chérubin, whose mind teemed with ideas and who enjoyed great favor with the duke, had suggested to Francis that they organize at Thonon itself a feast of the Forty Hours even more grandiose than the Forty Hours at Annemasse.

On May 2, 1598, Philip II of Spain and Henry IV of France signed the Treaty of Vervins. There was thus, it would seem, to be a long period of peace for Savoy; the Chablais would henceforth be protected from the incursions from Geneva. The population could live without fear of reprisals and make their return to Catholicism, and Charles-Emmanuel would have his hands freer to aid, if he wished, the missionaries of the Chablais.

The provost immediately sought to profit from the advantages of the new state of affairs. In July several pastors—"mature men, well experienced in pastoral care"—were placed in some important parishes. Francis organized a movable team of missionaries, who canvassed the countryside while he sustained them with his word and even—if necessary—with his presence. On occasion he even shared their misadventures and their dangers.

The Forty Hours at Thonon

The Forty Hours at Thonon were prepared eagerly but very seriously: profane splendors were not permitted to eclipse the properly spiritual exercises and ceremonies. Finally, on September 20, after many material, financial, and diplomatic difficulties were resolved, the Forty Hours were begun. This was not an easy thing: Cardinal-Legate de Médici (the future Leo XI) would make a stopover on his return to Italy from France, and the duke, with his court, wished to attend the event!

These difficulties of organization were such that the date of the Forty Hours had to be postponed several times, and finally the decision was made to observe them twice.

The first observance took place on September 19, 20, and 21, with Bishop de Granier presiding. Duke Charles-Emmanuel arrived at Thonon September 28, and the cardinal-legate, with a grand cortège, arrived on September 30. The bishop and his clergy came all the way to Allinges to meet him, where the cannons of the fortress thundered in his honor; the duke advanced "with five hundred men"; the cardinal was right on time at the church to celebrate Mass. At the city hall, after the bishop had given the account of the mission, the duke took the provost by the hand and led him before the legate. "My Lord," he said to him,

> he whom I am presenting to you is the apostle of the Chablais; you see here a man blessed by God and sent from heaven to us. Inflamed with great zeal for the salvation of souls, he came into this province with the utmost courage and not without great peril to his life, to spread the word of God and plant the Cross of our Lord. As for myself, I have brought my sword here in order to reinforce his holy enterprises, but there is no one who can deny that all the praise for this good work is due only to him.

What must Francis have thought while listening to this panegyric? Perhaps he looked back upon his arrival, four years earlier, in a hostile, threatening Thonon—his preaching before six or eight persons more courageous than the others; his Masses, which he was obliged to celebrate in the protection of the fortress of Allinges; the duke's silences; the thievishness of the Knights of Saint Maurice; and all that he had endured . . . But was he a man to fall back upon his memories? Instead he gave thanks to the omnipotent God for all that he was seeing and hearing today.

For three days the Forty Hours was a feast that surpassed all expectations. Everything was splendid, according to the baroque taste of the time: decorations, banners, music, fireworks, songs, processions, sermons, bells, and the like. Father Chérubin was the great creator of these solemnities, for which he possessed an incontestable charism. "He astonished everyone", the duke wrote to the Pope.

In the morning and afternoon of Thursday, October 1, the cardinal, Bishop de Granier, and Francis received the abjurations from the pastor, Pierre Petit, M. de Fores, ten or twelve gentlemen, some distinguished personages, certain groups, entire families . . . The next day, the rhythm was accelerated still more. The secretaries finally inscribed only the names of the heads of families. In eleven days (because the lines got longer and longer) 2,300 names were registered, according to the list that is preserved in the Vatican Archives.

The nights of October 2 and 3, the erection of a great cross on the city square crowned these festivities. Everything was terminated in the night, with a final sermon by the provost. He preached on the Eucharist.

The cardinal-legate, dazzled, left Thonon on October 3 for Le Valais. He had personally reconciled three hundred converts, but he left to the bishop—the duke assured him—more than three thousand converts to reconcile. But this took place before the serious events that we must narrate here.

Truly to understand these events, it is important not only to put ourselves back "in the point of view of the times", as they say, but to grasp the conflict that was unleashed in Francis' heart, between the jurist and the apostle of Jesus Christ. It was only four or five years since Francis had terminated his law studies, but, like all jurists of that era, he had adopted the principle that was the foundation of the religious politics of the states: "One Faith, one King, one law" (*cujus regio, ejus religio*). Francis had even undertaken, as early as 1595, to draw up a memorial that would serve as an introduction to the *Code* of his great friend Antoine Favre; it is a severe, harsh memorial that reveals to us an unexpected Francis de Sales, an intransigent jurist: Protestantism was, in his eyes, not only a heresy but a political schism, which broke the nation in half. Francis had been bitterly conscious of the disastrous consequences of heresy in Savoy, in Paris, and, above all—since his missionary apostolate—in the Chablais: these spectacles were not carried out to soften his principles of law! Let us recognize it frankly. The "Introduction" of the *Code Fabrien* (Favre) contains some pages that we would find insupportable today (cf. Pl., LXIX). But from the time he entered the Church, the Protestant problem settled on Francis under a new light. As the apostle, he would seek the restoration of unity by conciliation, or rather by reconciliation. He saw clearly the mistake of the two parties, but he was convinced that a common return to the sources of the Christian Faith—the Bible, the Gospel, the Fathers—could bring together minds, and soon afterward, hearts. He had a total faith in the efficacy of the word of God whenever it was accepted by a sincere heart.

This tension between the jurist and the apostle explains the complexity of his attitude in the days that followed the departure of the cardinal-legate.

On October 5, the duke assembled his council in order to examine how Catholicism was to be officially restored in the Chablais. Francis explained his program there, and it was approved: reestablishment of the former pastors and restitution of the former possessions of the Church to the new pastors, removal of the minister Viret (who had been illegally maintained in Thonon and had already left there), replacing the master of the Huguenot school with a Catholic, returning the rights of the bourgeoisie to the Catholics of Thonon, and forbidding any Calvinist to exercise public office. On his own initiative the duke added another very serious decision: he insisted and demanded "that the exercise of the contrary religion" be "forbidden to all".

This last point aroused a tumultuous opposition on the part of the Calvinists. The duke, in order to reduce it, summoned to the city hall—probably around October 12—the council, the nobility, and the bourgeoisie. Bishop de Granier, Francis de Sales, and Father Chérubin were present. The duke energetically harangued his audience and declared that he desired to bring back "all his subjects" to the Church. He summoned them, he said, in order to know their final decision and to become acquainted with "his good servants and his good subjects". As the Huguenots resisted, the duke hurled his thunderbolts: "Let those who wear the white cross over their heart, who are of our religion or who desire to belong to it, stand to my right, and let those who wear the black outlines of heresy and who prefer Calvin's schism to the Church of Jesus Christ pass to my left." The division was made.

Then, turning toward his left, the duke declared: "Is it you, then—unfaithful to God and to your prince—who wish to usurp my place? I would have you know that I am your sovereign and your master!" Then, refusing any intercession, the duke called upon the recalcitrants: "You may go, but within three days, get out of my states." We observe that the situation is becoming purely political; the Faith had nothing much to do with these princely actions. Francis, nevertheless, did not protest.

The honest thing is to look at the other panel of this sad diptych. While the duke was thus separating "the sheep from the goats", a witness shows Francis going toward several resisters and inviting them "by gentle and pleasant persuasion" to pass to the right of the prince. Those who remained obstinate obeyed the duke's orders and took refuge at Nyon, on the other side of the lake. Francis did not abandon them: he soon obtained safe conduct for and renewed dialogue with them. He succeeded in convincing several among them, and not the least important. To minimize the fact, it is sometimes said that this exile scarcely concerned "twenty persons, about ten families". The number is unimportant: a single exile for a religious motive is too many. It is more important to mention the fact that is certain: that the Protestants desired to abjure—once they made that decision—only before Francis, because they knew the heart of their "adversary".

Without playing on the paradox, might we not maintain that the Protestants of the Chablais, by abjuring in the hands of Francis de Sales, were achieving a great victory from their side? Francis—without conceding any of his conviction that Calvinism was creating a very detrimental division to the unity of the state, and in proportion to his advancement in his apostolic career—for converting hearts, would count less and less on the force of arms, diplomatic finesse, and even theological disputes, but more and more on the power of the word of God: the Bible, the Gospel, the Fathers. The apostle would take precedence over the jurist; the provost's harangue would sweep him over the *Code Fabrien.* We are unable to follow this evolution throughout its curve! But at least we can try to point out the great moments. His plan for pacification in 1616 would undoubtedly represent his most generous effort. But it seems undeniable that Francis must owe this progress to his personal contacts with the Protestants of the

Chablais: Pierre Poncet, Seigneur d'Avully, and still others—even Theodore de Bèze. He discovered among them, in turn, some serious convictions, an honest research, and frequently a sincere piety. The war of arms, libels, and public discussions soon appeared unproductive to him. Truth and charity alone would "reconquer Geneva".

At the Forty Hours at Thonon, Francis, the missionary of the Chablais, garnered the fruit of his works and of his sufferings. There was reason to hope, he thought, that the entire province would be converted: "And so, winter having fled, spring was smiling; everywhere one saw rising 'the precious and resplendent tree' of the living Cross; from every side the Church was making her songs heard like the voice of the *turtle,* and, renewed and *flourishing* again, the *vines* were exhaling their *perfume.*" Thus Francis—he was thirty-one years old!—described the situation in the Chablais in 1598, in a report addressed to Clement VIII in 1603. But the Chablais was still to cost him much more concern.

5

"A RARE BIRD ON THE EARTH"

(The expression is attributed to Henry IV in 1602. Is it one of those "historic" statements that was never uttered? However it may be, Henry IV so strongly appreciated Francis de Sales—and his language was so familiar—that this eulogy has every chance of being authentic.)

1598–1602

Bishop de Granier's Substitute for the "Ad Limina" Visit

Around October 20, 1598, Francis de Sales left Thonon to go to Sales and to make final preparations for his trip to Rome. He brought into focus for the duke, and in concurrence with Bishop de Granier, a report concerning the Catholic revival in the Chablais. This was a juridic plan, in which things were envisaged according to the medieval conception of Christianity. The duke signed this report on November 12.

About November 12, 1598, Francis departed for Rome. He would deal there with all the affairs of the diocese. He was accompanied by the "vicar-general", M. de Chisse, nephew of the bishop, with the particular charge of asking Pope Clement VIII for the nomination of Francis to the dignity of coadjutor. Rolland was also with them on this trip. The travelers took the Saint Bernard route to Modena, where they joined Favre, who was on his way to Rome to defend the interests of Anne d'Este in the complicated succession of Hercule d'Este, the duke of Ferrara. The group reached Rome around mid-December.

Pope Clement VIII granted Francis an audience after the Christmas feasts. The Pontiff's reception was extremely cordial. He was well informed about Francis, and Cardinal de Médici had recently told him about the Forty Hours at Thonon. Francis submitted Bishop de Granier's requests concerning the Chablais; the Pope entrusted the study of these to three *commissaires*. This study would have to be both minute and lengthy because—considering the political situation of the moment—the decision had to be made whether or not it was expedient to include or exclude Geneva in the treaty of Vervins. Henry IV, the duke of Savoy, and the Pope were indulging in very subtle diplomatic warfare on this point!

There was nothing more to do but await the decisions. Francis took advantage of his enforced leisure by visiting all the holy places in Rome. It was thus that he had contact with Baronius, who had just succeeded Philip Neri at the head of the Oratory of Divine Love, and with Giovenale Ancina, with whom he formed a firm friendship. Through them he got to know this institution, and he became enthusiastic to the point of forming the project of introducing the Oratory in France and in Savoy.

Francis Faces an Examining Board of Cardinals and Theologians

On March 15 M. de Chissé obtained a second audience and presented the request for the coadjutorship to the Pope. The Pope showed immediately that he was very favorable. He summoned Francis and told him that he agreed to Bishop de Granier's desire, but he asked Francis to prepare to submit to the customary canonical examination: he, himself, Clement VIII, would preside over the jury. Imagine the embarrassment of Francis and de Chissé! By an indult of January 10, 1451, those chosen by the duke of Savoy were exempt from this examination. To submit to it here would be an offense to the duke. In fact, the ambassador of Savoy protested. Finally, everything was arranged. "It is only for my personal contentment", the Pope said, "that I desire this test, and to make better known the learning of the future bishop, which would make him recommendable to all the Sacred College."

On Monday, March 22, 1599, Francis presented himself at the

pontifical palace. The hall was "filled with distinguished personages". Eight cardinals were seated around His Holiness, among them Cardinal de Médici, Cardinal Borghesi, Cardinal Baronius, and Cardinal Borromeo; twenty archbishops and bishops; generals of religious orders. Father Bellarmine was prominent among the theologians responsible for debating with the candidate. This was indeed an honorary jury! They posed, it appears, thirty-five very difficult questions. Everything went marvelously well. The Pope did not conceal his satisfaction—so much so that at the end of the examination, omitting all protocol, he stood up, walked toward Francis, embraced him, and said to him, quoting the Book of Proverbs: My son, "drink water from your own cistern, flowing water from your own well. Should your springs be scattered abroad, streams of water in the streets?"

This success elsewhere embarrassed Francis. What tales would they tell about this in Annecy? He wrote to his cousin Louis on March 26: "I am grateful that God did not permit us to be confused during the examination. . . . I assure you that M. le Grande Vicaire came away from the consistory more joyful than I. This faithful friend is only too eager to describe to Savoy the signs of paternal kindness with which the Pope honored me, which oblige me—more than ever—to be a good son and a good servant of the holy Roman Church, but whatever our friends write, remember that friends often exaggerate our good traits whereas our enemies exaggerate our faults" (E.A., XII, 6).

At the end of March 1599, our travelers were preparing to return to Savoy. On March 24 Pope Clement VIII had signed the decree granting to the bishop of Geneva a great many of the favors he was requesting, and he named Francis de Sales bishop of Nicopolis (in Bulgaria) and coadjutor of the bishop of Geneva. On March 25, Francis assisted at the Pope's Mass in Saint Peter's. There he received "some particular favors from our Lord", the meaning of which he consigned to a little notebook from which we take the text:

Having received the Blessed Eucharist from the hand of the Sovereign Pontiff on the feast of the Annunciation, my soul was consoled interiorly, and God granted me the grace of giving me great lights concerning the mystery of the Incarnation, making me know in an inexplicable manner how the Word took a body, by the power of the Father, and by the operation of the Holy Spirit, in the chaste womb of Mary, truly wishing himself to *dwell among us,* so that he would be a man like us. This Man—God also gave me an elevated and delightful understanding of *Transubstantiation,* of its entry into my soul, and in the ministry of the pastors of the Church.

March 31, 1599, Francis left for Savoy through Loretto and Turin. At Turin, where he arrived around April 15, Francis had much to do. This was because the Knights, made aware of Pope Clement's decisions to command them to restore the ecclesiastical benefices necessary for the reestablishment of the parishes and pastors, and for the maintenance of pastors and preachers, raised many objections, even at the ducal court. But they got nowhere. They soon perceived that under the benignity of the prelate were hidden the rigor of the jurist, the justice of the apostolic man, and a hardy love of the poor.

The Coadjutor of Bishop de Granier

Francis did not arrive in Savoy until June 1, 1599. For three years the "titular bishop of Nicopolis" was going to live in the shadow of Bishop de Granier—a shadow that he loved, and one, so to speak, that he created. Through poverty of finances and humility of spirit he did not ask for the publication of his bulls of the episcopacy, which he received finally on July 15, 1602. "He even refused to be called bishop"; he did not wish "any other vestments, or any other name or rank than that of provost of the cathedral" (A.S., 198–99). But he could not prevent the people from venerating him: in the eyes of all, he was the missionary who "converted thousands of souls".

It was, as it was proper, in the name of the ruling bishop that the coadjutor—nothing honored this name better—dealt with all the outstanding affairs. These affairs, for the most part, concerned the Chablais, where joys and disappointments alternated. The parishes were organized little by little but not without difficulties, because the knights of Saint Maurice were raising many obstacles to the restitutions that the duke had imposed on them.

But Francis was tenacious. He went forward, trusting in the "right hand of the Most High" and "the power of Christ". He wanted to make of Thonon the "bulwark" against Geneva: he sought to establish a Jesuit school there. The Pope approved and promised financial aid, but the provincial lacked Jesuits; its realization would only be modest and fleeting. He also envisioned a community of eight priests, inspired by the spirit of the Oratory, but this project would stagnate for lack of men and lodgings. At Thonon there was also to be a "hospice" to receive the converts from the neighboring areas, in particular from Geneva, who would be banished from their homelands and deprived of their possessions; but how would they live? The allocations were supposed to come from Rome. For all these projects Francis strove as actively as possible, appealing to Rome through the nuncio and to the ducal court. One man—whom he greatly loved and whose zeal he appreciated—helped him, but annoyed him with the impracticability of his personal projects. This was Father Chérubin, who envisaged the creation of a vast complex: an "inn" that would attract youth from every country, the "learned and the artistic" of the surrounding towns, in order to teach them "all the arts and sciences, literature, and languages". In order to finance this they would make an appeal to the generosity of all the Catholics of every country, through the mediation of a "league". Clement VIII seemed favorable to this tremendous project, and, by the bull *Redemptoris* (September 13, 1599), "erected and instituted in perpetuity" a house that would be called the "Inn of All Sciences and Arts", under the patronage of "our Lady of compassion", and he named his "dear son, Francis de Sales", prefect of this "Holy House". Francis, all the while admiring this project, clearly perceived the difficulties that it raised. Not until 1602 did its realization begin.

The French Invade Savoy

Events were going to complicate the situation even more. It is impossible to explain here this imbroglio, which Duke Charles-Emmanuel had created by his over-craftiness. Here are at least the main points of the quarrel between Henry IV and the duke. Taking advantage of the internal difficulties in France, at the end of the reign of Henry IV, the duke took possession of the marquisate of Saluces. In 1598, at the time of the peace of Vervins between France and Spain, the problem of Saluces had only been temporarily resolved. In December of 1599, the duke went to Paris to regulate it permanently. At the Treaty of Paris the duke pledged himself to give to France, in place of the marquisate, Bresse, Bugey, and the districts of Gex and Valromey. The duke put off executing his pledges and fomented a conspiracy with Brion, but Henry IV sensed the treachery. In August of 1600, war broke out between France and Savoy. Bernese and Genevans were soon supporting France and again penetrated the Chablais. The French victories were terrifying. Soon Savoy, torn into two or three strong factions that were not long in falling, was invaded. Between October 5 and 8, Henry IV appeared at Annecy.

On that day the positions of Bishop de Granier and his coadjutor were very tenuous. Annecy was in fact the territory of Duke Henry of Genevois-Nemours, and Duke Henry was, at the same time, the subject of the King of France and the duke of Savoy. In the conflict that then had Henry IV and Charles-Emmanuel opposing each other, the duke of Nemours had remained neutral. On October 5, he therefore hastily received the King—victorious over his duke. The *"Vert-Galant"* was accompanied by the Marquise de Verneuil, and he dined unabashedly in the Château d'Annecy "with his beautiful mistress in full view of everyone". This same October 5, at Florence, the official marriage, by proxy, of Henry IV and Marie de Médici was celebrated!

Bishop de Granier's embarrassment was great. Was it necessary for him to go to greet the King? He finally resolved to do so in order to intercede for the Chablais, devastated once more by war. "For the love of God, of our Holy Father the Pope, and in consideration for you as well," the King replied, "nothing will be introduced in the province of the Chablais contrary to what has been done for the Faith, and this I promise you on my blood oath."

Several days later the King set out again for the countryside, because Duke Charles-Emmanuel did not admit defeat. In fact, some powerful heretics were already governing in the Chablais, and they wanted to reestablish the exercise of the false religion and to have the ministers who followed them mount the pulpits again.

Peace was finally signed at Lyons on January 17, 1601, between the plenipotentiaries of the duke of Savoy and those of the King of France. Charles-Emmanuel kept Saluces, but he was obliged to restore Bresse, Bugey, Valromey, and the district of Gex to France. The King restored to Savoy the "mandate" of Gaillard between Ternier and the Chablais. What would become of Catholicism in these regions (of which several depended upon the bishopric of Geneva-Annecy), at a time when the King had no scruples about having notorious Huguenots govern in his name?

During these uncertainties, Francis saved the Chablais a second time. He personally scoured the territory at the risk of being arrested by the King's soldiers; he rekindled courage, supported the missionaries who were dispersed through fear of the Genevans and the Bernese, and comforted his pastors, "most of whom remained in their parishes, although a few of the more timid had withdrawn to see how things were going to end". He confronted the occupation authorities and engaged in several juridic and diplomatic battles. Nonetheless, in May 1600, the book that Francis had written in response to an old pamphlet by the minister la Faye, namely, *The Defense of the Standard of the Holy Cross of Our Lord Jesus Christ,* finally appeared at the Pillehote bookstore in Lyons. This response came too late; its success was not what might have been expected, but it effectively helped many souls to remain faithful under the new tornado that was buffeting the Chablais.

Taking stock of the situation during the years 1599 to 1601, in a letter dated March 18, 1601, to Nuncio Riccardi, Francis was able to offer him this "consolation".

If . . . at Thonon and at Ternier . . . we suffered much under the government of M. de Montglat, the Huguenot, and through the diverse ambushes of the Genevans (at Ternier, especially, they had behaved tyrannically and committed such desecrations and indignities to sacred things that they cannot be mentioned), nonetheless, in spite of all that, among such a great number of converts, we found only four who had relapsed, and these were of low status. Thus we have been gratified that their conversion was indeed the work of the right hand of the Most High, since *as an aftereffect* they celebrated the Christmas feast days with a fervor that was totally unusual.

Francis would soon (June 28, 1601) be able to announce to the nuncio that "in spite of the war, the number of converts had increased since Christmas", and several months later (December 21, 1601) he informed Msgr. Tartarini, successor to Nuncio Riccardi:

> Our progress . . . is very gratifying, not only at Thonon and at Ternier—because that is already old—but also quite recently in the districts of Gex and Gaillard, which extend as far as the gates of Geneva. In the second of these districts, last week the bishop of Geneva reconciled eight churches for the use of several thousand souls brought back to the Faith since Pentecost. In the first, which submitted to the King of France, three parishes have been erected, in which three of our canons have been installed to preach; they are producing much fruit. . . . Some others are being converted, and others are disposed to conversion.

Thus Francis dreamed of realizing at last, in Thonon, his project of the "Holy House" . . . without any further illusion about the obstacles that he would have to hurdle. "But," he said, "it is above all necessary that we soon put our hand to work earnestly and seriously, because good intentions are of little use. If this good cannot be carried out at once, let it at least be done little by little, starting with the most essential projects, such as the school, the seminary, and so on, successively."

The Death of M. de Boisy

In this year of 1601, at the request of Bishop de Granier, Francis preached the Lenten sermons at Annecy. Although even at the start of the year Francis' father—now an old man of eighty years—was very ill, Francis agreed to take the preaching assignment. On Friday, April 6, he had selected as his theme Martha's words to Jesus: "Lord, he whom you love is ill" (Jn 11:3). At the moment he was going to mount the pulpit, the Reverend Aimé Bouvard informed him that on the previous evening, M. de Boisy had "very gently rendered his spirit to God". Francis, joining his hands and raising his eyes to heaven, adored God and did not hesitate to stand in the pulpit, where he maintained such composure and delivered his sermon so well that no one even suspected that he was so troubled. After finishing his epilogue, he changed appropriately and startled the congregation with these words: "Coming to you, I learned of the death of the person to whom I am most obliged in this world: my father is dead. I ask two things of you: one is that you excuse me for a day or two so that I may render him the last duties; the other is that you will please pray to God for the repose of his soul." Then they saw that he was weeping.

Before dying, M. de Boisy summoned all his children who were then at Sales, and he "left them his son Francis for their father". This was a weighty burden that would be added to Francis' responsibilities as coadjutor: Gallois, the eldest, was married and living as a country gentleman; Louis, twenty-three years old, was completing his studies in Italy; Jean-François, twenty-two years old, was destined for an ecclesiastical career; Bernard and Janus were still in school; Gasparde had married Melchior de Cornillon in 1595; and Jeanne was still a child seven years old. For the present, Mme de Boisy would continue to live in the Château de Sales. And, thanks to Francis and Louis, the family continued to live in perfect union.

Lent ended; Bishop de Granier and his coadjutor set out to visit the parishes of the Chablais that had been stricken by the war and to reorganize them.

Bishop de Granier Sends Francis to Paris on a Diplomatic Mission

Now the bishop found himself confronting a delicate problem: Henry IV had shown himself very favorable to reestablishing Catholic worship in the district of Gex, which signified that pastors for the twenty-six parishes of the region were to be reinstated, but—caught between the favorable attitude to the Catholics and his concern about not displeasing Geneva—the King said nothing about restoring to these pastors the benefices stolen by the Protestant pastors. But on what would these priests live if they did not recover those revenues? Bishop de Granier asked at Rome that His Holiness exert some pressure on the king; Rome entrusted the affair to the nuncio at Paris. But the nuncio was not well informed as to the religious situation in that distant and modest land of Gex; he would have to have a competent counselor. Bishop de Granier, whose health was very poor at this time and who for three years had become accustomed to entrusting his most serious cares to his coadjutor, dispatched Francis to Paris to negotiate with the nuncio and the King.

Diplomat and Missionary

This diplomatic mission, which might have been only a limited and ephemeral episode in the life of the future bishop of Geneva, would have considerable effects on his destiny. During the nine months of his stay, Francis, the humble Francis, was going to conquer the King, the court, all Paris—and in return the King, the court, and Paris would make of him a celebrity of national dimension.

On Wednesday, January 2, 1602, Francis de Sales took, for the second time in his life, the Paris route. He was accompanied by Canon Déage and Antoine Favre, who had been called to Paris for the lawsuit of Anne d'Este. Tuesday, January 22, the little troop entered the capital.

In memory, perhaps, of his student days, Francis took lodgings on the rue Saint-Jacques. How Paris had changed in fourteen years! Nonetheless, he again found the walls with the fortified gates, and its thousand chapels and churches. The Collège de Clermont had been closed and its teachers expelled after the treason of Chatel against the King. What must have been Francis' prayer before the Black Virgin of Saint-Étienne-des-Grès!

Francis busied himself with his mission at once. Upon his arrival he presented himself to the nuncio, Msgr. Innocent del Bufalo, who proved himself to be well-disposed to Francis' homeland, but who clearly foresaw that nothing could be done in behalf of the Catholics of Gex unless they first won over to their cause M. de Villeroy, to whom the King had confided France's foreign affairs. On February 8, the provost was formally introduced to Villeroy by the nuncio, and they held a long and difficult conference. Francis wrote that same day to Bishop de Granier: "Well, I have had to argue persuasively in behalf of our claims. Nonetheless, in the end, I gave him my fundamental request, whereupon he told me that the council would give us justice and right and that we should not doubt that."

This was without taking into account the political eventualities: Spain, France, Savoy, and Geneva were soon to enter a complex diplomatic pact, and the Genevan delegates knew how to profit from it very skillfully. Matters dragged on.

At least this enforced stay in Paris was of very great apostolic and humanistic profit for Francis: it uprooted him—once and for all—from any regional particularism and made him confront the great problems of the world and of the time. When he would leave Paris, he would do so having experienced the most brilliant court in Europe, with its grandeurs but also with its intrigues and its power plays. He would have preached to and enthralled beneath his pulpit the most demanding of audiences, often as frivolous as they were sensitive. He would have been involved in the astonishing religious renewal that was then at work among the high Parisian society: "Saints, veritable saints, and in great numbers, everywhere", said Bremond (Br, I, 95). Francis would leave a firm impression on many minds and hearts.

Lent and the Louvre

Everything originated—if we judge from natural causes—from the fact that at Paris, Francis sometimes visited the home of the princess of Luxembourg, the duchess of Mercoeur: "There was there", Francis observed, "a nostalgia that I could not miss because it was hereditary to me: my father, my grandfather, and my great-grandfather had all had the honor of being reared there as page boys, and they had spent much of their life in that house of the very illustrious princes of Martigues who had been the father, the grandfather, and the great-grandfather of the duchess." But it so happened that shortly before Lent of 1602, "by luck the Queen's chapel in the Louvre was in need of a preacher". The Duchess de Longueville, cousin of the Duchess de Mercoeur, was supposed to provide a preacher, and so Francis was petitioned. Having nothing much else to do but await the outcome of his diplomacy, Francis did not see how he could refuse to accept: "I have been compelled, through courtesy, to preach in the Queen's Chapel three times a week", he wrote on March 9, 1603, to M. de Quoex, "before the princesses and courtiers, because I was unable to refuse the pleas and commands that were made to me".

"But," he subtly added, "this is undertaken without impeding the canvass that I am gradually making in order to influence the mood of those in control of the Gex affair, the primary matter demanding my attention." In spite of having been improvised, this Lenten series was nothing less than an unequivocal success. Antoine Favre wrote, very elated, to Bishop de Granier: "He is considered to be the best preacher that France has had in a long time in this important post." This was the era, moreover, when du Perron (the future cardinal) and Father Coton (the Jesuit) were triumphing! But Francis preached, as was his custom, with a totally angelic simplicity, without resorting to grand vocal effects or "fancy gestures"! He was also not unaware that—either through curiosity or politics—some Protestants had slipped into his audience. Such a one was this Dame de Predreauville, so well informed about her Calvinism that the most learned elite had failed to convert her. However, after having heard Francis in the pulpit and in private conversation, she abjured to the stupefaction of "the whole city of Paris". And her family soon followed her example. Francis, however, had said nothing in his sermons against Calvinism. This experience confirmed him in his conviction that the solution of religious conflict resulted less from learned discussions than by the explanation of the truth, totally inspired by love. He said: "Since I have always said that whoever preaches with love preaches enough against the heretics, even though he does not say a single word against them. . . ." And du Perron acknowledged it in an echo: "If it is a question of convincing the Calvinists, I could go to the limit with them; if it is a question of converting them, lead them to Monsieur de Genève."

A little incident added the final touch to Francis' high rating in Paris. Lent ended, and the Duchess de Longueville had a "very beautiful purse filled with shiny gold ecus" delivered to Francis, who refused it. Never in the memory of the courtiers had they witnessed a comparable detachment!

The Bishop and the King

Around this time there occurred an event that gave a more favorable turn to the negotiations. Henry IV, having heard of the great praises heaped upon the preacher at the Louvre, "wished to see him in the pulpit". Francis therefore traveled to Fontainebleau, and on Quasimodo Sunday, April 14, 1602, he preached before His Majesty. The King even played a trick on his Protestant friends, the delegates from Geneva: he invited them to come with him to hear Francis their bishop! The King "gave evidence of his pleasure" with the sermon and with the preacher. After the sermon he granted Francis a long audience. This was a stroke of luck. Francis wrote to Quoex on April 18:

> I have just returned from Fontainebleau where—if I had not been so fortunate—all my negotiating would have been ruined. I have accomplished so much, however, that I have regained some good hope. In two or three days I should have the resolution of the affair. This may not be—perhaps—as satisfactory as we would like, but we must snatch from the fire whatever can be saved. This will still be much more than what the experts speak of. The pace of affairs in this court is so difficult that when one thinks he has extricated himself, he finds he is more entangled.

Decidedly, the future bishop of Geneva was attending a rough school. From disappointment to hope, from hope to disappointment, things dragged on until September . . . and the gain, in fact, would be meager. Giving an account of his mission to Pope Clement VIII, Francis would draw up this disillusioned balance sheet:

> It seemed that nothing was contradicting our hope for the desired success. But, oh, the wretchedness of our times! After having made so many visits for the sake of this negotiation, we have scarcely gained the authorization to celebrate the sacred mysteries in three localities, with the concession, to this effect, of an annual revenue for our priests. As for the rest, the King himself epitomizes for us the harshness of the times: "I would desire more than anything else", he says, "the entire reestablishment of the Catholic religion, but my power is not my pleasure", and similar remarks. And so it is that after nine full months, I have been compelled to put an end to negotiations without having achieved virtually anything.

"Without having achieved virtually anything": the statement is correct, perhaps—although severe—concerning the plan for the negotiations. As to the spiritual plan, on the contrary, Francis had accomplished much; he had observed and learned a great deal more.

The Spiritual Radiance of Francis

He preached "more than a hundred times" in several churches; he heard confessions; he made converts; he visited convents and monasteries; he helped some of them, such as the celebrated royal abbey of Montmartre, in their reform. He was sought after everywhere, and he did not know how to refuse. At Paris—taking into account the difference in situations—he was still doing missionary work in the Chablais.

Above all, he was presented by Pierre de Bérulle, at that time a simple priest and eight years his junior, at the mansion of Madame Acarie, whom Bremond does not fear to call "a new Teresa" (of Avila). We must study this encounter: it marks, in fact, a capital moment in the formation of Francis as the spiritual master. It is not enough to say or to note that—in this Acarie circle—Francis made the acquaintance of "what Paris considered the most devout". We must also add that these persons, to whom France owed her "spiritual spring" in the seventeenth century, found themselves representing— each in his or her way—all the most important currents of Catholic spirituality. Indeed, we can affirm, without risk of exaggeration, that the *Treatise on the Love of God* would not be the perfect "grammar of the spiritual life" that it is, if Francis had not lived several months— and almost daily—in the intimacy of the Acarie circle. "He went there almost every day on foot, from the rue Saint-Jacques as far as the street behind the Church of le Petit-Saint-Antoine, in the mud which was everywhere in Paris."

Whom would he encounter in this "company"? First there was Mme Acarie herself. This brilliant woman of the world, the daughter and the wife of magistrates, who was called "la belle Acarie", lived—in the world and under the tyrannical authority of her husband—an extraordinary mystical life: ecstasies and other supernatural phenomena were habitual with her. She was saddened by these states, strove to resist them, and remained confused by them. She feared that this was only diabolical delusion. As soon as she came to know Francis de Sales, Mme Acarie had complete confidence in him, and she would have liked him to guide her. But he, knowing that she already had a good director, remained silent and very reserved. He only agreed to hear her confession, and he never questioned her concerning the extraordinary graces that the Holy Spirit showered upon her. Later, he would experience a kind of regret for this: "Oh, what a fault I committed when I did not profit from her very holy conversation: because she had freely revealed to me her whole soul, yet because of the great respect that I bore her, I did not dare to inquire about the least thing." Not that he himself had not experienced, on several occasions, these privileged states in which God renders himself exceptionally present to the heart, but each experience, in these kinds of graces, is original; each soul has something to learn from the souls of others and to teach other souls.

At least it was in this Acarie group that the resolution to introduce the reformed Carmel of Saint Teresa of Avila (who had died twenty years previously) was revived. At the conference in which this was discussed, Francis spoke last, and his favorable advice predominated. The Pope and the King agreed. In 1604 the first French Carmelite convent was founded in the suburb Saint-Jacques. Later, Mme Acarie's three daughters entered the order; she herself, when her husband died, asked for admission in the capacity of a lay-sister, and it was in this humble employment that she died in Pontoise in 1618, under the name of Marie de l'Incarnation.

One of the most illustrious members of the Acarie circle was the youthful Bérulle. With him Francis planned to introduce the Oratory of Philip Neri into France. There was also Benedict of Canfeld, of English origin, who was fully conversant with northern mysticism; Dom Beaucousin, vicar of the Chartreuse de Paris and spiritual director of Mme Acarie; André Duval, doctor of the Sorbonne; Jacques Gallemand, one of the most versatile artisans of the religious renaissance in France; Asseline; Marillac . . . In the Acarie circle there thus flowed certain spiritual currents coming from Spain, Italy, the Rhineland, and France. The abstract, mystical Rhineland tendency was dominant; they felt very much attracted by the "ultra-contemplative life" of direct union with the Divine Essence, even beyond the humanity of Christ. Francis de Sales plainly took the position—right from the start—in favor of Teresan mysticism, in which the solid, evangelical virtues were much preferable to visions, revelations, and ecstasies. His original spirituality was reaffirmed. With an astonishing certitude he discerned in each of these tendencies what was good, viable, and salutary, but he clearly marked their limitations and even the dangers of excess and deviation. He harmonized them and, beginning with his activities and letters of this time, we see him orienting those men and women who asked for his advice with a firmness that found its perfect expression in the *Introduction to the Devout Life* and the *Treatise on the Love of God.* How could one of our great historians of French spirituality write of this Francis of 1602: "He kept silence, observed, admired, criticized, kept a watch on himself, worked diligently, and absorbed the atmosphere . . . in this School of Saints, which he entered in order to graduate", Br, I, 74–76.

When, at the end of September 1602, Francis departed for Savoy, he left behind some profound friendships. These friends watched him go away with great regret. And the King was not the last to wish to detain him. The admiration—we might even say the sympathy—that Henry felt for Francis de Sales is one of the most curious features of their relationship. Everyone quotes these words of the King speaking of the coadjutor from Savoy as "a phoenix of bishops", or again, "he is a rare bird on this earth". These theatrical expressions do not reveal the affection of Henry IV for Francis. The two men had certain qualities in common: finesse, wit, good common sense that went right to essentials, a "round simplicity", and a certain charm that no one could resist . . . only, they each made different uses of these shared qualities!

Maurice Henry Coüannier would have liked, he said, "to have overheard a dialogue between these two conquerors". He is not alone. Whatever Henry IV was, one fact is certain; he would have been happy to have enticed Francis de Sales away from the duke of Savoy and to have annexed him to the hierarchy of France. After all, did not a part of the diocese of Geneva—minimal, it is true—belong to the realm? Henry IV considered this project very seriously. He said of the coadjutor: "He possesses all the virtues to the sovereign degree of their perfection. I know of no one more capable of restoring the episcopal state to its pristine splendor." But Francis diplomatically refused the royal proposition: "He was", he said, "called to the diocese of Geneva; he was indebted to his fatherland, which had nourished him and reared him until now."

The King tried in vain to insist and to beleaguer Francis through those whom he knew to be influential and related, such as the duchess of Mercoeur and Princess de Longueville. Nothing came of this. The King "gave him his word that he would name him to the first vacant archbishopric, and he assigned him a generous pension while awaiting it". Francis was indeed embarrassed; he extricated himself from the situation with a very . . . Salesian . . . dexterity: "Sire, I thank Your Majesty with all my heart for the thoughtfulness that you have condescended to bestow on me. I accept, yes, I accept with a very great affection your royal liberality, but thanks to our Lord, I am now in such a position that I have no need of this pension. Consequently, I very humbly beg Your Majesty that your present be kept within the safekeeping of your treasurer, and I shall avail myself of it whenever I shall have need of it."

The King was a good sport. He said, "Now that is the wittiest refusal that I have ever heard." Several years later, the tenacious Henry IV would again attempt to attract Francis de Sales to France. He was thinking of making him a cardinal and—it was said—he would gladly have seen him archbishop of Paris! Francis, around 1608, was ready to obey . . . if Pope Paul V had wished it (E.A., XIV, 9–10).

As he was passing through Lyons, on September 29, 1602, Francis learned that Bishop de Granier had died ten days previously. For the coadjutor this was a very "sad blow". He wept copiously.

The Episcopal Consecration of Francis in the Church at Thorens

Francis' lot was thus fixed: he had "to undertake the laborious and dangerous burden of a bishop". "Let God's will be done", he wrote to a friend on October 21, 1602. "I am still as I was formerly: I no more desire to be bishop now than I desired it in the past. If it comes to me, it will have to be borne; if not, I shall feel so much better." How could the episcopacy not come to him? The consecration was set for December 8. "I have received the episcopal consecration on the day of the Conception of the Virgin Mary, our Lady, into whose hands I have confided my lot", he would write on January 10, 1603, to Msgr. Ancina, bishop of Saluces.

Francis chose Thorens for the solemnity of his consecration to satisfy a pious desire of his mother. "The reason is that that was where my mother and my brothers lived. It was also the desire and the request of the people, and—beyond that—there is my natural inclination to my fatherland, which seemed to merit this from me to see me anointed pontiff, even as it had seen me born and made a Christian."

He wished to prepare himself for this grace of consecration by making a long retreat.

> He wrote to Father Jean Fourier of the Society of Jesus, who was at that time in Thonon, begging him to do him the favor of coming to Sales to serve him as director in the review that he wished to make of his entire life. Being thus delivered from all other thoughts, Francis remained for the space of twenty days almost in solitude, and by continual prayers, fasts, mortifications of the body, and similar disciplines, he prepared himself for the general confession of his sins; after which he prescribed for himself a manner of living with the advice of his wise director.

Mother de Chantal affirmed having seen and read these rules of life "written by his own hand". They constitute, in themselves, a short treatise on the apostolic ideal such as the Gospel and the Church propose it: poverty, fasting, almsgiving, prayer, confession, relations with his "people", and—at the center of all this life of union with God and of love of neighbor—"the most Holy Sacrifice of the Mass, which he would celebrate every day, unless prevented by some extreme necessity. . . . It would not be inappropriate that—on days that are called days of devotion—he should celebrate Mass in the churches where the particular devotion was to be observed, so that the people coming to it might always find their bishop at their head, as on the solemn feasts of those churches." The retreatant insisted that Father Fourier put his signature on this rule of life.

On December 8, "they began early in the morning to walk from Sales to Thorens". The little parish church had been decorated and tapestried by Mme de Boisy as much as she could. The "prelates for the consecration" were Vespasian Gribaldi, archbishop of Vienne (France), primate of the Gauls; Thomas Pobel, bishop of Saint-Paul-Trois-Châteaux; and Jacques Maistret, Carmelite and bishop of Damascus (in partibus infidelium). Mme de Boisy was seated in the first pew, and behind her the nobility of Savoy were assembled. The ceremony proceeded according to ritual. But just as Francis was on his knees before Vincent Gribaldi, "the consecrator", his face became resplendent, as it had formerly in the chapel at Loretto, "not without great astonishment to everyone". What happened?

Mother de Chantal relates to us "the very words" that she gathered from what Francis himself told her. "In this action of his consecration it seemed to him, naïvely, that the most adorable Trinity was interiorly imprinting on his soul what the bishops were doing exteriorly on his person. It even seemed to him that he saw the most Blessed Mother of our Lord, who placed him under her protection, and the apostles Saints Peter and Paul were protecting him." A supranormal phenomenon or a high level of faith? What is certain is that for a month after this "consecration", Francis spoke only "like a stranger from another world"; and, on December 14, 1602, at the ceremony of his solemn enthronement in the cathedral church in Annecy, during the sermon that he preached to the people after Vespers, he was suddenly "as though rapt in ecstasy, and he recounted—without being aware of it—the marvels that had happened to him at the time of his consecration".

In order to form as objective an idea as is possible about this moment of fervor, we ought to read attentively what Francis would write ten years later, on the anniversary of his consecration, to Mother de Chantal: "I said in my sermon that it has been ten years since I was consecrated, that is to say, that God has taken me out of myself in order to take me to him and then give me to the people, in other words that he had converted me from what I was for myself into what I was to be for them." He would speak in 1619 of the "burning sensation in his heart" that he experienced at that time.

December 8 . . . Thirteen days later there occurred what the historians call the Escalation of Geneva. On the night of December 21 or 22, the duke unleashed the attack that he had minutely prepared. It failed; a chance blow caused it to collapse. The fight in itself was only a scuffle. But its diplomatic reverberation was considerable: they must have feared, some of the time, that the war was involving western Europe anew.

For the new bishop, this was the source of grave difficulties that he would soon have to confront.

6

FRANCIS DE SALES, PRINCE–BISHOP OF GENEVA

In the Steps of Jesus Christ in the Manner of the Apostles

"Francis de Sales immediately applied his mind to the great and demanding affairs of his diocese", we are told. It is more precise to add the qualification "in the manner of the apostles, and especially of his two great models, Saint Peter and Saint Paul". Francis took his place—then and there—in the field of the Heavenly Father, and how zealously he would work! But Francis was convinced that action is not productive unless the apostle allows himself to be "seized" entirely by Christ. We know, through Francis himself, his intimate dispositions during this first year of his pontificate. One of his friends, Antoine de Revol, had been promoted to the diocese of Dol (he was not yet a priest), and he sought Francis' advice. On June 3, 1603, Francis answered him in a long and admirable letter, which deserves to be quoted in its entirety: "You are entering the ecclesiastical state at the summit of that state. I shall say to you what was said to a shepherd chosen to be king of Israel: *'Mutaberis in virum alterum'*, you must become someone totally different in your interior and in your exterior. And to bring about this great and solemn transformation, you must turn your mind inside out and restructure it completely."

Francis had entirely too much spiritual experience to believe that this ideal of the bishop that he held for himself could be realized without mistakes and a "multitude of imperfections". He had written to M. de Bérulle a few days after his consecration: "There is no remedy:

we shall always need to wash our feet, since we walk in the dust."

We see from this how Francis de Sales gave himself totally to his diocese. For twenty years he would consecrate to it his days and nights, his labors and his vigils. If, by necessity, he had to be away from it, it was always with regret and not without fear that his absence might prove harmful to it. Whenever this happened it was invariably to render some service for it either "by the command of the Pope or of "His Highness" the duke, who was very proud—and jealous—of his bishop . . . to the extent of being disturbed by the esteem shown him by Paris and the King of France! In any case, Francis himself felt no desire to be anywhere but in his own sheepfold. There was so much to be done in this diocese of Geneva-Annecy!

A Reformer-Bishop

Francis had an acute consciousness of the secret malaise that was undermining the Church and that touched the Christian people more or less profoundly. Later, in 1619, he would confide his anxiety to Mother Angélique Arnauld in a long conversation.

> My daughter, these are the subjects for tears. . . . We must weep and pray in secret that God will place the Church where men would have no idea of putting it. . . . We must ask him . . . to reform the abuses that have slipped in through the conduct of the Church's ministers, and to send her holy pastors animated with the zeal of Saint Charles Borromeo, who will strive to purify her by the fire of their zeal and by their learning, and *to restore her without stain and without blemish* in matters of discipline as well as of faith and doctrine.

The allusion to Saint Charles Borromeo was significant:

> Francis de Sales' devotion to the saintly and intrepid bishop of Milan was long-standing. Fresh from his doctorate at the University of Padua, he had wished to make a pilgrimage to Milan, the city where Charles Borromeo had died several years previously. And Francis took the great reformer as the model for his episcopate. But what a difference there was in their respective temperaments and in their methods: whereas the one was austere and authoritarian—even harsh

on occasion—the other was patient, persuasive, and amiably tenacious. ... Confronted by the problems of his diocese and Church, Francis would remain faithful to the spirit of his provost speech.

He would be able to say: "We must reconquer Christianity", just as he had formerly launched his war cry "We must reconquer Geneva", but he would immediately specify, "It is by *love* that our attack must be made!" Such sicknesses could only be cured by charity, prayer, penance, and the care of the humble and the poor. The first commandment of the Bible and "the second, which is like it" would inspire and comfort all his activity.

The Bishop of Geneva's Daily Schedule

Faithful to the spirit of the Tridentine reform *in capite et in membris,* it was by his person and in his own household that Francis began the sanctification of his diocese. He led a very simple life-style in his modest bishop's house in exile on the rue Juivrie. It was a poor place: poor in personal resources (he had abandoned the family patrimony to his brothers); poor in episcopal resources (his bishopric did not provide him with more than a thousand golden ecus per year because his benefice—at Geneva—had been confiscated by the Calvinists); poor because he multiplied his almsgiving in secret and in public; poor quite simply because he wished to be so in order to "live like the apostles". He reduced the personnel of his house to the strict minimum, discontinued their "livery of bright color", and forbade the "turned-up moustaches" so much in style at the great houses, but he wanted their uniforms to be like his own—"neat and very clean"—and to be worn for a long time. His table was frugal, his dinner service common: whenever he received a piece of silverware as a gift, he would use it only on those days when he was entertaining guests whom he wished to honor. He had no carriage: he made his trips on horseback or on foot if he was traversing the mountains. In 1610, when Antoine Favre put his beautiful town house—"it was the most beautiful mansion in the city of Annecy at that time"—at Francis' disposal, Francis reserved for himself only a modest bedroom. "I shall walk all day in my capacity as bishop of Geneva, and I shall retire at night as Francis de Sales."

Above all he prayed, and, as was his custom, he did not separate penance from prayer. He devoted a whole hour to prayer, sometimes more. As much as he could in keeping with his episcopal resolutions, he reserved for himself two hours for reading "something suitable to my profession". But when his obligations or the service of souls impeded him from adhering to this rule, he knew how to leave God for God, or rather how to find God again in love of neighbor. Each day, around nine o'clock, he said his Mass. This was generally in the intimacy of his oratory in the bishop's house, but he also loved those days that were called "devotion days" so as to be with his people and to celebrate with them in a church or a chapel in Annecy. He had a love of beautiful liturgy, and if he officiated pontifically, he proved to be strict in the observance of the rubrics. Mass was, in his eyes, the summit of particular devotion and of public worship. To celebrate Mass and to celebrate it well, in all its ecclesiological dimensions, was, in his opinion, the primary duty of a pastor.

Thus began for Francis de Sales "his works and his setbacks". The business affairs that devolved around him were, to be sure, numerous, complex, and delicate. But there was also that correspondence, which seemed endless! Harrying and harassing. His secretary insisted that when Francis was in Annecy he wrote twenty letters per day . . . and in his own hand. And the various interviews and "counselings"! Confession consumed a considerable amount of his time, because he always welcomed the penitents whom, he feared, the other confessors might rebuff: the "wretched, diseased, and other foul-smelling" persons. Francis preached, catechized, and disseminated the word of God. *The Complete Works of Saint Francis de Sales* in twenty-six volumes may fill the shelves of our libraries, but they preserve only a tiny handful of Francis' activities. His catechetical instructions, notably, do not figure among them, nor do his individual instructions in the confessional or at the bishop's house. And that is a great shame: there we would see the real Francis de Sales at the time of his episcopate. He was "loving" not only toward the upper classes and the gentle, noble ladies—"gourmandes of spiritual direction"—but also toward the humble people who did not know how to read or write or speak well, and he was particularly kind to children. We would encounter among this anonymous crowd Jacqueline Coste, the servant at the Geneva inn who would enter the service of the first Visitandine; Pernette Boutey, "one of his great friends", the matron from the mountain village and mother of an exemplary family in her simplicity and strictness; "Huguette", the daughter of the baker in Annecy; Sister Simplicienne, whose religious vocation he would authenticate; and more.

As for the catechism classes, he "took pleasure in them" and, as it happened, "so did his young pupils". Did not he, the bishop of Geneva, "go so far as to become a child with the children"? These modest lessons were so well inaugurated in his cathedral that they soon attracted many adults—so many that the bishop had to have recourse to some willing helpers and divide the clientele among three churches. Wasted effort! Everyone wanted to be a member of his group. Mme de Boisy herself came to see and hear her son. "Madame," he told her, "you cause me some distraction when I see you at my catechism lesson with all our little children, because it is you yourself who taught it to me."

At such a pace, Francis achieved a tremendous popularity without seeking it. So true was this that his entire person radiated a peace, a goodness, and a charity that won all hearts. Whenever he appeared in the street, the children surrounded him, and the poor approached him. He neglected no one. All the same, he knew how to be firm when he had to be; he was not afraid to apply iron and fire to otherwise incurable wounds. The "Valentines" (the lovers who celebrated the feast of Saint Valentine a little too recklessly!) in Annecy experienced this. They grumbled, they resisted, but his gentle tenacity finally won them over.

The Aura of the Miraculous

It was inevitable that an atmosphere of holy legend would surround the bishop. Poor Francis! He mistrusted nothing so much as this "cult of the personality"; he only wanted to be loved so as to bring souls to love God. But how do you prevent people from crying miracle when

God, at Francis' prayer, accomplished some cure or granted some favor? It is possible that popular fervor exaggerated this, but the dossier of these extraordinary facts is so copious, and the greater part of the witnesses so serious, that the severest critic cannot eliminate all of them. What could Francis do? Nothing, except to prevent his friends, at least, from ganging up on him. "You do not write as I would wish", he wrote to Baroness de Chantal on November 25, 1607, "either to my mother or to Mme de Charmoisy, when you say 'our good and holy bishop', because in the place where these good women ought to be reading *simple* bishop they read *saintly* bishop. I am well aware that in the time of Saint Jerome they used to call all bishops saints by reason of their responsibility, but that is not the custom now." Did Mme de Chantal correct herself? Well, on January 24, 1608, Francis raised his voice: "I must forbid you to use this word *saint* when you are writing about me, my daughter. I am more *sot* than *saint:* besides, canonization is not your function."

Francis, on the contrary, was conscious of his weaknesses. He had to admit that his body grew weary and that his mind could be distracted by so many activities. Then he had recourse to retreat in God. It was not five years after he became bishop when he wrote to a friend this note, in which humor tempers a certain sadness: "I shall spend this Lent in residence at my cathedral and in rehabilitating my soul, which is almost totally fragmented by so many worries it has suffered. . . . It is a clock that is out of order; it must be dismantled piece by piece, and after it has been cleaned and oiled, it must be reassembled to make it chime more accurately." This is, after all, merely the implementation of a resolution that he had made at the time of his consecration: "Every year, for the space of eight days— and even more when feasible—he would attend to the recollection and the cleansing of his soul."

Francis de Sales' Apostolic Vision of the World

This care for union with God and assistance to neighbor properly forms the basic framework of the twenty-two years' episcopacy of Francis de Sales. The events that we must present are only the putting into practice of these fundamental dispositions. Before explaining them, and in order to permit the reader to find his way through their intricacies, let us make some rough sketches of the world view that was formed—little by little—by this astonishing apostle.

— The gospel is addressed to all, no matter what their social origin, their profession, or their tasks may be. The call is universal, though the response may differ and be differentiated. And all Christians, in spite of their differences, are supposed to form a community of faith and charity, an *ecclesia,* a Church, as in the time of the apostles and around the apostles.

— As in the time of the apostles, there exist in the Church and in every church two hierarchies: the *one of function,* the Pope, the bishop, the priests, the deacons; the *other of fervor,* of spiritual generosity, of charity. The two hierarchies ought to coincide, but that is not always so with them. It happens too often, above all in a politico-ecclesial system where "benefices", certain posts, and the revenues of the abbeys stir up and attract the covetous, that those who ought to nourish the Christian people with the word and the sacraments of Christ are merely wretched shepherds. Francis de Sales, the bishop, was forced to restore evangelical order in his diocese. The solicitude of the "reformer" (he would prefer to say "rebuilder") obsessed him, especially regarding some monasteries of which certain ones, he said, were veritable "seminaries of scandals".

— Thus, by his preaching, his correspondence, and his two books and by all his daily public and private activity, he seeks to arouse in souls pure, authentic Christianity, a living faith, an efficacious and cheerful charity. This Christianity is not "new"; he draws from both the Gospel and the Acts of the Apostles, but he renews it in his presentation, adapts it to the new circumstances of the times and persons. He gives it a name that he borrows from the traditional language of spirituality, but which he reanimates and reinvigorates by restoring the meaning of its origins: *devotion.*

— But is not this group of Christians who will agree to live the word of God fervently going to constitute a kind of "elite", and be isolated from civil society, such as it is with its intrigues, its jealousies, its hatreds, its sins? Not so! This devotion, in order to be true Salesian devotion, must penetrate—in the manner of oil or of perfume—all civil society; all relationships among the powerful and the weak, the rich and the poor, the cultivated and the ignorant. It aims to infuse everywhere, apart from all religious opinion, a spirit of service, of exchange—let us latch onto the phrase dear to Francis de Sales—a "spirit of friendship". As much as it is possible. Salesian devotion is a "civil" devotion. Francis, himself, will merit a fine surname: they will call him "the conciliator", but it is up to every Christian to work at reconciling men with one another, to make them "live together".

In short, Francis de Sales, bishop and successor to the apostles, will strive to reinstate, as best he can, and according to the opportunities that Providence will offer him, the Kingdom of God, of a God whose name is "Love". He is convinced that no rock—no matter how hard—can resist this living seed. He will sow Love, he will break open "hearts of stone", and he will change them into "hearts of flesh".

Let us then see it in his work—not by getting lost in the infinite labyrinth of his activity, but in his principal and most significant enterprises.

1603: THE NEW BISHOP'S MOST URGENT TASKS

To pass too rapidly over this first year of the pontificate of Francis de Sales would be to deprive ourselves of knowing certain characteristic aspects of his personality.

Change of Strategy Regarding Some Protestants in Gex

In his diplomatic mission at the French court, Francis had experienced a partial setback, as we said. But this partial setback was accompanied by a partial success! He had notably obtained assurance that three parishes in the district of Gex (whence the deanery of Gex) would be restored to Catholic worship. In August 1603, Francis therefore returned to Gex in order to proceed to the execution of the royal ordinances. We can easily imagine the conflicts, discussions, and disputes into which the bishop was going to be hurled in this entirely

Huguenot area; it is even said that someone attempted to poison him. What is certain is that he contracted there a "high fever that lasted a long time". This "quarrel over steeples"—that is the way to describe it—became interminable, and Francis could not even see the outcome. What interests us in this biography is that Francis appears to us, at this time, in a new light: he acts and struggles no longer as a missionary in the territory, but as a *jurist* and a *diplomat.*

What brought about this change of attitude? At Gex he was on French soil, that is to say, under a very different legal system from the Savoyard legal system. The Edict of Nantes had been promulgated by Henry IV, who incontestably favored the Protestants and supported Geneva. On the other hand, he reestablished a peaceful coexistence between Huguenots and Catholics, which permitted the King to restore to the kingdom a semblance of unity. Given this situation, Francis de Sales strove to obtain, not that the district of Gex should benefit from the same legislation as the Chablais in Savoy—that is to say, from a total and absolute reestablishment of Catholicism—but that the famous "Interim" enjoyed by the Protestants in France should be accepted by Geneva in favor of Catholic worship. His diplomacy was no longer that of "all or nothing" but that of "giving, giving". It would certainly be an exaggeration to speak of a "liberal Francis de Sales", but it is, all the same, a Francis de Sales as *negotiator* who is revealed in this Gex affair, which could have dragged on for many years. In the course of these visits, Francis was closely observed both by France and by the ever-suspicious duke. Francis would even be accused and calumniated. In 1604, had he not been declared "prelate of the realm" by Henry IV? And then, in the early days of September 1609, there had been that picturesque horseback ride across Geneva.

Francis had received the command from the duke of Savoy to go to Gex in order to confer about religious interests with Baron de Lux. He therefore left Annecy on horseback, accompanied by twelve persons, one of whom was Jean Favre, one of his vicars-general. It was raining torrents. The little troop slept that evening at Saint-Julien. The next day there could be no question of crossing the Rhône, because the rains had dangerously swollen it. Thus we have this account, by Francis himself, of this typically Salesian escapade:

Not long ago, on our way to Gex, it came to me in my heart, after having celebrated Mass in a nearby village, that to pass through Geneva was the most direct route for me. I did so without any apprehension, but with a certain boldness in which was mixed more simplicity than prudence. When I arrived at the gates of the city, the customs officer asked who I was. I made my reply through my vicar-general that I was the bishop. And to the question "What bishop?" I had him answer, "The bishop of this diocese". The man recorded in his register these words: "Monsieur Francis de Sales, bishop of this diocese". I do not know if he understood the word diocese; in any case, he let me enter, and so I passed through the center of the city and was greeted with great respect by most of the men and women.

Francis was even dressed "in his episcopal regalia". Soon the council of Geneva, having learned of the incident, were divided as to how they ought to have dealt with Francis. Who was the most dumbfounded by this episode? The duke of Savoy! He even suspected Francis of being in "some kind of collusion" with his "miserable Geneva". Here is Francis' mischievous reaction:

This is how they have discussed the incident: "How did he get away with so much at Geneva? Who gave him the permission to pass through the city, particularly with such an infamous name as his, and in his capacity as bishop? Moreover, none of his predecessors has ever entered Geneva since the revolt without a safe conduct, or without being disguised, or without denying his position." But the real truth is that they have underestimated my spirit if they judge me to be so cautious and apprehensive that I am unable to demonstrate a little temerity. The opportunity, my innocence, but above all the Providence of God, were all in my favor.

The escapade might have been only a good joke played on the Genevans, but here is where it took on all its apostolic meaning. Upon his arrival Francis was asked by Baron de Lux: "My Lord Bishop, why did you take such a risk?" Francis replied: "My life is a very small thing when there is question of the glory of God and of the good of the Church."

The Gex affairs confirmed Francis de Sales in a conviction that had already stirred in his mind, particularly since 1602, in Paris. Protestantism was a factor with which he would have to deal henceforth, and the desirable reconciliation was not taking place either by military or diplomatic interventions or by oratory or by libels, even though all those were inevitable and, in certain cases, useful. Reconciliation was being achieved through serene, serious, in short, *religious, dialogue* in the most profound sense of the word. If we examine the details— infinite and sensitive—of Francis de Sales' contacts as bishop with the Protestants of Geneva and elsewhere, we easily document this change in attitude. We shall again become conscious of it in his letter of April 27, 1616.

Francis de Sales, Father Chérubin, and the "Pope's League"

We recall that, since 1598, the Roman court, Francis de Sales, Father Chérubin, and whoever was involved in the Chablais were in agreement about making Thonon the "stronghold" of Catholicism confronting Geneva—as a kind of apostolic "Allinges". On September 13, 1599, Pope Clement VIII signed the bull *Redemptoris,* by which he erected and established "in perpetuity this *Holy House* which would be directed by a prefect and seven secular priests". Apart from this priestly community, Thonon was supposed to shelter other important projects: a Catholic school, a seminary, a "hostel of all sciences and arts", a mission center entrusted to the Capuchins, and so forth.

Francis, at this time, was only the provost. The Pope's brief designated him as "Prefect of the *Holy House*". He quickly took account of the fact that this plan was utopian, that it was financially unfeasible, and that it would be necessary to proceed gradually.

But in September 1603, Francis, now bishop, was obliged to send to the Pope his resignation as "Prefect of the Holy House". He had to entrust the apostolic renewal of the Chablais to the priests and to the religious whom he had himself established there, and among whom—conspicuous for his innovative ardor—was Father Chérubin, the Capuchin who had been the organizer of the Forty Hours at Annemasse and at Thonon. From this time, two attitudes were going to be opposed in the relations of the Savoyard Catholics with Geneva.

The one was more calm, more patient, less provocative, in a word, Salesian. The other was more lively, more combative, and, it must be admitted, more temporal and more political—that of Father Chérubin. Francis turned to the Pope and the duke to ask them to designate a new prefect. The affair dragged on for reasons of personalities, and also as a result of the deaths of Clement VIII and Leo XI. Finally, Pope Paul V requested Francis to take back personal responsibility of organizing the Holy House "on the model of the Oratory in Rome". Now came problems about money, about churches, about habits, even about precedence. In the midst of all this hullabaloo, Francis strove to found an Oratory that would be an apostolic center, like that of Philip Neri but adapted to the Savoyard situation. All that he was able to realize, however, was to procure for the Holy House a congregation of eight priests and a school managed by the Barnabites.

For his part, Father Chérubin continued his apostolic pugnacity. In his initial plan, there was the foundation of the "Confraternity of Our Lady of Compassion"; through it, in effect, were supposed to come—from all Christianity—the funds to establish, maintain, and develop "the Hostel of All the Virtues" and, in general, to finance the entire Thonon project. But this financial enterprise very quickly raised some diplomatic difficulties. Henry IV did not look favorably on this international confraternity, behind which he suspected lurked a plan to regroup the political and even the military forces against Geneva. Alas! This was only too true: the "Pope's league" was not a myth, even if its design remained blurred. Was Father Chérubin *au courant* concerning this second project? And if he was, to what extent? It is difficult to make a decision about it; besides, he was in very good standing at the court in Rome. The devious duke of Savoy played his usual Machiavellian game of jumbling the cards! What is certain is that the Capuchins were accused—unjustly, in the opinion of certain persons (around 1608–9)—of not being strangers to the duke's adventurous intrigues, and that Father Chérubin took refuge in Turin, where he died on October 23, 1609. His audacity during his final years ought not make us forget the tremendous service he rendered to the Chablais mission. Francis de Sales preserved a faithful friendship with this companion of his hardest hours in the

Chablais. It is said that on his trip to Turin in 1613, he went to pray at the tomb of the Capuchin, and that he wept. "To the dead man," wrote the historian of the Capuchin order, "this was the best and most solid praise."

The Bishop and His Priests

The diocesan synod of Annecy was held in 1603, as it had been each year since 1582. Taking notice of the deplorable state of his clergy—and, consequently, of his people—Bishop de Granier had taken this initiative, a bold one for the time. The diocese of Annecy, like many dioceses, had great need of it: the *Synodal Constitutions* of 1582 are revealing! The evil came principally from the manner of recruiting clerics. The nobility directed its younger sons toward the Church, and these found in a livelihood clerical functions. As for the sons of the bourgeoisie or of the peasantry, they obtained—thanks to not-too-scrupulous patrons—profitable social promotion. Not a true vocation, and no formation in theology or in spirituality. Bishop de Granier had begun by dismissing the unworthy from the priesthood, by means of a rigorous examination of the candidates and the practice of competitive testing. Then he convoked each year, under penalty of a fine, all the pastors to a synod, a veritable deliberating assembly of some 250 priests, over which he personally presided. Here they practiced a sincere self-critique of the state of the diocese; here they elected the bishop's principal collaborators; here they decreed certain "constitutions". In 1603 the reform had produced certain fruit, but much remained to be done. Francis de Sales was totally convinced of this. As early as August 11, he convoked "all the clergy of the diocese" to a synod that would be held at Annecy on October 2.

This was because he had a very lofty idea of the priesthood. The priest, and above all the pastor, was one with the bishop; he was the father, the shepherd (*forma gregis*), the animator of the Christian community that was confided to his care. He participated in the bishop's mission as "lieutenant of our Lord", about which the *Controversies* speak so eloquently. The priests were truly responsible for this part of the bishop's mission, and they must accomplish their task in every apostolic initiative. Such was the spirit of Francis in his relationship with his priests.

He also brought the best of care to their formation. Despite a thousand difficulties, which gave rise to the impertinent interventions or schemes of influential persons, he reinforced the measures—examinations, competitive testing—for the allocating of appointments and benefices. In the Ordinance of Synods that he held in the course of his episcopate, we discover a Francis de Sales who is demanding, precise, just, and unafraid to threaten recalcitrants with canonical sanctions. We read, for example, in an ordinance of 1617, "Those who, in the near future, wish to be promoted to Holy Orders will be required to be drilled in the exercise of the orders that they have, and to bring a written certificate from their pastor, as to their age and good morals; in which the said pastors are exhorted and enjoined—on the part of the eternal Judge—to be conscientious and truthful."

Francis strove to establish a learned, cultivated, competent clergy. A seminary was, therefore, a necessity, and a seminary of high quality. There was no dearth of candidates for orders; in less than two years—from 1605 to 1606—Francis conferred tonsure on more than 570 young men in the course of his visits. But the diocese was too poor to support a seminary. He could deduct nothing from the episcopal income; the chapter's funds did not suffice to feed the canons; "as for the rich abbeys and priories, no one could touch any of them at all, because those who held them held them firmly, and because most often these benefices were rendered anemic following certain diverse assessments that were imposed on them". Francis groaned; he implored the generosity of Rome; he even considered soliciting a general contribution from the pastors of the diocese. Until the end of his life, he would struggle tenaciously to fulfill his desire, because, in his eyes, "there is not a diocese in the Christian world that has greater need of a seminary for clerics than that of Geneva". He would fail.

To alleviate this serious lack, Francis urged his clergy to study "everything good", as he himself had done during the time he spent in Paris and in Padua and as he continued to do every day. Learning for a priest is "the eighth sacrament of the hierarchy of the Church". "Ignorance in a priest", he said, "is worse than malice."

Knowledge of Scripture and of the Fathers is necessary for the personal holiness of the priest, and "it provides enrichment to his speech". Better still, Francis, during the first three years of his episcopate, assumed the role of professor of theology in his own house, where he lectured to the canons and the priests of Annecy. When the proliferation of his duties obliged him to discontinue this (in 1607), he inaugurated a monthly conference for the clergy in order to deal with "certain current questions" and to mold them, in particular, as confessors.

From Francis' efforts to endow his diocese with a quality corps of priests there remain some precious testimonies. Such are the regulations for instructing catechism, or even that astounding "Memorial for Confessors", in which Francis placed at the disposal of all his priests his long personal experience in the confessional. And what consideration! "Remember that the poor penitents call you *Father* and that you, in fact, are supposed to have a paternal heart in their regard, receiving them with great love, patiently enduring their rusticity, ignorance, weakness, stupidity, and other imperfections, always allowing yourself to help and support them as long as there is some hope for amendment in them. . . . The responsibility of pastors is not strong souls, but the feeble and the debilitated." And to define the apostolic attitudes of the priest in this truly divine ministry:

> Have a great cleanness and purity of conscience. . . . Have an ardent desire for the salvation of souls. . . . Have the prudence of a physician. . . . Above all, be charitable and discreet. . . . When you encounter some persons who—because of their serious sins . . . are excessively overwhelmed and troubled in their conscience, you must lift up their spirit and console them by every possible means, assuring them of the great mercy of God, who is infinitely greater in pardoning them than are all the sins in the world in damning them, and you must promise to assist them in all that they will need from you for the salvation of their soul!

"The 'touchstone' of a very good confessor", he says in another fragment, "is that he be *compassionate* to vice in others, and implacable to it in himself."

It was even more by his example than by his counsels and writings that Francis created, before the eyes of his clergy, the model of Jesus Christ, the priest. Just as he wished to be close to them, so he greatly desired to make them his personal friends, in spite of the social distance that at that time separated the bishop from the simple cleric! On the occasion of his episcopal visits to the parishes, he inquired about the material and spiritual situation of each pastor, remembering those years when he had been the "pastor of Thonon"—pastor without a church, without a rectory, without a curate!—and where he had experienced in his feelings and in his flesh what the pastoral life demanded of the priest in terms of courage, zeal, and grace.

Let us recall, in passing, a characteristic pastoral trait of Francis de Sales. He advised many of his priests to collaborate with their lay parishioners in seeking to discern among their flock certain generous souls—they might even be simple and uncultivated—who might commit themselves to true "devotion", and to dedicate to their formation all the time necessary. Just as he, the bishop, was establishing a new spirit for the diocese by giving his priests a real share in its responsibilities and spiritual benefits, so did he desire that the pastors in their parishes would collaborate with certain "devout" lay folk.

One day he would have a sad opportunity to demonstrate the extent of his love for his priests. Denis de Granier, Bishop de Granier's nephew and a canon of the church of Geneva (1602) who had been ordained a priest by Francis de Sales (1611), apostatized in 1620 and left for England. We can judge Francis de Sales' emotion when, by mistake, he opened the letter in which Denis de Granier announced his defection to Bishop Jean-François de Sales, Francis' brother and coadjutor.[1] Francis immediately wrote his brother a magnificent letter in which he revealed his paternal and priestly heart:

> O God, my dear brother, what sorrows I felt in my soul when I read this letter. Indeed, it is true that in all my life I have never suffered such a distressing shock. Is it possible that this soul is to be thus lost? . . . If you write to him, assure him that all the waters in the seas surrounding England will never extinguish the flames of my love, so

[1] Concerning Jean-François de Sales, cf. below, p. 240.

long as there may remain some hope of his return to the Church and to the way of his eternal salvation.

Francis de Sales brought his passion for unity—for *friendship*—into his relations with his priests, insofar as he was able, and in accord with the grace proper to each.

7

"THE GOD OF ENCOUNTERS"
1604: Lent at Dijon

To Avoid a Lawsuit between Bishops

There was nothing more commonplace in Francis de Sales' apostolate than to preach a Lenten series. How many Advents and Lents, how many sermons had he preached? And all the while carrying out how many administrative and diplomatic assignments? He very nearly had no intention of giving the Lenten sermons at Dijon. However, it provided an opportunity for a meeting that would prove to be the decisive occasion in the life, soul, and influence of Francis de Sales.

To put it precisely, it was because of "business" concerning the district of Gex that Francis had accepted the suggestion of the municipal magistrates of Dijon to preach this series of Lenten sermons. Among these business matters he had to deal with a young archbishop, twenty-five years of age, who was an excellent legal writer, already supplied with several benefices in the duchy of Burgundy, who had "preempted" the deanery of Gex from King Henry IV, although the king had already conceded this deanery to the diocese of Geneva! The name of this young prelate was André Frémyot, bishop of Bourges, and he was the brother of Baroness de Chantal! That one bishop should go to court against another bishop was something scandalous in Francis' judgment. Perhaps the matter might find an issue through more pacific means? Under the cover of a preaching assignment he might be able to regulate things more amicably.

To go to Dijon and preach the Lenten sermons was not as simple as

Francis had figured. The duke of Savoy took umbrage that his bishop had accepted the magistrates' invitation "without his approval". Francis apologized: "I very frankly admit the poverty of my spirit, which — regarding all things at their face value — was unable to foresee this consequence." Father Fourier, that friend and confidant of Francis, succeeded in convincing the duke of the uprightness of Francis' intentions and of his "inviolable fidelity". The duke finally gave his consent.

Francis arrived at Dijon in the very earliest days of March. The sermons were preached in the *Sainte Chapelle* of the ducal palace. It was a chapel larger than many churches, and as splendid as one could wish. The dukes of Burgundy who had had it built had wished it to be worthy of their power and wealth.

"A Lady of Quality, Dressed as a Widow"

Lent began. The crowd was pressing around the pulpit, so great was the reputation of the preacher. Soon Francis noticed that a lady of quality, dressed as a widow, had taken her place for the sermon in front of the pulpit, and she listened "very attentively to the word of truth". Who was she? The simplest thing was to ask Archbishop André Frémyot, who was remarkably well acquainted with the entire society of Dijon. "Monseigneur de Bourges (that was the young prelate's bishopric), smiling, was able to tell him who she was, and our blessed father was extremely gratified to learn that she was his sister, because these two prelates had already mutually begun to contract a great and holy friendship." Bishop Frémyot renounced his claims to the deanery of Gex.

By what chance was Jeanne Frémyot de Chantal attending the Lenten series in Dijon? (She was the widow of Baron Christophe de Chantal, who — after the accidental death of her husband, whom she "had loved madly" — had retired to her father-in-law's château in Monthelon with her four children.) Her father, President Frémyot, knowing of her tremendous distress and of the unhappy life that she led at Monthelon (the old Baron Guy de Chantal maintained a servant-mistress and her five children there), had "suggested to her that she come to spend Lent with him" in Dijon. And Baron Guy, as tyrannical as he was, did not dare to oppose this appeal.

The marvel is that Francis de Sales and Jane de Chantal—who were not even acquainted—recognized each other! Had each of them "seen" the other in thought or in a vision or in some kind of premonition? Jane had seen "Francis in the form of a shepherd of a great flock of sheep, to whom God would confide the care of guiding her"; Francis had seen Jane as becoming the foundress of a religious congregation that he would have to create one day. They both had, moreover, ample opportunities to become better acquainted because President Frémyot, one of the most important personages in Dijon since the recapture of the city by Henry IV, considered it an honor to invite to his table sometimes the preacher from the *Sainte Chapelle* who had conquered the minds and hearts of his fellow citizens overnight. The bishop of Bourges and Madame de Chantal attended these dinners. "Personally," she said, "from the very moment that I had the honor of meeting him, I admired him as an oracle. I called him 'saint' from the depth of my heart, and I considered him such."

Here we have no need to be very precise all at once because we are going to witness the birth, development, and flowering of one of the greatest friendships that ever bound a director and his disciple. After having read and reread all that the most objective history tells us, and especially the correspondence that passed between them, we can conclude, if we are loyal, that this friendship is of the radically spiritual order, and directly so from its origin. It is the work of him whom Father Fichet, one of the first biographers of Jane de Chantal, names magnificently "the God of encounters". That this friendship had had its repercussions in the mind, the sensitivity—in brief, the heart—what could be more normal since it is a question of a man and a woman, but this does not impede in any way this friendship from being spiritual. Francis, in the *Introduction to the Devout Life,* addressing himself to persons in the world, explains it luminously:

> O Philothea, love one another with a great, charitable love, but only have a friendship with those who can communicate virtuous things with you, and the more exquisite the virtues that you will put in your relationship the more perfect will your friendship be.... If

your mutual and reciprocal communication is made from charity, devotion, and Christian perfection, O God, how precious will your friendship be! It will be excellent because it comes from God, excellent because it tends toward God, excellent because its good is God, excellent because it will endure eternally in God. Oh, how good it is to love on earth as we shall in heaven, and to learn to seek for one another in this world as we shall do eternally in the other. ... I am speaking of spiritual friendship through which two or three or several souls intercommunicate their devotion, their spiritual affections, and make of themselves one spirit among them.

This text is the indispensable key for correctly reading the letters that Francis de Sales wrote to Jane de Chantal, but also to many other Philotheas—and even to some men such as Antoine Favre or Duke de Bellegarde! Let us add that Francis enjoyed an extremely affectionate temperament. He himself will admit this in a remarkable letter. It is addressed to Mother de Chantal but concerns another sister:

I love this poor girl with a perfect heart. This is a great point; there is not a soul in the world, it seems to me, who cherishes more cordially, tenderly, and—to say it in all good faith—more lovingly than I, because it has pleased God to make my heart so. But, nonetheless, I love independent, vigorous souls that are not female, because this so great tenderness confuses the heart, disturbs it, and distracts it from loving prayer toward God; impedes the total resignation and the perfect death of self-love. Whatever is not God is nothing for us. How is it possible that I feel these things, I who am the most affectionate in the world, as you know, my dear Mother? In truth, I feel this, nonetheless, but it is marvelous how I accommodate all this together because it is my opinion that I love nothing at all except God, and all souls for God.

"It is marvelous ... " Why is it that good biographers—even Catholic, even ecclesiastic—have cast suspicion, however lightly, on the friendship of Francis de Sales and Jane de Chantal, and that they have left to Sainte-Beuve (little inclined to indulgence) the honor of this scathing and decisive statement (apropos the letter of Jane to Dom Jean de Saint François): "Those who have been able to allow themselves some frivolous and indifferent banter concerning the relationship of this holy bishop and this virtuous woman have not read—I like to believe—this piece" (Lundis, bk. VII, 3d ed., Garnier, p. 285). Alas! The fact is well known that everyone judges the heart of others according to his own heart, and the "spiritual mystery" always escapes notice. That is why the duke of Savoy never believed in the bishop of Geneva's political loyalty.

The True Problem

In fact, the biographer's astonishment lies elsewhere. A letter from Francis to his Jesuit friend Father Nicholas Polliens, March 24, 1610, declares apropos the Visitation that he is in the process of founding: "Our Congregation is the fruit of the trip to Dijon, which I could never take at its natural face value, and my soul was secretly forced to penetrate another result which bore so directly upon the service of souls that I preferred to expose myself to the opinion and the mercy of the good than to the cruelty of the calumny of the malicious." The sentence appears to be a bit obscure, but it can clearly be inferred from this that, at Dijon, Francis had the supernatural inspiration to found a new congregation. "At Dijon", therefore—thanks to Mme de Chantal, this was then something completely disconcerting, for it went beyond the "natural face" of things.

Because what could have been the likelihood that Mme de Chantal might establish a new congregation? She was thirty-two years old, but she was a widow with four children to rear: the eldest, Celse-Bénigne, was ten years old; Marie-Aimée, six years; Françoise, five years; and Charlotte was a baby of three years. If, according to the custom of the time, Celse-Bénigne could dispense with the maternal presence, it was unthinkable that she might abandon her three small daughters. To whom would she confide them? She was obliged, on the contrary, to confront a very thorny material and moral situation: she had to maintain not only Bourbilly, her husband's estate that she had rescued from ruin, but Monthelon as well, the estate of Baron Guy de Rabutin-Chantal, an old man who would end his final days sadly. And had not her eccentric father-in-law insisted that she live in his hovel under the threat that he might contract marriage in spite of his seventy-five years, and thus disinherit her four children? How could the idea of a religious vocation germinate in the heart of Jane?

Jane de Chantal and Her Director-Dictator

Certainly Jane was a fervent Christian; she had a thirst for prayer, for mortification, and she devoted herself unstintingly to the poor. But even this fervor was the source of a dolorous spiritual complexity. Upon the advice of several friends in Dijon, she had placed herself under the guidance of a religious who enjoyed a great reputation for holiness, but who deserved rather to be called "dictator" than "director" of souls. Had he not required her to pronounce four strange vows: "The first, that she would obey him; the second, that she would never change him; the third, to keep secret whatever he would tell her; the fourth, not to discuss her interior life with anyone but him"? In fact, Jane was a captive, chained with the most formidable chains there are: spiritual shackles!

At the time, Francis wisely refrained from speaking to Jane about the project that God inspired in him in Dijon. All the more so since this project was still enveloped in fog for him. He would advance, therefore, at God's pace, step by step.

Before all else, Francis would restore confidence and hope to this desperate soul. How else explain this enigmatic note that he addressed to her "at the first dinner" after having left Dijon: "God, it seems to me, has given me to you. I grow more certain of this with every hour; that is all that I can tell you. Recommend me to your good angel." Then began a correspondence, of which, unfortunately, Jane destroyed the greater part of her own letters, but those of Francis reveal unmistakably in what an interior distress his correspondent was floundering.

Francis Restores Mme de Chantal's Spiritual Freedom

With what a deft hand he set about untying the "ropes" that bound Mme de Chantal. "The strictness of the spiritual director from Dijon did not preclude confidence and communication with another— provided the promised obedience remained firmly in its place." She was thus to have scruples about asking Francis' advice: "Make use of all that God has given me for the service of your spirit", he wrote her. "I am totally yours, and you are no longer to think about in what quality or in what degree I am so. . . . Obey your first director filially and freely and make use of me charitably and frankly. . . . Guard against anxiety, melancholy, scruples. You would not want to offend God for anything in the world; that is quite enough to live joyously."

This breath of freedom that finally penetrated her prison revived in Jane the desire to place herself entirely under the guidance of Francis. More especially since Father de Villars, superior of the Jesuits in Dijon, told her: "I tell you that not only should you detach yourself from this first guidance and place yourself totally under that of Monseigneur, but I also tell you that if you do not do it, you will be resisting the Holy Spirit." Poor Jane! One director was a lot; three were too many! Francis pressed her from afar and took advantage of an opportunity, the month of August 1604, to meet Jane again. Letters—even the clearest letters—did not suffice; a direct conference was necessary.

Mme de Boisy was scheduled to make a pilgrimage to Saint-Claude, in the Jura, in order to fulfill a vow. Francis was to accompany her, as well as his little sister Jeanne de Sales. Jane de Chantal and two friends, Madame la Présidente Brûlart and her sister Rose Bourgeois, abbess of Puits d'Orbe—who had been captivated by the Lenten sermons of March—were to meet the pilgrims at Saint-Claude. The interview took place between August 24 and 28, 1604. It was liberating for Jane. Francis assured her that her four previous vows "were worth nothing whatever except for destroying the peace of a conscience", he heard her general confession, and then handed her this note, signed by himself: "I accept, in the name of God, the responsibility for your spiritual guidance, and will do everything possible, with all care and fidelity, and as much as my episcopacy and my previous duties will permit me."

As for herself, and without Francis asking it of her—and even, it seems, without having first mentioned it—Jane made "to the Divine Majesty, a vow of obedience to the bishop of Geneva, beyond the authority of all legitimate superiors". Francis prescribed for her a little "rule of life", which he recommended to her thus in a letter written several days later: "If you should happen to omit something of what I am ordering you, do not become scrupulous about it, because here is the general rule of our obedience written in large letters: *We must do all through love and nothing through force; we must love obedience more than we fear disobedience.* I leave you liberty of spirit. . . . I wish that if a just and charitable opportunity comes for you to omit your exercises, this will be a kind of obedience for you, and that this omission will be supplied by love." There was no mention of a religious vocation or the project of a new congregation.

Jane de Chantal on Her Way toward Pure Love

The following year (1605), Mme de Boisy invited Jane de Chantal to come to Sales "around the Pentecost season". Jane arrived in Savoy on May 21 and stayed ten days. In the course of their conferences Francis presented his project to her. But with what prudence, what "vagueness"! Two dialogues have come down to us. First the marvelous exchange: Francis said to her one day, "Are you, then, really in earnest about wanting to serve Jesus Christ?"

"Really in earnest", she replied.

"Then, you would consecrate yourself totally to pure love?"

"Totally," she answered, "so that he may consume me and transform me into himself."

"Do you consecrate yourself to him without reservation?"

"Yes, I consecrate myself to him without reservation."

Francis then invited her to "despise the world". Jane acquiesced.

"To conclude, my daughter, you wish, then, only God?"

"I wish only him, for time and for eternity."

Another day, however, he said to her: "Several years ago God communicated to me something for a way of life, but I do not want to tell it to you for a year." Jane did not insist; besides, did not "several years" signify that this divine communication was prior to their meeting? Her impatience was to belong "totally to God". Also, she had asked him this question one day: "O my God! My Father, ah! Will you not uproot me from the world and from myself?" The *Mémoires* tell us that he gave a slow, grave, and cryptic response: "Yes, one day you will leave everything, you will come to me, and I shall empty you completely and you will be stripped of all for God."

Two more years passed (1605–7), during which they corresponded but during which there was no question of the religious life and even less of founding the Visitation. Nonetheless, the desire of a total gift to God was constantly growing in the heart of Jane, and it was she who clearly envisaged the eventuality of "entering religion". August 6, 1606, Francis, with remarkable spiritual discernment, got to the "point" of this thinking. After having assured Jane that he had frequently asked himself the same question, and that he had prayed much "at the Holy Sacrifice and elsewhere", and after having had others pray for this intention, he declared:

> What have I learned up until now? That one day, my daughter, you will have to leave all, that is to say—lest you understand it differently from me—I have learned that I must one day counsel you to leave everything. I say "everything", but whether this means to enter religious life is a big question; I am not yet at the point of having advice about that; I am still in doubt about that, and I see nothing before my eyes that invites me to favor it. For the love of God, understand me well: I do not say no, but I say that my spirit has not yet been able to find reason to say yes. . . . And know that in this investigation, I have made myself so detached concerning my own inclination for seeking God's will that I never do it very strongly, and, nonetheless, *Yes* has never been able to stop in my heart, so much so that up until now I would not know how to say it or pronounce it, and the *No,* on the contrary, is still found there with much strength.

In order not to misconstrue this declaration by Francis, we must, we believe, give to the word *religion* its canonical meaning at that time: it was a question of a well-established religious order with solemn vows and pontifical cloister such as the Carmel, which had just been established in Dijon and which Mme de Chantal and her friends frequented. It was another form of religious life that Francis de Sales was considering. The question that he was still asking himself at this moment was this: Should he advise Jane de Chantal to enter a great existing order or make of her the foundation stone of the new congregation of which he was dreaming? On February 11, 1607, he was still writing to her: "I shall think about it very hard, and I shall say several Masses to obtain clarity from the Holy Spirit, because you see, my daughter, this is a masterstroke, and one that ought to be weighed *with the shekels of the sanctuary.*"

Light at Last

Be that as it may, in the first months of 1607, the light that Francis was imploring from God was given to him, and he decided to reveal his project to Mme de Chantal. He therefore invited her to come to Annecy. She arrived there four or five days before Pentecost. It was not until Monday of Pentecost, June 4, 1607, that Francis took her aside after Mass, "with a grave and serious visage, and the manner of someone wholly engulfed in God", and said, "Ah, my daughter, I have decided what I wish to do with you."

"And I, my lord and father, am resolved to obey."

Daughter of Saint Clare? Hospital sister? Carmelite? Whatever Francis proposed, Jane declared herself "totally ready" to acquiesce. It is true that there was still only a question of the "religious" with which she was well acquainted. Then Francis announced to her quite simply the plan that he had for our Institute. Instantly she "experienced a great interior sense of agreement". She said yes. As she began to grasp the risks of the project she sometimes was seized with severe feelings of insecurity. This woman "with clear and pure", farsighted spirit who was not satisfied unless all her affairs were in order—here she was thrust into the unknown! A kind of vertigo would seize her at certain times, even after the Visitation had been established!

And three points still disturbed her emotions: Did she have the right to drag her children into this risk? Or to desert her father and her father-in-law? And did not the bishop speak of installing the first house of the new Institute not in Dijon, the capital of Burgundy, but in Annecy, that modest city outside France? For her, this would be some sort of exile!

Moreover, the bishop acknowledged that he was well aware of all these difficulties and that he "did not see any way out of them". But at the same time he affirmed that "Divine Providence would do it by means unknown to creatures". Whence came this assurance? Jane believed it on his word.

Jane's stay in Annecy was prolonged twenty days after this dramatic interview. When she left for Burgundy, it was agreed that nothing would be done for several long years—six or seven at least—and that in the meantime they would observe absolute secrecy about the project.

Correspondence of a Spiritual Friendship

After the Lent in Dijon, Francis' correspondence with his Philotheas expanded considerably. But it had existed at least since 1602. That year the Parisians discovered that Francis de Sales was a marvelous director of souls; numerous persons and communities had had recourse to his counsels. And naturally, when he had left the capital, they wrote to one another. In fact, we must go back still further, and—to make it brief—point out the remarkable correspondence that was exchanged as early as 1593 between Francis de Sales and President Favre. Theirs was a truly exemplary friendship that lasted until death. It characterized perfectly the concept that Francis had formulated concerning friendship and spiritual direction: there is no friendship without "communication of the highest gifts of the spirit and of the heart"; no spiritual direction that does not become very close friendship.

In order to appreciate more exactly the tone and the style of Francis' letters to Jane de Chantal, we may study his very affectionate letters to Antoine Favre, which he soon extended to Favre's entire family. Antoine is his "very dear and gentle brother", "his brother always and ever more dear"; Mme la Présidente Favre is his "sister"; their children are his "nephews and nieces", his "sons and daughters". In 1594, for example, he asked his friend's sons to send him "a new letter because the one that you wrote me is all worn from the repeated reading that I have made of it". Or again, he wrote to Jacqueline Favre, who entered the Visitation at the very foundation of the Institute and was burdened with heavy responsibilities, and Francis called her in his letters "My very grown-up daughter": "You are well aware that you are my beloved grown-up daughter, and that nothing will remove the rank that you hold in my heart" (1615). "It seems to me that it has been a long time since you have written to me, and, all the same, love is never mute, even filial love, which always has something to say to the father."

There is a style, even a vocabulary, in his letters of spiritual friendship, which is not at all the same as that in the *Introduction to the Devout Life* or in the *Treatise on the Love of God.* Francis had a remarkable gift for "personalizing" each letter. No correspondent is identical to another; or more exactly, a correspondent is never identical to oneself, and the art of the good director is to address himself to his directee as though he or she were present at the moment. This principle is not only a guidance tactic; it is even more a fundamental counsel of the spiritual life. "Live from day to day . . . " "Go in good faith, under the Providence of God, having concern only for the present day." We "must accept ourselves such as we are here and now". "Do not desire to be what you are not, but desire to be very well what you are. Here you have the *key word* and the one that is least understood in spiritual guidance." "You must render a tenderly loving account of your state and its demands for the love of him who wishes it so."

This attitude of Francis in spirituality does not allow any fatalism or anything that resembles resignation, failure or negligence. It is for him, on the contrary, the condition of an efficacious spiritual combat. In fact, to accept oneself is to accept the will of God for us, in order to carry it out with the most love we can give it.

Francis de Sales wishes us to welcome this will of God *with heart;* he wishes us to accomplish it *with heart.* In the intimacy of his correspondence—even more than in his writings—he bases all his spirituality on the *heart.* Our relation to God ought to be an incessant *heart to heart,* and thus also our relations among ourselves. But let us be very careful to give to the word *heart* its Salesian meaning: the heart designates here, as in the Bible, that which is most profound, most inalienable, most personal, most divine in us; it is that mysterious center where each encounters God, acquiesces to his appeals or refuses to do so. "I shall never give up wishing that you will be the daughter of the heart of God, who has given us hearts so that we may be his children, by loving, blessing, and serving him." Francis likes to finish his letters with this wish: "May God be your heart." Or even, "Let our Savior be the heart of your heart."

This gives their true meaning to certain expressions that astonish us and, perhaps, annoy us when they do not shock us in the letters of Francis de Sales. Whenever he wrote to one or other of his Philotheas, he would say things like: "My heart and yours, it is all one", or "our very unique heart"; "Oh, my daughter, truly most beloved of my heart" (Mère de Chastel); "It is with all my heart that I cherish your beloved soul" (Soeur Marie-Aimée de Blonay); and other such expressions that sound sentimental to our ears, yet he gives them a totally different meaning: Francis perceives the hand of Providence in all true friendship that binds us. Thus nothing limits the love between two hearts that are united, solely because each is united to "the paternally maternal heart" of God (L.S.F., 525). And Francis thinks of the "friendship of the Virgin Mary: 'I am firmly resolved not to wish for more heart than that that she will give me, this sweet Mother of Hearts, this Mother of holy love, this Mother of the heart of hearts.'"

And so we explain the affectionate tone of Francis de Sales' correspondence. How impoverishing it is to see in it only the fact of temperament. It is, on the contrary, the concern of faith and of spiritual doctrine. It is true that we can easily be mistaken about this, because these letters, in general, were written "without time to breathe or relax", "without reflection", in the midst of worries and cares of all kinds. His spirit flowed through his pen. Moreover, what makes the original charm of this spiritual correspondence has to be the images and sentiments that rush forth so freely. Humor is mixed with the most profound thoughts; it goes from the anecdote to the intimate confidence. This is so true that his correspondence is for the biographer the best and most sincere *Spiritual Journal* that Francis de Sales has left us.

The mission of the Chablais permitted us to discover a combative Francis de Sales, a man who stood his ground and was audaciously defiant—and who was a lawyer and diplomat as well. The spiritual correspondence reveals to us a marvelous "friend of souls", whose psychological finesse relies upon a mystical doctrine that is sure of itself.

8

THE BISHOP AMONG THE PEOPLE OF GOD

1605–1608

These three years of Francis de Sales' episcopate must be grouped together because they were marked by a similar activity: Francis spent long weeks, even months, roaming over the most precipitous mountain roads and paths to visit these parishes in his diocese and thus have a direct contact with his far-flung pastors and people. To this we must add the Lenten sermons that he preached at La Roche-sur-Foron (1605), at Chambéry (1606)—although that city belonged to the diocese of Grenoble—and at Annecy (1607).

The missionary of the Chablais, at such times, showed beneath the violet robe of the bishop, but his activities were carried out in very different conditions. These populations were traditionally Catholic; it was again a question of converting them, but of converting them from a Christianity that was often formal, ritualistic, and mixed with ancestral superstitions to a true life of faith. Francis had the great concern of convincing the pastors that their care for souls had to be closely aligned to teaching catechism and teaching the Faith.

"A Complete Sphere under a Single Star" (Sainte-Beuve)

These years from 1605 to 1608 permit us to discover even better the breadth, richness, and fullness of Francis de Sales' personality: at this time he combined within himself the most contrasting gifts. The bishop who traveled, on horseback or on foot with a meager escort, across the plains and mountains was a prelate who already belonged to the universal Church. Pope Leo XI (Alexander de Médici, the former legate to Thonon) would have elevated Francis to the cardinalate and would have undoubtedly summoned him to Rome had not death abruptly interrupted his pontificate (March–April 1605). Francis was also a theologian, not a specialist in theological research but an "accomplished practitioner" of mystical theology, so well informed about the great quarrels of his time and about matters of faith that Pope Paul V consulted him in order to put an end to the conflict *De Auxiliis* (1606). Francis investigated new solutions for the problems—at that time acute—of religious life. He went directly to the essential, to the truth, to the sincerity of total adherence to God. He was only forty years old! But he was decidedly a complete genius in whom all kinds of qualities and virtues were balanced and blended into one another. To this was added his marvelous attractiveness: his goodness, patience, and affability drew hearts to him.

Pastoral Visitations

The diocese of Geneva-Annecy was, territorially, one of the most vast of that era: in 1606 it numbered 450 Catholic parishes and 150 Protestant parishes (in the areas of Vaud and Gex). On its terrain were numerous "chapels", five abbeys, six conventual priories, four Carthusian monasteries, and five convents of "mendicants".

Francis, caught up in urgent business matters, particularly concerning Gex, had only been able to plan his visitations in 1604. He would only really begin them on October 25, 1605, but on November 26 he was obliged to return to Annecy, "after having scoured the fields for six weeks without stopping in any place for more than a half day". In a letter to the Baroness de Chantal, dated December 5, 1605, he wrote: "Since my return from the visitations I have experienced some catarrhal fever; our doctor did not want to order me any other remedy than rest, and I have obeyed him." The winter ended, and he resumed his trips. He remained on the road about five months this time, and he returned exhausted on October 21. From October 7 to November 23, 1607, he visited the valley of Thones, the region of Parmelan,

and the shores of Lake Annecy. He visited the several remaining un-
visited parishes in 1608 and 1610. He was fortunate if he found a few
days of leisure in a life that was becoming more and more encumbered.

Let us not imagine that these were tourist jaunts. The romantics
and the sportsmen had not yet made the mountains fashionable! We
can believe that the pilgrim-bishop was responsive to certain panoramas,
but for him and his little entourage the route—or rather, the paths and
their soil, the ravines, the slopes, the stepping-stones and the rushing
streams—was more challenging than scenic! Some of these remote
parishes had never seen a bishop's miter! "During these past days,"
Francis wrote to the Baroness de Chantal in July 1606, "I have seen
some awesome mountains all covered with thick ice, about ten or
twelve miles distant." These awesome mountains, no doubt, were
Mont Blanc!

Francis experienced some dread about these trips. In the beginning
of October 1605, just before setting out again, he wrote to the
Baroness de Chantal: "I am going on this blessed visitation in which
I see at the end of the field crosses of all kinds. My flesh trembles, but
my heart adores them. Yes, I salute you, small and great crosses. I
salute you and kiss your foot, unworthy of the honor of your shade."
Six weeks later he wrote to his correspondent:

> I have preached regularly every day, and frequently twice a day. Ah!
> How good God is to me! I have never felt stronger. All the crosses
> that I had foreseen initially have only been olive trees and palm
> trees; everything that seemed like gall to me has proved to be like
> honey or something better. I can say, in all truth, however, that
> except for the time when I am riding horseback or waiting to fall
> asleep at night, I have had no leisure to give any thought to myself
> or to consider the direction of my heart, so closely did important
> preoccupations crowd upon each other. I have confirmed a countless
> number of people.

Francis knew in advance that the spiritual trials would greatly
surpass the physical sufferings during these visitations. Certainly these
were "good people", these mountain people of Savoy, but "ignorance"
—common to the Christian countrysides of every region in Europe—

was singularly aggravated by the geographic situation. Certain villages or hamlets and certain towns lived in a kind of isolation from the rest of the world, cut off by high mountains or snow. "Uncivilized and uncouth" is how Father de Quoex characterized them. "They have never, so to speak, heard anyone speak the Christian religion." Besides, it was necessary, in order to reach them, frequently to employ only their dialect, and so Francis was obliged to do this "in several places". To all of this were added many superstitions, magic, charms, and sorceries . . . ingrained in their spirit for generations: here and there Francis even had to cope with some who were "possessed".

In general, the receptions were less dramatic; thus, it was the enthusiasm with which the parishes received their bishop and the love shown by his people that comforted Francis. "O my dear daughter," he wrote to Mme de Chantal on October 2, 1606, "what good people I have found among such high mountains! What honor, what welcome, what reverence for their bishop! The day before yesterday I arrived in this little town (Bonneville) in the dead of night, but the inhabitants lit so many torches and so many fires that it was like daylight. Ah! How well they deserve another bishop!"

It is true that Francis did not husband either his time or his strength in the service of his people:

He preached and taught catechism and did not neglect to visit the smallest chapel; he conferred the sacrament of confirmation, heard confessions, and personally distributed Holy Communion to his people. He lent an ear to the complaints of all with great patience and ordered what he deemed necessary. He was informed about the excesses of some ecclesiastical and secular persons and about public sins and sinners, and he made corrections when there was need with a severity nicely seasoned with natural gentleness. . . .

Temporal administrations, reconciliations, lawsuits, and differences—nothing was overlooked, so that after the visitation souls and affairs were found to be at peace. Francis had a great concern for the pastors, and he was interested in their material situation; he sustained or stimulated their zeal, leaving them his directives so that they might serve their flocks even better. "In short, he was that good shepherd and bishop who lays down his life for his sheep."

The letters that Francis found time to write to several of his correspondents throw some light on the feelings that these visitations inspired in him: "The inhabitants tell me that a shepherd, going out to search for a missing ewe, fell into a very deep crevice in which he froze to death. O God! I ask, was the ardor of this shepherd so warm in his search for his sheep that this ice did not freeze over his body? And why then am I so lax in searching for my sheep? Certainly this softened my heart, and my heart—all frozen—melted somewhat."

With what eyes Francis regarded the scenery! "I saw marvels in these places: the valleys were filled with houses, and the mountains were completely covered with snow down to their bases. The poor widows and the humble village women—like the low valleys—are so productive, whereas the bishops—so highly elevated in the Church of God—are all ice! Ah! Will there not be a sun strong enough to melt what benumbs me?"

A pious remark? Not at all. And to convince us, here is an anecdote that dates from this same trip to the region of Chamonix.

In 1605, while preaching during Lent at La Roche-sur-Foron, Francis had made the acquaintance of a "simple village woman", a widow named Pernette Boutey, who lived in Amancy, a small market town near La Roche. She had married Pierre Dumonal, "a rather irksome husband", but, by dint of patience, Pernette succeeded in maintaining a true harmony in her home. When Francis met her, she was managing a business in dry goods and drapery. Always "careful and farsighted, never idle," she was "very generous to the poor, always on good terms with her relatives and friends". She attended Mass every day, even though the church was very distant, and if she was unable to go to church, she prayed at home "for the space of two hours"—in short, a Philothea before Philothea! Francis was astounded. He looked upon Pernette as a great friend of God, and he recommended himself to her prayers. But in June 1606 someone came to inform him that Pernette was deceased. To the stupefaction of those present, Francis displayed great emotion and "wiped his eyes two or three times". He asked his secretary to make inquiries as to the life and death of the dead woman. This was quickly done, and in July he wrote to the Baroness de Chantal: "Just now, someone brought me a report on the life and death of a saintly village woman of my diocese who died in June. Do you think that I should write about her? One day I shall send you an excerpt because—to tell the truth—there is something—I don't know what—good in this little tale of a married woman who was, thank God, one of my great friends, and she often recommended me to God."

This story had an unintended epilogue. About this time—indeed, well before he even envisioned writing the *Introduction to the Devout Life*—Francis had begun to write an important work on charity. On February 11, 1607, he told Mme de Chantal about it confidentially. "Whenever I happen to have a quarter of an hour free, I spend it writing an admirable life of a saint about whom you have not yet heard me speak." He was speaking of the *Life of Holy Charity*. "This is a long-term project, and one that I would not have dared to undertake had not some of my confidants urged me to do so." Francis promised her: "You will see a good portion of it when you come to Annecy." This was the germ of the *Treatise on the Love of God*. But Francis slipped into his letter this unexpected confidential remark: "I shall be able to interpolate in some corner of it the story of our humble village woman."

And so the memory of Pernette Boutey haunted Francis in this first draft of his great book. Others have even advanced the hypothesis that it is the story of this humble village woman that may have inspired him to take up his pen! It would seem ironic that the *Introduction* is due to a noble lady, Mme de Charmoisy, and the master work may be due to a humble village woman! With Francis de Sales anything is possible.

After the visitation of 1606, Francis wrote poetically: "I have encountered God very often in the calm and warmth that exist amid our highest and harshest mountains, where many simple souls cherish and adore him in all truth and sincerity and where the goats and chamoix run hither and yon on the treacherous ice to announce his praises!"

Sometimes Francis involuntarily admitted that these pastoral rounds weighed heavily on his shoulders, but he knew well enough how to react: "There is a little miracle that God works every night", he wrote to the baroness in 1608. "When I go to bed at night I am unable to move my body or my spirit because I am so exhausted, but in the morning I awake more eager than ever. Presently, I have no control whatever over order, measure, or reason (I tell you this because I would not want to conceal anything from you), and nevertheless here I am feeling very strong, thank God."

It was not his health or his tiredness that upset Francis on these trips: it was his "heart", the state of his soul. It seemed to him that, in spite of his efforts to animate his apostolic work with an authentic love of God, something within him was "distracting him". And so, right after his return, he plunged into a retreat.

"This is the day for my farewells, before leaving tomorrow at daybreak to go to Chambéry where the Father Rector of the Jesuits (Fr. Fourier) is expecting me as a guest for these five or six days of Lent that I have reserved in order to compose my poor spirit that is so disturbed by so many affairs. There, my daughter, I intend to review myself thoroughly and to replace all the jumbled pieces of my heart with the help of this good Father who is so genuinely concerned about me and my welfare."

The results of these visitations were considerable. Everywhere the people saw him exercise the sacerdotal functions, and with such devotion! Thus, in a single day—it was in the church in Chilly—he conferred all the sacraments except extreme unction. He preached, he catechized, he met and reconciled the people, and he advised the pastors. "He put things back in order wherever he went": canonical order is understood, but above all the order of charity.

As early as January 1606 he could write: "The heart of my people is almost totally mine at present", and in return "I feel a little more loving than usual." They could indeed tempt him with the cardinalate or incardination in the French clergy. But what were those honors for this man with so eminently pastoral a heart? Undoubtedly, he would obey a papal command. "It is true", he wrote—not without humor— "that I am in my own country and among my own people with as much security as I deserve, and what is even more dear to me, with as much rest as my responsibility can permit and that seems to me to be secure enough." Beneath the humor lay a great, concealed love.

Beginning in 1608, Francis was no longer able to visit the parishes except sporadically. "The affairs of this diocese are not waters, they are floods." Wherever he could not go personally, he would send some of his canons or some priests whom he trusted and who would give him detailed reports of their visitation. But if his presence seemed necessary, he forced himself to put in at least a hasty appearance. Then, too, all the pastors knew that at Annecy the bishop's door—and even his table—were always open to them.

The Florimontane Academy (1606–1610)

Decidedly, Francis de Sales does not cease to surprise us. At the end of 1606, during which he devoted six months to visiting parishes and also found time to preach the Lenten series at Chambéry, "the city of princes and of the august senate", Francis, in collaboration with his great friend Antoine Favre (at that time residing in Annecy as president of the council of Geneva, a powerful and influential institution), created an Academy, that is, a society of scholars and literary men. From where did this idea come to them? No doubt from the very flourishing academies in Italy, perhaps even from the Academy that Calvin had founded in Geneva; or else the "academies" that the student Francis de Sales had known at the Collège de Clermont in Paris. In any case, the coincidence of the people's missions and the foundation of an Academy is pregnant with meaning.

This Academy would last only three years (winter 1606, 1607, 1610), but thanks to the personalities of the two founders, it enjoyed a considerable influence. They baptized it la Florimontane "because the Muses flourished amid the mountains of Savoy", and they "selected for its emblem an orange tree with this device: flowers and fruit".

Never was an academy less . . . academic. To be sure, they were vigilant about securing among the members only doctors and scholars of incontestable quality, and these would even have special meetings, but these gentlemen would be there to "communicate" (a word dear to Francis de Sales) their knowledge in the "general assemblies" to "all these good masters of honorable arts such as painters, sculptors, carpenters, architects, and so on". It was expressly recommended in the constitutions of the Academy that "the style of speaking or of reading should be serious, polite, simple, and should not in any way suggest pedantry"; they should teach "well, much, and efficiently". Finally "the students—if there was something that they did not understand—were to ask questions about it after the lesson was finished". What were the subjects of these lessons? " . . . Theology, politics, philosophy, rhetoric, cosmography, geometry, or arithmetic. They would also study the embellishments of languages, especially of French." We learn that in the first year they gave a course in the art of navigation and in music theory. What was the atmosphere like in this Academy? "All the members of the Academy were to maintain a mutual and fraternal love." There was also this formula, which has the tone of a motto: "All things will come to the one who does his best."

The meetings were held in the home of Antoine Favre, at first in the Clos du Céans, then, beginning in 1608, in a vast mansion on the rue Sainte-Claire. The six Favre children joined in greeting those who came to teach or learn, which further accented the friendly atmosphere. To the cultural goal was joined a moral and civil aim that was deemed equally important. "All disturbers of the public peace"—by this we infer "heretics" and "enemies of the fatherland"—were not to be admitted into the Academy, which Francis and Favre dreamed of making "a forum of exemplary life".

The registers of the Florimontane Academy have, unfortunately, disappeared; however, we do know the names of several of its members. Let us at least mention the name of Honoré d'Urfé, who, after his misadventures at Ligueur, retired to his manor at Virieu-le-Grand. It was in this winter of 1606 that he was preparing to publish the first part of his saga *l'Astrée*. Claude, the son of Antoine Favre, was only twenty years old, but he would become celebrated among the first members of the *Academie française* under the name of Claude de Vaugelas.

In 1610 Antoine Favre was promoted to president of the senate of Savoy and was obliged to leave Annecy for Chambéry. Francis de Sales was too engulfed in responsibilities to maintain the Florimontane Academy alone. It declined, then disappeared.

But beyond the institution there was an "idea force" that animated Francis de Sales. He would delegate to others what he was no longer able to do himself. In 1614, he would succeed in having the Chappuisien College in Annecy taken over by the Barnabite Fathers: they would open the courses and lessons to the laity. Certainly, the project did not have the scope of the Florimontane Academy, but some excellent work was accomplished there . . . under the aegis of Francis! One of the youngest—and most brilliant—professors in the College, Don Redente Baranzano, was in contact with Galileo, and in spite of the official opposition of theologians as illustrious as Bellarmine, Baranzano dared to defend the opinion of Copernicus. In 1617 he published his *Uranoscopia seu de Coelo,* without the authorization of his superiors. The Father General of the Barnabites was furious and censured the author, wanted to withdraw him, and demanded of him a written retraction, which was published in 1618. But in 1619 the second edition of *Uranoscopia* appeared in Paris. In this affair Francis de Sales had the merit of thinking clearly and the courage of defending Baranzano as early as 1617. He asked his general not to withdraw him from Annecy. And when, the following year, Baranzano published his *Novae Opiniones Physicae* through the Pillehotte company in Lyons, Francis approved and praised the book. Meanwhile, in these years from 1615 to 1623, the Galileo trial was being prepared at Rome. In this affair, in which the theologians and exegetes were going to be bogged down for several centuries, Francis de Sales staunchly took the position right from the start in favor of astronomy. This taking of a stand went even beyond that of Baranzano and Galileo. Francis de Sales' solid theology permitted him to reject from the outset every conflict between science and faith. God, Creator of the universe and the light of human reason, is the same as the God of revelation. In the dawn of modern times, Francis, thanks to the serene profundity of his faith and of his spiritual experience, rises like a precursor.

The Quarrel "De Auxiliis" (1606)

For Francis de Sales, conciliation—and even more, reconciliation—was one of the most essential ministries of the priest and especially of the bishop. At Annecy and in the parishes that he visited, this was one of his major concerns. "Ever since my return from the visitations," he wrote in 1607, "I have been so pressed and rushed making appointments [meaning reconciling plaintiffs] that my house was full of plaintiffs who, by the grace of God, were, for the most part, restored to peace and repose. . . . We must yield to the needs of the neighbor." He succeeded so well in this role that he was given the surname of "conciliator". Not that he always satisfied the two parties; his arbitrations also earned him several tenacious hatreds. He himself, to his great regret, was sometimes subject to lawsuits. At least he did all that he could to bring the quarrelers, plaintiffs, or enemies to "peace and repose".

Francis' temperament played an important part in favor of his pacifying activities: everyone recognized his goodness, serenity, and equity—but also his judicial expertise acquired at Padua and enriched by his friendship with President Antoine Favre and other great jurisconsults, and finally his willingness to work among men in the manner of Jesus Christ: to pardon and to succeed in getting the people—above all Christians—to pardon one another. For Francis the request in the Pater Noster was not a prayer devoid of meaning. If we believe him in his letters and sermons, the forgiveness that Jesus accorded his executioners from the height of the Cross was one of the most useful as well as one of the most mysterious examples.

These three "gifts" of Francis were manifested in the affair *De Auxiliis,* which, at that time, risked tearing asunder the unity of the Church. The question actually did not date from the sixteenth century but from the very origins of Christianity. How could God, with his grace, aid human liberty to choose the good without ruining it—and how could human liberty preserve, under grace, the possibility of choosing evil without thwarting God's infallible aid? Luther and Calvin had just given a particular focus to this ancient problem, and Francis, in whom the least movement of ideas found echo and resonance, suggested that this problem would be more and more bound to the emancipation of human reason, to scientific progress, to the evolution of political and social law; in brief, that it was and would always be would always be central to the theme of the amazing intellectual and moral renaissance that had given birth to classical humanism. What? Are we not to consider the crises in Paris and Padua as a providential preparation for this? The solution that Francis was going to propose to the Pope and to the Church in the debate was not a theoretical, conceptual solution but one that had matured in him in the fire of his long suffering; it was a solution that had conquered and lived and was still living. It was, if we wish, the projection of his personal experience onto the universal plan.

In Francis' time the quarrel *De Auxiliis* had reached its most acute stage. The partisans of the Jesuit Molina and those of the Dominican Bañez confronted each other violently for twenty years. The Papacy had been obliged to take a hand in the controversy since 1598 and to organize a commission to settle the conflict. Things dragged on, and Pope Paul V decided to put an end to it. On September 14, 1605, he summoned the champions of these opposing theses before the commission. "And there," according to the report of a historian, "until March 1 of the following year, there took place the most bitter struggle, the most violent assault of arguments for and against, that had ever been seen, without the question being any more clarified or anyone being able to claim victory." Politics were involved: the King of Spain backed the Dominicans; Henry IV, the Jesuits.

In this imbroglio Bishop Anastase Germonio, who was close to the Pope and who knew of the latter's admiration for Francis de Sales, had the idea, at the end of 1606, of consulting Francis.

Unfortunately, Francis' response is lost. But many documents and his own experience reveal its tenor: it is the same solution that he would explain in the *Treatise on the Love of God* (bK., III, chap. V):

God willed primarily with a true will that even after the sin of Adam, *all men should be saved,* but in a manner and by a means suitable to the condition of their nature endowed with free will (*liberty*): that is, God willed the salvation of all those who would contribute their consent to the graces and favors that he would prepare, offer, and distribute to this end.

Now among these favors he willed that *vocation* (the call to the Christian Faith and life) should be the first, and that it should be so accommodated to our liberty that we might accept it or reject it at our pleasure. And to such as he saw would receive it, he would furnish with the sacred desire for repentance, and to those who would acquiesce to that desire he determined to give *holy charity,* and to those who were in charity, he intended to supply the helps needed to persevere, and to those who would employ these divine helps, he resolved to impart final perseverance and the glorious felicity of his eternal love.

Does this position constitute a dogmatic solution to the problem of liberty and grace? Or ought we to consider it as neither one nor the other but rather that it passes beyond one and the other by harmonizing them. It is situated—and this is by a very Salesian theology—in the plan of revelation, of immediately evangelical truths; it synthesizes the incontestable gifts of Christian revelation: it maintains the mystery of grace in the heart of the certainty of the Christian life.

In any case, Francis' response was read to Pope Paul V, who ordered that it be communicated to the Congregation *De Auxiliis.*

While writing to Bishop Germonio Francis declared that "the dispute over this question was extremely dangerous and had in its extremes certain heresies. . . . Starting from this there were many other things to cause anguish in the Church and to which she had better show concern rather than the clarification of this question, which would bring no good to the Christian republic but would cause it much harm. . . . And as for these very subtle minds of the Dominicans and the Jesuits, they would always agree sufficiently."

Paul V acted in the manner that Francis de Sales suggested. On August 28, 1607, "he imposed silence on one and the other" and sent each home. He "forbade" the parties to call each other names or to censure each other; "each was to remain free to support with good will the thesis that seemed the more true."

The Dominicans and the Jesuits did not disdain the inspirer of the pontifical decision, and at least they were in agreement about thanking Francis de Sales. On September 12, 1607, Francis received a diploma of affiliation in the Order of the Friars Preachers from the Father General of the Dominicans, Luigi Istella. "From diverse places he also received several beautiful and estimable letters from the most celebrated Jesuits."

The Death of Young Jeanne de Sales (1607)

In 1607 Francis was obliged to slacken his pastoral visits some-what. Two events detained him longer in Annecy: he preached the

Lenten sermons there, and he had to preside at the funeral of Duchess Anne d'Este, widow of the duke of Nemours. This was also the year when, around Pentecost, Baroness de Chantal spent twenty days in Annecy, and when—we recall—Francis announced to her his project of a new Institute. They parted foreseeing that this project would not be realized until after many years owing to the great familial responsibilities that encumbered the baroness.

God would move more quickly than the farsighted Francis de Sales and Jane de Chantal.

When leaving Francis de Sales at the end of May 1605, the baroness brought Francis' sister, Jeanne de Sales, "the little heart and delight of her mother", with her to Burgundy. Mme de Boisy had resigned herself to this sacrifice in order that her daughter might receive a quality education and "acquire a taste for devotion". The girl was entrusted to Rose Bourgeois, abbess of Puits d'Orbe, but the atmosphere of the cloister proved more than the girl could bear. Mme Brûlart, sister of Rose Bourgeois, took the child to her home in Dijon; this was another setback. In 1607 Baroness de Chantal, upon her return from Annecy, brought Jeanne de Sales to her own home to be raised with her own daughters. Shortly before autumn, President Frémyot went to spend a few weeks of vacation on his estate in Thoste. Jane and her little troupe of children joined him there. But they had hardly arrived when Jeanne de Sales died suddenly.

The baroness' grief was tremendous, so much so that she made "a vow to give one of her own daughters to the house of Sales" in order to return to Mme de Boisy the daughter that she had been unable to care for.

In Savoy there was weeping; Francis went up to Sales to console his mother. He was personally very afflicted by the death of this little sister, "whom he had baptized with his own hands" after his priestly ordination. "Alas, my daughter," he wrote to the baroness on November 2, 1607, "I am only a man, nothing more. My heart is more moved than I had thought. . . . But as for the rest, O! *Vive Jésus!* I shall always hold onto the will of Divine Providence; it does everything well and disposes all things for the best. . . . In the midst of my heart of flesh, which has had such a shock from this death, I perceive very palpably a certain warmth, tranquility, and gentle repose of my spirit in Divine Providence, which spreads in my soul a great contentment amid its grief." And returning to the baroness' secret offer, he dared to criticize her for her courageous sacrifice:

> You see I have not been pleased that you have offered either your life or the life of one of your children in exchange for that of the dead girl. No, my dear daughter, we must not only be willing for God to take us, but we must acquiesce that this be in whatever place it may please him; we must leave the choice to God, because it belongs to him. . . . In temporal losses, O my daughter, may God touch whatever string of our lute that he chooses; he will never make anything but a good harmony. Lord Jesus, without reservation, without if, without but, without exception, without limitation, let your will be done in father, in mother, in daughter, in all things and everywhere. Ah! I do not say that it is a fault to wish for and pray for their preservation, but to say to God: "Leave this one and take that one", my dear daughter, *that* we must not say.

This letter of November 2, 1607, is admirable. Never did Francis, in his numerous letters of condolence, reveal himself to be more human or more evangelical.

9

A WRITER
"WITHOUT TIME TO CATCH HIS BREATH"
1608–1609

The years 1608 to 1609 appear, at first glance, to be uneventful (I almost said banal) in the life of Francis de Sales: in 1608 he preached the Lenten sermons at Rumilly, he was preoccupied with the current affairs of his diocese, he was faithful to his episcopal obligations, and he made several short pastoral visits. These were the years, however, when he was editing and publishing a book that would enjoy a very great success well beyond the frontiers of Savoy: the *Introduction to the Devout Life*.

The Marriage of Bernard de Sales and Marie-Aimée de Chantal

During her stay at Annecy in 1607, the baroness had let slip a pleasant remark, but one to which she attached no importance. Returning from the procession of the Blessed Sacrament, she felt tired and decided to go upstairs to her room for awhile before dinner. At once several gentlemen appeared to assist her, but she accepted only the arm of Bernard de Sales: "You are all very kind, but this one is my choice", she said. Mme de Boisy, who was yearning for an alliance between her family and that of the baroness, envisioned her dear Bernard married to Marie-Aimée de Chantal. There was no such idea in the mind of the baroness: to begin with, both grandfathers in Burgundy would not accept such an alliance and besides, Marie-Aimée was only nine years old. In spite of the customs of the time, that would really be rushing things too fast!

The following October 8, 1607, young Jeanne de Sales died suddenly and the baroness had impulsively vowed to give one of her daughters to the house of Sales. It would be Marie-Aimée. Negotiations were to be held soon, and at the beginning of October 1608, Francis—taking advantage of the mission he had been given by the Pope to attempt to reform the abbey of Puits d'Orbe—brought along his young brother Bernard to arrange the betrothal. Bernard, the charming Bernard, knew how to captivate everyone—and above all the heart of Marie-Aimée. They were soon celebrating their engagement. The contract was signed on February 9, 1609, and the official marriage was celebrated in Burgundy on October 13, 1609.

The Service of Souls: Philotheas and Theotimuses

The contacts that Francis had with his people in the confessional, in individual conferences, in the course of his pastoral visits, in all his activities, unceasingly quickened his desire to furnish souls—desirous of attaining evangelical perfection—with a "guide" for the spiritual life. He worked, whenever he could (during his rare leisure moments), on this *Life of Holy Charity*, about which he had already spoken confidentially to Mme de Chantal in 1606. On all sides, he discerned souls capable of carrying out literally their "act of charity", of loving God with all their heart, all their strength, and their neighbor as themselves. These souls were asking for counsel and direction. But how could he respond to so many letters or grant so many private conferences? Then he had the idea—at least as early as 1602—of editing the short "treatises on spiritual matters", which would explain the essence of his direction and which Philotheas and Theotimuses would be able to communicate to one another, free to adapt them to their personal cases. "Madame," he announced on May 3, 1604 to the Baroness de Chantal, "I am sending you a manuscript touching upon the perfection of the life of all Christians. I have drawn it up not for you, but for several others; nonetheless, you will see whether you can find it profitable." On the same day, he addressed the same text to Mme la Présidente Brûlart and to her sister, Rose Bourgeois.

But among the beneficiaries of these precious, brief treatises would figure, at the end of Lent in Annecy, in 1607, Louise de Chastel, wife of Claude Vidomne de Chaumont, Seigneur de Charmoisy, Marclaz et Villy. Louise was twenty years old at this time. This young woman from Normandy was a very pleasant person, a bit of "an exile" in Annecy, but one who valiantly endured her exile out of love for a husband whom she adored and who adored her but whose duties as "regular gentleman" to the duke of Nemours required his frequent absence. Before her marriage Louise had lived in Paris as a maid of honor to Catherine de Clèves, dowager duchess of Guise, and she had tasted deeply of court life. The beautiful scenery in Savoy did not compensate for the splendors of the Louvre; likewise, her husband's lands were a nest of lawsuits that had to be regulated.

She met Francis de Sales at her first contacts with Savoyard society because the Saleses and Charmoisys were cousins; Francis and Claude were the same age. But it seems that, for three years, Louise had only that respect mixed with admiration for the bishop that was shared by everyone else.

A striking detail: it seems that "Philothea" first sought to profit from Francis' wisdom on the feast of Saint Timothy, January 24, 1603. And still with great reserve! On that day, having heard the bishop preach, she was interiorly urged to confess to him. Then she would sometimes lead her two children, Henry and little Frances, to him. Francis had a presentiment as to what this soul was capable of; he gently encouraged her to fervor, but for four years Louise—although very virtuous—seemed to have "no taste for devotion". It must be added that she was absent from Annecy rather frequently, visiting Paris or some of her estates. However, Francis did not lose heart. "There is a great possibility", he wrote her on May 20, 1606, for example, "that I may be prevented from speaking to you about the training of the heart and soul; it is because I do not only love yours, but I cherish it tenderly before God who, in my opinion, desires much devotion from it."

Finally, during Lent 1607, the young woman yielded to the call from God and placed herself resolutely under the bishop's direction. He announced it to Mme de Chantal: "I have just found in our sacred nets a fish that I had desired for four years. I must confess the truth: I have been delighted about her; I should say extremely so. I recommend her to your prayers so that our Lord may establish in her heart the resolutions that are placed there. She is a lady, as good as gold and infinitely fit to serve her Lord; if she perseveres she will do so with fruit."

The Misadventures of a Little Book and Its Author

In order to introduce this new Philothea to the devout life, Francis edited several "exercises". But suddenly, in March 1606, Mme de Charmoisy was obliged to leave Annecy for Chambéry: she had to undertake a long and difficult lawsuit before the sovereign senate. Francis recommended to Louise that she confide her soul to Father Fourier, rector of the college and Francis' friend. But she brought with her the papers with the "exercises" that Francis had edited for her: "I have been very careful", said Francis in the preface to the *Introduction* "to instruct her well. . . . I gave her some notes (*mémoires*) in writing so that she might have recourse to them as needed." When Father Fourier became acquainted with these *mémoires,* he was astounded. As early as March 25 (that is, fifteen days after Mme de Charmoisy's arrival in Chambéry), he wrote to Francis: "My Lord, how shall we persuade you to have Mme de Charmoisy's treasure printed? You must, in my opinion, review the whole thing, rearrange it, give it a title and a preface, with the author's name, in order that its worth may be more assured and more universal, all for the glory of God."

Docile as a schoolboy, Francis obeyed. Later he confided to Bishop Pierre de Villars: "It was Father Fourier who urged me so strongly to publish this writing. After I had hastily reviewed and revised it with several small improvements, I sent it to the printer." In fact, it was Father Fourier who would take the manuscript to the publisher, Pierre Rigaud, in Lyons, and it was also to Father Fourier that Francis—overburdened with business—would entrust the care of supervising its printing. Francis signed the preface on August 8, 1608; the book appeared in Rigaud's display window in December.

This was not the end of Francis' tribulations, because the book was in immediate demand in France and abroad, among Catholics and Protestants alike, both at court and in the city. A second edition had to be prepared early in 1609. In mid-February 1609, Francis wrote to Mme de Chantal, who was planning to come to Annecy: "Bring me all the letters and notes that I have ever sent you, if you still have them, because if the *Introduction* has to be reprinted, it will help me a lot if I can find among them some things on this subject."

Poor Francis! Life in 1609 scarcely left him those periods of solitude so necessary to a writer; nevertheless, he "reviewed, corrected, and augmented" his book with several chapters. He adapted his counsels in such a way that they were suitable not just for women but also for men: Philothea was extended to the masculine, just as Theotimus would soon be to the feminine! About September 1609 Pierre Rigaud gave the public the second edition of the *Introduction*. Disaster! They had worked so feverishly that three chapters had been "omitted inadvertently". As early as December 1609 they had to think about a third edition. Just as many pirated versions and translations were multiplying, unknown to the author. It was not until 1619 that the "last edition, reviewed, corrected, and augmented by the author— during his preaching at Paris" appeared. This time Francis seemed satisfied.

What was the reason for the success of Francis de Sales' "little book"? A great evangelical wind was suddenly passing over souls, a vivifying, pure, exalting breath that descended from the highest summits and retained all its purity. Every man and woman wanted to embrace it. Henry IV saluted with joy the publication of the work; Marie de Médici presented a copy of it, in a sumptuous binding studded with diamonds, to James I, King of England, who found it so much to his liking that he "carried it on his person for six entire weeks". In Geneva and the district of Vaud, "there was not a respectable house or a person of honorable condition who did not have this book". During Francis' lifetime, the *Introduction to the Devout Life* would have forty editions . . . without counting the clandestine versions. Today we give up counting them.

---

[1] At Paris, at the House of Joseph Cottereau, rue Saint-Jacques, at la Prudence.

A "Great Confusion of Affairs"

1609 was a year laden with events that greatly preoccupied the heart and the time of Francis de Sales. He wrote to the archbishop of Vienne: "There is probably not a bishop within a hundred leagues of me who has such a great confusion of affairs as I." Let us mention the most delicate of these "affairs".

There was, first of all, a weighty pontifical mission in June: Paul V ordered Francis to undertake, a second time, the reform of the Benedictine Priory of Saint-Germain de Talloires. The task was thorny: at the time of the first attempt at reform, had not the recalcitrants forced the prior to seek refuge in the neighboring village? They had even fired three pistol shots at him to warn him to keep quiet! This second visit was less dramatic. The bishop "summoned the monks and told them to embrace the monastic observance or to get out of the monastery within three days"—which was done—and they returned to their monastic observance.

Another event, on the contrary, must have rejoiced the heart of Francis. On August 30, in the Cathedral of Saint John in Belley, he consecrated Bishop Jean-Pierre Camus de Saint-Bonnet, who was twenty-five years old and who entertained an admiration for his elder peer in age and episcopate that took up rather a lot of Francis' time. Later Bishop Camus would write: "I was so new in this function that everything seemed darkness to me." And he counted on Francis to dissipate this darkness. All his life Francis—by dint of honor and affection—bore the weight of this friend, whose heart was even more bubbling with fantasy than were his countless novels. "You see, Bishop," Francis sometimes reminded Camus, "you are indeed right to do me honor because, although I have been called upon for the consecration of several bishops, it was only in the capacity of assistant, whereas for you I have been your consecrator, and so you are my unique consecration, apprenticeship, and masterpiece all in one."

The day after the consecration of Bishop Camus, on August 31, 1609, Francis received the "command from His Majesty [the King of France] to dispatch himself immediately to the district of Gex in order to confer about religious interests with Baron de Lux. Francis obeyed with such alacrity that he dared, as we have seen, to travel through Geneva.

This royal mission accomplished, Francis prepared to carry out another "at the command of His Holiness". The Pope entrusted to him the task of arbitrating a litigation that opposed the archduke of Austria (acting in behalf of the count of Burgundy) against the clergy of the province apropos the exploitation of rock salt in the Franche-Comté city of Salins. The affair would be regulated at Baume-les-Dames.

To get to Baume from Gex, Francis chose his dates and planned his itinerary so as to be at Monthelon on October 13, 1609, and there bless the marriage of his brother Bernard, Seigneur de Thorens, to Marie-Aimée de Rabutin-Chantal.

He was informed that two days later, on October 15, he, President Frémyot, and the bishop of Bourges would discuss the vocation of Jane de Chantal. The latter had opened her heart to her father the past June 24. The President had balked dolorously; finally, he asked his daughter "to make no resolution until he had spoken" with Francis. The hour for the interview had sounded.

Jane de Chantal "Obtains Permission" to Pursue Her Vocation

The interview between Francis and Benigne Frémyot was held on the prearranged date. Bishop de Bourges, strongly opposed to his sister's vocation, attended the interview. First they carried on their discussion with Jane absent. We do not know what was said, only that—as always—it was Francis who won the hearts of his questioners. They wished, however, to hear Jane herself before giving their definitive assent. Jane then entered and submitted to a "barrage of interrogations and remonstrances" on the part of her father and her brother. She replied to all their objections, notably on the subject of her children. She gave "an accounting of the state in which she had put her children's financial assets and how she would leave them free of lawsuits, disagreements, or debts (which was rare at that time!)". As for Celse-Benigne, he would remain under the guardianship of his grandfather Frémyot until the day when—according to his desire—he would be admitted to the court of France.

Marie-Aimée had just married two days ago and would, in the near future, be settled in the Château de Sales. Jane would retire to Annecy in order to guide this "young wife" in the conduct that she would have to maintain in her new position and in her housekeeping", and Jane would rear the two youngest girls, Françoise and Charlotte, at her side.

All this—inasmuch as Jane would not yet be a nun—seemed wisely organized! But when the time came, where would the new congregation be founded? The President wanted it at Dijon, the archbishop in his city of Bourges or Autun; Annecy was only a very little city . . . and outside the realm. Jane pleaded and assured them that "the kind of life she would embrace would allow her, for some time, enough freedom to provide general care for the welfare of her children". Francis, who had not said a word throughout this debate, promised that for the first several years Jane could make the trip to Burgundy whenever necessary. President Frémyot and the bishop of Bourges finally laid down their arms. "This woman", said the President (quoting the Bible) "has searched all the corners of her house."

The old Baron Guy de Chantal would have to be informed of all these decisions; the President assumed that responsibility. The debauched old lord was so overwhelmed that Benigne Frémyot himself asked his daughter not to hasten her departure but to postpone the date to spring.

With everything so organized, Francis again took the route for Baume-les-Dames on October 31, 1609. He brought with him the young Baron de Thorens, Bernard, "married as yet in name only". The President, the archbishop, and Mme de Chantal accompanied him as far as Baume. After hearing Mass in the chapel of the celebrated hospital, they separated "among the poor of our Lord". At Baume-les-Dames "arrangements were made to the satisfaction of all". On November 18, Francis returned by crossing the Franche-Comté above Annecy: he had promised to preach the Advent sermons there.

Decidedly, we must come to a clear understanding as to how to classify Francis de Sales as a spiritual writer. He was that, certainly and eminently. But he was a writer who scarcely found the privacy to write. It was in the fire of apostolic action that he began to write. The fact is evident for the *Introduction to the Devout Life,* but let us not forget that at the same time he was working on this *Life of Holy Charity* that he held close to his heart! How, then, was he able to manage all those tasks at the same time? Francis gives us the secret himself in the preface to the *Treatise on the Love of God:*

> I shall tell you, dear reader, that like those who engrave or cut precious stones, who, when their sight becomes tired from keeping it continually fixed upon the fine lines of their work, are glad to keep before them some beautiful emerald so that by looking at it from time to time they might be relaxed by its greenness and restore their strained eyesight to its normal condition—just so in this pressure of business that my office daily exacts from me I have always some little projects of some treatise of piety that I look at when I can, to revive and relax my mind.

10

THE "INTRODUCTION TO THE DEVOUT LIFE"

1609 . . . and Still Continuing

It is fitting for us to pause and consider this "poor little book", as Francis called it, because—although it first appeared in December 1608, practically in 1609—it remains very much alive today: the editions continue. Just what is there in this book that so fascinates our minds and hearts in a world that is so different from that at the beginning of the seventeenth century?

It concerns a word that we are going to develop: it responds and continues to respond to the fundamental religious desire of the human heart.

Three Key Words

Before we explain further, let us note the three words of the title: *Introduction* . . . Philothea (let us thus name the Christian soul) is still waiting at the gate, and Francis is going to try to help her penetrate, step by step, the Christianity to which she aspires. Philothea is instructed in her religion, she knows her catechism, and she practices her duties, but between her life and her faith there is more or less the distance that separates life and death. One day Francis wrote: "What good are these half-dead hearts?" *Devotion* is one of the most sacred words in spiritual language, but—it must be recognized—it is also one of the most insipid and one of the most boring in contemporary language. Perhaps it was a little less so in the time of Francis de Sales. He admits in the very first pages of the *Introduction:* "The world vilifies holy devotion as much as it can. It pictures devout persons as having discontented, gloomy, sullen faces and claims that devotion brings on depression and unbearable moods." It is true that each author, and even each Christian, lists under this same word some very diverse ways of practicing devotion.

> Almost all those who have hitherto written about devotion have been concerned with instructing persons wholly withdrawn from the world or have at least taught a kind of devotion that leads to such complete retirement. My purpose is to instruct those who live in town, within families, or at court, and by their state of life are obliged to live an ordinary life as to outward appearances. Frequently, on the pretext of some supposed impossibility, they will not even think of undertaking a devout life.

It is not, therefore, condition, profession, or age that opens the way to the devout life. It is the interior call, the "desire" to "aspire to the love of God". And God addresses this *call* to all Christians, and even to all men and women. This *call* is universal; it comes from the foundation of the gospel: "You shall love the Lord your God with all your heart, and your neighbor as yourself, for the love of God."

What, Then, Is the Devout Life?

Francis devotes the first three chapters of his book to describing "devotion" carefully. Because it is important to be precise about the *goal* and to define clearly this life to which he "tends and intends" to introduce Philothea, "it is essential that we know what the *virtue* of devotion is, inasmuch as there is only one true devotion, but a quantity of false and vain devotions".

Here is the illuminating text. Let us follow it in its progressive articulations: "True and living devotion presupposes the love of God; it is nothing other than true love of God." This is a capital declaration that immediately separates all the adulterated and dangerous forms of devotion. When, then, can we call the love of God *devotion?* Answer: "When it has reached that degree of perfection whereby it not only makes us do well, but it makes us do so carefully, frequently, and promptly." Let us note these three adverbs; they recur unceasingly under the pen of Francis de Sales in order to qualify devotion. They are even enriched with synonyms: "quickly . . . openly . . . affectionately . . . actively . . . diligently . . . " It is the leitmotif of this first chapter.

In brief, *devotion* is a certain "style", a way of practicing the love of God and the love of neighbor. "Devotion is nothing other than a spiritual agility and vivacity by means of which charity effects its activity in us, or we through it, promptly and affectionately." Devotion is the contrary of "devotions". "Just as it pertains to *charity* to enable us generously and universally to practice all the commandments of God, it pertains to *devotion* to enable us to do so promptly and diligently." All the commandments? How can this lighthearted availability be limited to these divine "orders"? "Beyond this, devotion provokes us to do promptly and gladly as many good works as we can, even when they are in no way commanded but only counseled or inspired." And in order not to mislead us, Francis sums up his thoughts thus: "Charity and devotion are no more different from one another than flame is from fire, inasmuch as charity—being a spiritual fire—when it is greatly inflamed is called *devotion,* thus devotion adds nothing to the fire of charity except the flame that renders charity prompt, active, and diligent, not only as to the observance of the commandments of God but also as to the exercise of the heavenly counsels and inspirations." Francis could be still more precise: "If charity is a plant, devotion is its flower; if charity is a costly gem, devotion is its luster; if charity is a precious balm, devotion is its perfume."

There is nothing less abstract or formal than *devotion.* Like charity, it varies for everyone "according to his occupation and vocation": "Devotion ought to be practiced differently by the gentleman, by the artisan, by the valet, by the prince, by the widow, by the young girl, by the married woman . . . and not only that, but it is important to accommodate the practice of devotion to the strength, affairs, and duties of each individual. . . . Devotion spoils nothing when it is true, but it perfects everything." It is forever and everywhere. "It is an error—indeed a *heresy*—to want to banish the devout life from the company of soldiers, from the shop of artisans, from the court of princes, from the household of married people. . . . Wherever we may be, we ought to aspire to the perfect life." In August 1609 Francis wrote to his friend des Hayes that he had written this book "always having in mind the people who live amid the pressures of the world".

So now we find ourselves well oriented; we know where Francis de Sales wishes to lead us. And the "people" are not mistaken by plunging into this little book. It is as if religion were suddenly—for them—liberated from a yoke, as if they were finally able to hope to love God totally while living their daily lives. Was this, then, a revolution? There were some objectors, but for the great majority it was not. As early as 1580 four great spiritual currents were proposed to souls desirous of loving God: one, prolonging the Middle Ages, insisted that one could not attain true devotion except by renouncing the world and shutting oneself in a cloister; a second was that of the "easy devotion" inspired by the "wisdom" of the humanist Pierre Charron; a third came from the Rhenish-Flemish mystics, and it reserved the love of God for a contemplative elite. (Francis de Sales knew this firsthand in 1602 as a member of the Acarie circle.) Happily, for the "great number" another current was formulated a few years previously: it came from Spain and Italy. Among its representatives, two, above all, won Francis' preference: Luis de Granada (*The Guide for Sinners* and the *Memoirs of the Christian Life*) and the Theatine Lorenzo Scupoli (*The Spiritual Combat*). To tell the truth, Gerson in France had—from the beginning of the fifteenth century—inclined toward spirituality in the sense of a "universal devotion". His celebrated cry *"Monachatus non est pietas"* ("Devotion is not the prerogative of the monk") became proverbial. Francis de Sales was very well acquainted with these tendencies of spirituality, but he had several times carried out the Spiritual Exercises of Ignatius of Loyola, during which he had heard "the universal call" that Jesus Christ launched in the gospel to all men, and he knew that the most humble souls could give to this appeal the response of "the distinguished", namely, those who threw themselves resolutely, generously, joyously into following the Lord Jesus and who wished "to distinguish themselves in his service". *Devotion*—such as Francis de Sales intended it—was born of his personal experience and of the confidences of his Philotheas.

The Itinerary of the Devout Life

By what itinerary was Francis going to "introduce" Philothea initially in the devout life, and then help her to make progress in it? He tells us himself in his preface:

> I have divided this *Introduction* into five parts, in the first of which I attempt . . . to convert Philothea's simple desire into a total resolution, which she does after her general confession, by a solid protestation, followed by a most Holy Communion in which, giving herself to her Savior and receiving him, she enters happily into his holy love. (All the words and gestures of this first step ought to be pondered.) This done — in order to lead her still more forward — I show her two great methods of uniting herself closer and closer to the Divine Majesty: the use of the sacraments, through which the good God comes to us, and holy prayer, through which he draws us to himself, and in this I employ the second part. In the third, I make her see how she must practice certain virtues more pertinent to her advancement. . . . In the fourth, I make her discover a few of her enemies' ambushes, and I show her how she must be dedicated to extricating herself from them so as to pass onward. Finally, in the fifth part, I make her withdraw a little from herself in order to refresh herself, catch her breath, and renew her strength so that she may afterward reach her goal more happily and advance in the devout life.

Such is the reader's "peephole" that Francis himself offers us in order that we may grasp his project.

The Outstanding Characteristics of Salesian Devotion

Alas! It is essential that we also "find our way" in our book. We are unable to present the richness of this spiritual text. At least it is fitting — so as not to be too incomplete — to point out the outstanding features of this spirituality.

First there is the importance Francis accords to the *baptismal commitment:* the "solid protestation" with which the itinerary of devotion opens is nothing other than that. Francis makes explicit reference to it two times: "I avow a second time and I renew the sacred profession of fidelity made in my behalf to my God at my baptism, renouncing the devil, the world, and the flesh . . . , converting myself to God I desire, propose, determine, and resolve irrevocably to serve him and love him now and eternally."

Francis did not separate the union of life with God from baptism, a union that is realized in the light, more-or-less "foreshadowed by faith", and of which the Eucharist is the sign and the nourishment. In the Eucharist one gives oneself to the Savior, and one receives him. The *Eucharist* — which Francis, like a good theologian, calls "the most holy, sacred, and most sovereign Sacrifice and sacrament of the Mass" — is "the sun of the spiritual exercises, the center of the Christian religion, the heart of devotion, the soul of piety. It is the ineffable mystery that encompasses the abyss of divine charity, and through which God — really applying himself to us — magnificently communicates to us his gifts and favors." Here all the words convey — and we especially remember: *The Eucharist is the heart of devotion.*

A third characteristic of the *Introduction to the Devout Life* is that it is bathed in an atmosphere of *spiritual liberty.* Playing upon the expression celebrated by Saint Paul, Francis introduces Philothea to *the liberty of heart of the children of God.* Thus, for example, when it is a question of prayer: to him who objects that Francis' counsels presuppose that Philothea has the gift of prayer, and that this gift — as experience proves — is not dispensed to each and every one, he replies: "Almost everyone can have it, even the most ignorant, provided they have good directors and that they are willing to work to acquire it, as much as it deserves. And if one finds that he does not have this gift to any degree . . . the wise spiritual father will easily help him make up for the lack: liturgical prayer, ejaculatory prayer, attentive spiritual reading, even "sighs" are there in order to relieve the difficulty of meditation."

Three Questions

Three questions, however, can be legitimately asked apropos the *Introduction.*

Francis states positively that he is speaking to certain people taken up with "the worries of the world", then to certain lay persons. And the priests and religious? No, he does not exclude them. Let them profit from it if they wish, according to their position and vocation! But they have access to more-learned books, better adapted to their state.

Another more subtle question is this. Was not the devout life, by intending to serve as a substitute for the monastic and contemplative life, not going to create—by its relationship to the simple Christian life—a new elitism? On the contrary, Francis de Sales asks Philothea to be present to the world, to her family, to her relations, to others, not only as if—but better than if—she were not devout. *Salesian devotion transfigures life; it does not mutilate it.* It is, according to Mother de Chaugy's beautiful expression, a *"well-mannered devotion".* Baroness de Chantal's servants gave a happy account of this: "Madame's first (spiritual) guide made her pray only three times a day, and we were all annoyed by it, but the bishop of Geneva makes her pray at all hours of the day, and this disturbs no one." A question of the hand, a question of the heart.

Finally, certain people ask, is not the divine call to devotion, such as Francis de Sales defines it, a privileged grace, already mystical? The answer depends upon the conception of the mystical that each of us has made for himself. Let us rather let Francis himself explain how he conceives these things; let us reread his three astonishing chapters on poverty—a problem still of much concern among Christians today (pt. III, chaps. XIV, XV, XVI). Philothea, like every disciple of Christ, must take into account the first Beatitude—that of the empty hands— "Blessed are the poor in spirit, for the Kingdom of heaven belongs to them", and understand that to those who have their spirit set on riches, the Kingdom will be closed. Philothea must not fix her spirit on terrestrial things. "Let it always be superior to them, above them, not in them." Let her be free from excessive love of wealth, "that prodigious fever that renders itself all the more insensitive, the more violent and ardent it is".

This does not signify that Philothea will neglect to "preserve or increase her temporal goods whenever a just opportunity presents itself". Quite the contrary. Francis tells her: "Have much more care about rendering your goods useful and productive so that the worldly do not get them." Why? Because "the possessions that we have are not ours; God has given them to us to cultivate." Philothea must be a faithful steward. God wishes it so.

Let us be on our guard against counterfeits. And Francis indicates to Philothea several infallible criteria of sincerity in the practice of poverty.

First of all, alms: "Always leave some portion of your means by giving it to the poor with a good heart."

Better still: "Love the poor and love poverty, because by this love you will become truly poor.... Love equalizes the lovers." And let this love be true. "Go frequently among the poor; take pleasure in seeing them in your home and in visiting them in their homes. Converse with them willingly; be much at ease, so that they may approach you in the churches, in the streets, and elsewhere. Be poor in your language with them, speaking to them like their companion."

What a merciless "conductor" this gentle Francis de Sales is! "Do you wish to do still more, Philothea? Do not be content to be poor like the poor, but be poorer than the poor." And how is that done? *"The servant is less than his master;* therefore, make yourself the servant of the poor; go to serve them in their beds when they are sick, I say with your own hands; be their cook, and at your own expense; be their seamstress and their laundress."

Finally, let Philothea profit from the thousand little occasions when she is lacking something useful or necessary. "Be very glad for these opportunities; accept them with a good heart; suffer them gladly."

Above all, if "some inconveniences occur that impoverish her— either from much or little"—storms, fires, floods, lawsuits ... "Oh, then you have the true season for practicing poverty, receiving with gentleness these losses of money, and adjusting yourself patiently and constantly to this impoverishment."

It may happen that this "diminution of money" goes as far as real poverty. "If you are really poor, Philothea, be so even in spirit.... You are in good company: our Lord, our Lady, the apostles ... were all poor.... Embrace it, therefore, as the dear friend of Jesus Christ who was born, lived, and died in poverty." Inasmuch as this poverty is a poverty "despised, rejected, reproached, and abandoned" among the worldly, it is "truly poverty".

This is a typical example of the way in which Francis makes

Philothea walk on the paths of devotion. Or rather, he does not lead her; he teaches her to guide herself according to the way God leads her. He teaches her to interpret and transfigure according to the spirit of the Gospel all that she encounters: joys and trials. "But, what we receive purely from the will of God is always very agreeable to him, provided that we receive it with a good heart and for love of his holy will: where there is less of ourself, there is more of God."

In these successive stages of her detachment, does Philothea—in order to act and react as devout—have need of being sustained by an exceptional grace? Francis de Sales is very cautious about entering this needless debate. It suffices for him that she has the spirit and the force of the gospel. For him a great principle dominates human existence: God has his gaze on each of us—what he calls a "Providence"—and, at each moment, in each situation, he helps the soul to acquiesce to his "tenderly paternal" will.

The Style of the Introduction to the Devout Life

By its content the *Introduction* was extremely close to the aspirations of Francis' contemporaries. It was, to use Vaugelas' expression, "the necessary book". How else explain its lightning success in the bookstores as well as its impact? Henri Bremond declared: "It marks a memorable date in the history of Christian thought and life." Its impact was all the more keen because the book possessed the familiar and simple tone of correspondence. Everyone reads it as though it were a letter that was addressed to him personally.

The style of the *Introduction* has delighted and still delights the most demanding critics, with few rare exceptions. These eulogies are repeated in the works of literature. I shall quote only these few words of Sainte-Beuve, who is, in my opinion, among the critics the one who best perceived Francis de Sales' literary secret:

> He crowns and represents to our eyes this doctrine in which the dogma melts and slips away ceaselessly, by a multitude—indeed, a cascade—of comparisons, all of them prettier than each other. . . . So much brilliance and smiling on the surface must cling to the founda-

tion itself and reveal it.... It is important to have seen to what excess everything with him festoons and flourishes.... Although he led a practical life, totally apostolic and episcopal, Francis de Sales is a writer.

Never has the word "style" had a greater fullness of meaning. We must take it in its most aesthetic but also its most touching sense. Francis de Sales has profoundly understood his era, its malaises, its needs, its appeals; he perceived the responses that some—in the name of theology—and others—in the name of humanism, of the Bible, of the Reformation, of mystical experience—attempted to give to these appeals. He assimilated, assumed, and transformed these responses the way a bee makes its honey from all the flowers in the garden. It was his personal response, the response surging from his profound personality. It was essential for him to be very sure of his theology, of his thinking, of his language, to dare to reveal himself in this way. The truths that he explains are neither scholastic nor didactic nor literary: they come from the heart and speak from the heart. They instruct and they charm.

How was the same man able to write the *Controversies* and the *Introduction?* Francis himself, in a letter to his friend Pierre Jay (1620 or 1621), gives us the secret of his new style: "We are fishers, and fishers of men. We must therefore use for this catch—not only care, labor, and patience but also bait, industry, lures, yes, even if I dare say it—holy ruses. The world is becoming so delicate that in future we shall not dare to touch it except with scented gloves and perfumed bandages, but what does it matter, provided that man be cured and finally be saved" (E.A., XX, 219).

Before passing on to the month of June 1610, which will witness the birth of the Visitation, it is good to note that the *Introduction* preceded the event by eighteen months. By July 1610, the book was in its third edition!

THE ANNECY VISITATION
1610–1615

Bereavements in the de Sales and de Chantal Families

In early 1610 two bereavements struck Jane and Francis. At the end of January, Charlotte, Mme de Chantal's youngest daughter, a child nine years old, died suddenly at Monthelon in the arms of her mother. On March 1 Mme de Boisy died at Thorens. Francis was at his mother's bedside when he learned of Charlotte's death. On March 11 he wrote a long letter to the baroness:

> My mother came here (to Annecy) this winter, and in the month that she stayed here she made a general review of her soul and renewed her desires to do well, with a great deal of affection, and she went away more contented with me than anyone. . . . She continued in this joyful state until Ash Wednesday, when she went to Thorens, where she went to confession and received holy Communion with very great devotion, heard three Masses, and assisted at Vespers. In the evening—being in bed and unable to sleep—she had her chambermaid read three chapters of the *Introduction* to her so as to give her some good thoughts to ponder, and she had her maid mark the *Protestation* to be read the following morning.

But as she was getting out of bed, Mme de Boisy had a stroke. Francis was notified and he rushed from Annecy: "Upon my arrival, totally blind and almost unconscious as she was, she caressed me firmly and said: 'This is my father and my son', and she kissed me while enfolding me in her arms."

The agony lasted two days. Then Mme de Boisy

> rendered her soul to our Lord, gently, peacefully, and with a counte-
> nance and beauty greater than she had ever had in life. While
> remaining there still I must tell you that I had the courage to give
> her the last blessing, to close her eyes and mouth, and to give her the
> final kiss of peace at the moment of death. After which my heart
> swelled greatly and I wept over this good mother more than I have
> done since I joined the Church, but this was a spiritual bitterness,
> thank God.

And Francis then turned toward this other deceased for whom Mme
de Chantal was weeping: "Our poor little Charlotte is blessed to have
left his earth before it had hardly touched her. Alas! It was, nonetheless,
needful to weep a little for her because, after all, do we not have a
heart that is human and naturally sensitive? . . . God gives, God takes
away, *blessed be his Holy Name!*"

On January 20, 1611, President Frémyot, Jane's father, died in Dijon;
in June 1613 it was the old Baron Guy de Chantal's turn. Francis would
lose his brother Gallois on July 29, 1614. Gallois had become the legal
head of the de Sales family after Francis took Holy Orders.

Jane de Chantal Leaves Burgundy for Annecy

"Now, then, dear daughter, *you are coming to the mountains.* There God
will enable you to see the Sacred Spouse *who leaps over the mountains
and runs over the hills, who looks through the windows and peers through the
lattice* at the souls whom he loves!" And so, around March 25, 1610,
Francis sent from Annecy, to Baroness de Chantal, the invitation to
depart. Jane set out under the protection of Bernard de Sales; she was accompanied by Marie-Aimée, who was soon to arrive at her "dwelling",
and by a friend, Jeanne-Charlotte de Bréchard, who had decided to enter
the bishop's new Institute. Young Françoise was at her mother's side.

This departure has been recounted at great length; it has even been
considerably romanticized.

It remains true that, when Jane left Monthelon, "the poor made a
mournful crowd" and that Baron Guy, who had caused Jane so much

suffering, that old man—"more than eighty years of age"—"almost collapsed" and "was able to respond only with pitiful cries". All were losing their treasure.

From Autun, where she stayed for two days, Jane reached Dijon. On March 29 she made her farewells. The scene belongs to Salesian folklore: Jane has remained in legend as "the mother who stepped over the body of her son in order to become a nun"; this means forgetting that Celse-Benigne was a young lord who was already burning to make—within a few months—his entrance at court, and that, born a Rabutin, he had from his childhood a very lively flair for the theatrical; also that he had stretched himself not in front of the main door but before the door of the study where President Frémyot had taken refuge so as to hide his sorrow while Jane was bidding farewell to relatives and friends. It was he, her father, who was most to be pitied and who was the most noble in his heartbreak. He blessed Jane and said to her: "Go, then, my dear daughter, to where God is calling you, and let us both stop the flow of our just tears in order to do greater homage to the divine will and also so that the world may not think that our constancy is shaken."

Celse-Benigne would soon leave for Paris, where he would reveal himself to be one of the most elegant, most ostentatious, and most foolish of young men: he would become the pride and the torment of his mother, but he would one day admit that if his mother had remained in the world, she would not have been able to give her attention to him. Everyone is free to feel pity, according to his heart, for the lot of the "poor child twice an orphan".

When it was learned that Jane and her little entourage were approaching Annecy, Francis de Sales "and about twenty-five persons—as many lords as ladies—mounted horses and went out to meet them". It was April 4, 1610, and Palm Sunday. Jane and her little company were received in the home of President Favre, whose daughter, the beautiful Jacqueline Favre, had been "gripped" by God in the course of a worldly festival organized "for the pleasure of seeing her dance"; Francis had accepted her among the foundresses of the new Institute.

The Easter celebrations over, Jane de Chantal led Marie-Aimée to the Château de Thorens and remained with her "in order to help her take charge", because the good Madame de Boisy was no longer there.

It was planned that the new Institute would be inaugurated on the feast of Pentecost, May 30. Francis had a great devotion to this mystery of the beginning of the Church.

The "Bethlehem" of the New Institute

They settled in a little house that the Baron de Cuzy had acquired in the Perrière suburb and "made it suitable for lodging a dozen persons plus the addition of a little oratory". This house was called "the Gallery House", because it comprised a rather vast room — a gallery — whose bay windows opened onto the lake, the mountains, and the gardens along the shore. It was understood that Mme de Cuzy, who believed that she was called to the religious life, would be included among the group of foundresses, while her husband would become a Capuchin! A sum of money, donated by the Baron and Baroness de Cuzy, would permit the nuns to live. But suddenly Mme de Cuzy fell ill and saw in this illness a sign that God did not approve of her vocation. No more Gallery House, no more money. Where would they settle? How would they live? Francis had distributed his inheritance among his brothers and sisters; Jane de Chantal had just divested herself of all her goods and would receive only a small pension "by way of an alms" from her brother, the archbishop. Jacqueline Favre had ten brothers and sisters; Charlotte de Bréchard could no longer hope for anything from her father. As for the house, this was arranged: M. de Cuzy had not yet handed over the sum stipulated by the ex-proprietor; the name of the bishop was substituted for the baron in the sales contract. Francis paid several ecus on the spot; he would give the rest in payments. But the daily bread? They would implore the bounty of the Father, who feeds the birds of the sky!

When Mme de Chantal came down again from Thorens to Annecy on Saturday, May 29, she learned that the inauguration of the Institute was postponed. The date was fixed: June 6, the feast of the Blessed Trinity, which coincided with the feast of Saint Claude!

God wished that even before being founded, the new Institute should learn to take no thought for the morrow.

These setbacks, after all, would scarcely have any importance if a letter in which Francis related his misadventures to Father Nicholas Polliens did not reveal to us his feelings at this critical moment:

Amidst all that, I had to suspend the plan to erect a reformed monastery (conformed to the reform of the monasteries according to the Council of Trent); and, nevertheless — in order to provide a place for a very decent retreat for a few souls who were firmly resolved and holily impatient to withdraw from the troubles of the world — I opened to them the door of a little assembly or Congregation of women and girls living together in an experimental manner, under some pious little Constitutions. We shall begin with poverty because our Congregation will not claim to enrich itself except by good works.

We see the direction of Francis' reply: from the plan of a "reformed monastery" he passed to "a little assembly or Congregation". But "the pious little Constitutions" were going to reveal the essence of his project: the "cloister", but a modified cloister; the Sisters "will go out for the service of the sick after the year of their novitiate"; "they will chant the Little Office of our Lady"; and here was their major occupation: "Besides, they will be occupied with all kinds of good practices, notably, that of holy and cordial interior union." This was simple. Too simple, no doubt! Francis foresaw that this innovation would not please everyone: "I know that I shall attract criticism upon myself, but I am not concerned about that, because who has ever done any good without it?" His goal would be attained: "Several souls will withdraw to be close to our Lord, and they will find a little refreshment and will glorify the name of the Savior. Without that they would remain with the other frogs in the marsh."

Francis added: "There you have the summary and first outline of this work." It was with these sentiments that Francis, twelve days later, would install his first three daughters in the little Gallery House.

The Evening of June 6, 1610

In the morning of this June 6, 1610, Mme de Chantal, Jacqueline Favre, and Jeanne-Charlotte de Bréchard heard Mass in the chapel of the bishop's residence, and they received Holy Communion from his hand. They spent the day visiting churches and the poor. In the evening they returned to the bishop's dwelling, because he had invited them to have supper with his brothers. The meal ended, Francis handed Jane a booklet of "pious little Constitutions" that he had drawn up, and he told her: "Follow this road, my daughter, and make all those follow it whom heaven has destined to follow in your footsteps." Then he blessed them "in the *name of the Father* who attracted them, *of the Son,* the eternal Wisdom, and *of the Holy Spirit,* who animated them with his loving flames". They then set out from the bishop's house for the little Gallery House. Bernard de Sales escorted Jane, his mother-in-law; Jean-François led Jacqueline Favre, and Louis (Jacqueline Favre's former suitor) brought Charlotte de Bréchard. The cortège had great difficulty covering the short distance that separated the two lodgings, so dense was the crowd. A woman was waiting at the door of the Gallery: it was Anne-Jacqueline Coste, that "peasant by birth, very noble of heart and desire", whom Francis had providentially encountered in Geneva at the time when she was the servant of the Calvinist innkeepers. Her courageous activity, her rustic faith, her charity would gladden and enliven those first days of the Visitation. Mother de Chantal would write about her after her death: "All in all, she was incomparable."

When everyone had withdrawn, the two young girls and the servant promised Jane de Chantal perfect obedience, and—after saying their prayers in common—they went off to bed. Beginning the next day, the novitiate of the three foundresses commenced under strict enclosure. The little family grew very quickly: at the end of a year the community counted ten members. Francis himself served as "spiritual master" to three novices. "They say the Office of our Lady and spend time in mental prayer", he wrote to a friend. "They have work, silence, obedience, humility, exemption from all ownership, and—as much as any monastery in the world—their life is loving, peaceful, and greatly edifying. After their profession, with the help of God, they will serve the sick with great humility." They passed the year of the novitiate, but not without Mother de Chantal's falling ill and "thinking she was going to die".

On June 6, 1611, Francis de Sales received the vows of the first three Mothers. On December 31, the first annual chapter of the new Congregation was held. At the end of the meeting Sister Marie-Jacqueline Favre asked of Mother de Chantal "permission to visit the sick". Starting the next day, the first day of the year 1612, the good people of Annecy were able to see two of the "bishop's Sisters" walking through "the slums and hovels of the city two or three times a week". But soon recruits were plentiful, and the Gallery House became too small; they were obliged to seek another lodging. They found a house in the interior of the city, near the ramparts. The resettlement took place on the vigil of All Saints, 1612: this was "the first monastery".

Thus the Congregation lived and grew. Francis de Sales and Mother de Chantal scarcely ventured to look beyond the walls of Annecy — and still less beyond the frontiers of the diocese.

Genesis of the Visitation of Holy Mary

When we consider the birth of the Visitation and its development in the course of the years 1610 to 1615, we discover this striking contrast between the firm security of Francis de Sales' fundamental intuition and his deliberateness and prudence in planning each detail of its completion.

Even the name of the new Institute, for example. At the start of the project his daughters had neither name nor patron. Then, being inspired by the foundation of Saint Frances of Rome, Francis had thought of calling them "Oblates of the Blessed Virgin". Afterward he preferred "Daughters of Saint Martha". The correspondence proves that he had settled on this name in 1607. Finally, "for more than one motive the Congregation desired as its patroness the Blessed Virgin of the Visitation". This choice dates at least from July 1, 1610, and the new Sisters called themselves "Religious of the Visitation of Holy Mary". Francis allowed several of his choice motives to filter down; one of these seems preponderant: "He found in this mystery", he said, "a thousand spiritual particularities, which gave him a special light concerning the spirit that he desired to establish in his Institute." And this name, as tardy as it was, henceforth clung to his heart: at the time of certain discussions with Archbishop de Marquemont, which we shall recall below, he would beg the archbishop of Lyons to agree "that in any case the name of the Visitation remain" (E.A., XXV, 340). In fact, the pontifical brief that would transform the Annecy Visitation into "formal religion" would call it a "Congregation of the Blessed Virgin Mother of God of the Visitation".

One point of the Constitutions has elicited and still elicits discussions among historians of the Visitation: the visiting of the sick in their homes. We shall not go into the basis for this debate, but here are some items to consider in the dossier.

It is undeniable that, starting with January 1, 1612, two Sisters of the Visitation went through the city of Annecy to visit the sick, to care for them, to bring them remedies and nourishment. Mother de Chantal herself was the first, with Sister Favre, to give the example. In doing this she was repeating her heroic charitable activities at Bourbilly and Monthelon.

Undoubtedly, the public health situation in Annecy (4,500 inhabitants in 1610)—which had at its disposal only "a poor little hospital" to accept the poor and the sick—prescribed that this "assembly of Christian young women and widows" should be concerned, like Philothea, with helping the unfortunate. But this explanation is insufficient: visiting the sick "constituted an integral part" of the bishop's initial project, without being, for all that, "the principal end".

Already in 1607, at the time when the Sisters were supposed to call themselves "Daughters of Saint Martha", Francis had written to Mme de Chantal that they would alternate between "loving contemplation at the feet of the Savior" and the "hard tasks of serving him well", and that they would share their hours, giving "a good portion to the exterior works of charity and the best portion to the interior (work) of contemplation" (E.A., XIII, 311).

In 1610, in his letter of May 24 to Father Polliens (thus even before the inauguration of the Institute)—which we have cited earlier—the founder makes himself more precise. The two axes of his formation are strongly marked in their proportion: the Visitation will have the cloister of a "reformed monastery", with, however, one exception: the Sisters "will go out for the service of the sick after the year of novitiate"; and besides, "they will occupy themselves with all kinds of other good exercises (besides the Little Office of our Lady), notably that of holy and cordial interior union". Francis would enumerate these "other good exercises" a few days later, in a letter to Philippe de Quoex: "An hour of mental prayer in the morning and one hour in the evening, and, for the remainder, a maintenance of work, silence, obedience, humility, and extremely strict abnegation of ownership as much in the monastery as in the world."

Not until July–September 1613 would Francis finally give his daughters some real Constitutions. His project was at the time totally mature, not only in reflection and prayer but also in experience. But on the point concerning "going out to serve the poor", we discover a capital text:

> If the Congregation were established in some large city (*some steps were already outlined for the establishment of the Visitation outside of Savoy*), going out to visit the particular invalids might be perilous. It would be up to the prelate of the place either to curtail all these visits or to limit the sisters solely to visiting hospitals and pious places or to the visitation of known homes, such as he would deem to be more appropriate. And even if there were some resources in the Congregation, they could make use of these solely for the preparation of food necessary for the sick, the poor, the suffering, because it is one of the more desirable advantages of simple congregations that they be able to be employed in diverse ways, according to the variety of places, time, and circumstances (E.A., XXV, 226).

Francis de Sales was no armchair strategist! The Visitation, for him, was a living creation, which God fashioned to the taste of his Providence, which ought to grow and evolve "according to the variety of places, of time, and of circumstances".

We must have this before our eyes in order to understand what was going to happen.

Francis de Sales and Archbishop de Marquemont: The Visitation as a Religious Order

In 1617 (September–December) Francis wrote a "Preface for the Instruction of Devout Souls on the Dignity, Antiquity, and Variety of the Congregations of Women and Girls Dedicated to God". An astonishing picture of the life consecrated to God, which starts from creation—"God created man in his image and likeness" (Gen 1)—it runs across the centuries and envisages all the ways in which the woman can consecrate herself to God! What erudition, but, above all, what a vision of "consecration"! To conclude, finally (it is true that the end of the text has disappeared): "In sum, if the spirit of devotion reigns in the congregations, a mediocre cloister will suffice to make good servants of God; if it does not reign there, the strictest cloister in the world will not suffice" (E.A., XXV, 291). This was to defend the option that he had established in the Annecy Visitation!

But in 1613, Msgr. de Marquemont, Archbishop of Lyons, had begun negotiations with Francis de Sales to have a monastery of the Visitation installed in that city. As early as February 1615 the matter was done. But Mgr. de Marquemont was a redoubtable canonist: the originality of the Annecy Visitation was not agreeable to him; he wished that the Lyons Visitation would be a "formal religion" (as they said at that time), that is, that the strict cloister would be imposed on it and that the Sisters would pronounce solemn vows. The two prelates met in July, then in September 1615. January 20, 1616, Mgr. de Marquemont sent Francis a learned and very critical note. To be fair, it must be said that this note was accompanied by a more accommodating letter, at least in its final passage: "If, after having recommended the affair to our Lord, you wish that I allow the visits to the sick to stand and that I conform to you entirely . . . , I shall tread my feeling underfoot . . . and I shall establish the Congregation, and I shall have the Constitutions published and printed word for word, as you will order, without changing anything at all" (E.A., XVII, 407). To which Francis replied at length on February 2, 1616: an admirable response of humility and respect, yet very firm.

Francis defended and legitimized his Annecy Visitation, put everything in place, even asked the archbishop to correct his language "in certain areas" of the *Notes* (had not the latter accused him of wishing "to lecture the bishops and to act like the Pope"!), but in the end—because he saw clearly that the archbishop would be more completely and agreeably satisfied if this Congregation were converted into a *formal religion, under the Rule of Saint Augustine* and with the same *Constitutions* that it now had, the bishop of Geneva acquiesced to this also, freely and generously, "because in this transmutation we could exactly preserve the goal of this Congregation" (E.A., XXV, 340).

Finally, Francis submitted to the demands of Bishop de Marquemont. He did so "with gentleness and tranquility — better still — with unparalleled sensitivity". This was because in founding his Institute he had intended and only intended one thing, "that God be glorified and that his holy love be diffused more abundantly in the hearts of these souls who are so happy to dedicate themselves totally to God" (E.A., XVII, 139).

Three points were fixed in the heart of the founder in these transactions: (1) that the Sisters were not to be required to recite the Divine Office but "the Hours of our Lady"; (2) that the Congregation be more accessible to older women for admission and that it have the right to admit into community widows predisposed for a long time to the religious life but still having "some business to regulate"; (3) that lay women be permitted to "make a retreat" within the cloister. Francis urged at Rome that these three requests be accepted, but without success. Only the "Little Office" was accorded him, and for a period of seven years.

The pontifical brief of April 23, 1618, finally elevated the simple Annecy Institute to a religious Order, and on Sunday, October 16, Francis promulgated the Brief in the Visitation at Annecy.

The Spirit of the Visitation

To grasp the spirit of a religious Order, one must live its Rule. Only the Visitandines can speak knowingly of the spirit of the Visitation. The historian only perceives something of the exterior. He has no experience; he can only transcribe certain impressions.

One phrase of Francis sums up all that we could say: a "thousand lights" concerning the evangelical mystery of the Visitation had come to him for his Institute. The spirit of the Order of the Visitation is nothing other than the spirit that animated the Virgin Mary at the time when she visited her cousin Elizabeth "in the mountains"; the spirit of adoring union with the Word Incarnate, the spirit of thanksgiving before "the marvels of God", of spontaneity and promptness in rendering the humble services of daily life. The most extraordinary divinity enclosed in humanity the most silent and the most commonplace. The essential!

Just as he had gone directly to the essential of the religious life when writing the *Introduction,* Francis de Sales went to the essential of the Christian life when founding the Visitation of Holy Mary. Certainly he appreciated, praised, and assisted all the forms of "religions" (this was how the great contemplative orders of his time were designated); but he wished them to be fervent, faithful to their Rule and to their vows, animated by an authentic charity. "The strictest cloisters do not make souls united to God." There is no need for more great austerities and mortifications, or more rigorous observances, or more lofty contemplation, or the most extraordinary ecstasies, but only charity. The whole exterior of the religious life is nothing if the hearts of the monks and of the nuns do not burn with the love and the spirit of Jesus Christ. One might say that Francis was obsessed in his concept of the religious life by the text of Saint Paul to the Corinthians: "If I should speak with the tongues of men and of angels ... if I should deliver my body to be burned, if I do not have charity, it profits me nothing" (1 Cor 13:1–8). In the *Book of Vows* he wrote on June 6, 1611, the day of profession for the first three Mothers: "The humble glory of the Sisters of the Congregation. We have only one bond, the bond of love. The charity of Jesus Christ presses us." In 1619, concerning a candidate "who has no use of her legs", he would write to Mother de Chantal: "Without legs, one can do all the essential exercises of the Rule: obey, pray, sing, keep silence, sew, eat, and—above all—have patience with the Sisters who will carry her, when they will not be ready and prompt to do this charity. . . . I see nothing that ought to prevent her reception, if she is not crippled in her heart."

To form the heart of his daughters according to this spirit, Francis brought all his care: he visited them frequently, spoke to them in community, directed them personally. Some Sisters, with more reliable memories, had the good idea of recording these "Conferences" as soon as the conversation ended. Twenty-one of them remain, of which only six belong to this period from 1611 to 1616. This is rather disappointing, but throughout these gracious, scattered colloquies we easily recover the "style" (in the sense in which we have already defined it) of the *Introduction* and of the *Treatise on the Love of God.*

As in the *Treatise,* we detect in many pages the influence of the experiences of the first Visitandines. "It has been a very long time", Francis declared in the preface of the book, "since I first planned to write about holy love, but that project was not comparable to what this opportunity (the charge of the Visitation) has enabled me to produce."

"Like Rays of the Sun"

That the Visitation had existed for six years under the Annecy form before maturing into "formal religion" and extending beyond Savoy matters much in the history of religious life in Christianity. We speak with just cause and admiration about the prodigious growth of the Order that followed this transformation: thirteen monasteries were founded by 1622, at the death of Saint Francis de Sales, and in December 1641 Mother de Chantal left eighty-seven houses. But the influence of the original creation of Francis de Sales on religious life is not limited to this assessment, beautiful as it is: from the eighteenth to the twentieth centuries certain congregations, institutes, and associations of men and women arose in the Church that claim kinship with him or were inspired by his spirit: contemplatives, actives, missionaries; educators . . . who could expect to identify them all? Would this *influence* have been possible if Francis de Sales had not first created and inspired a first "assembly" that—beyond all the traditional forms— lived simply with its total "oblation" to God? By aiming thus at the essential, Francis de Sales was able to be universal . . . to such a degree that it is possible to notice certain parallels between the Salesian conception of the religious life and that that Vatican Council II restored to honor: "The congregations and the religious", Francis had dared to write to Mother Favre on February 2, 1616, "are no different before the Divine Majesty" (E.A., XVII, 140). The ways may vary; the goal is identical.

12

THE "TREATISE ON THE LOVE OF GOD" 1616

Before presenting the *Treatise on the Love of God,* we must remember what a "turmoil of affairs" and events preoccupied Francis de Sales while he was writing the final pages of his book and seeing to its publication.

The Retreat during Pentecost 1616

The first event was not outwardly apparent; it was, nonetheless, very important. It had to do with the private retreat that Mother de Chantal made during Pentecost (May) 1616. Here, then, was Mother de Chantal "in solitude" at the Visitation. Francis was ill at the time, and unable to go to the parlor of the monastery to help his "dear daughter", he remained in his bishop's residence. They communicated by notes. Thanks to an unhoped-for bit of luck, Mother de Chantal did not destroy these brief messages—as she had nearly all of her letters to Francis—and so we are able today to pursue this admirable exchange. What did this mean to Francis? Since 1604 he had been directing Jane de Chantal and had accompanied her in her spiritual progress. He discerned in her that call to "pure and unconditional love", which is the summit, here on earth, of the spiritual ascension. In 1616 he judged that the moment had come to indicate to her in a clear way that God wished to establish her in "a perfect purity of heart" and to counsel her to make the leap decisively. It was in the message of May 21 that he finally wrote her:

Our Lord loves you, Mother; he wishes you to be totally his. Have no other arms to carry you except his, no other breast to repose upon except his and his Providence. Do not look elsewhere, and do not repose your spirit anywhere save in him alone. Keep your will so simply united to his in all that it will please him to accomplish in you, through you, and for you and in all the things that are outside you. Let there be nothing separating you from him. Think no more of the friendship or of the unity that God has effected between us or of your children or of your body [Mother de Chantal was very often ill] or of your soul or of anything else, because you have handed everything over to God. Clothe yourself with our Lord crucified; love him in his sufferings. . . . What you have to do, do no longer because it is your inclination but purely because it is the will of God.

Mother de Chantal understood all too well to what sacrifices God was calling her: "My God, my true Father," she replied, "how deeply the razor has penetrated!" Shortly afterward, she began to travel the great roads to found Visitations. Francis intervened only to regulate certain juridic or financial difficulties. He himself soon began to take long absences from Annecy, so much so that he and Jane would not meet except intermittently and briefly, and so no opportunity for a conversation would present itself during the last three years of Francis' life. Mother de Chantal, so Francis judged, had to assume alone all her lofty stature of foundress.

The War in Savoy

The second event was political and diplomatic. At the end of 1615 and the start of 1616, the duke of Savoy had taken up arms, this time against Spain, and he had required of his vassal the duke of Nemours that he raise a troop of three thousand men in his Genevan appanage. Louis de Sales, Francis' brother, found himself committed in the affair. But Spain had secretly hired Nemours' mercenaries and convinced him to use his troops to make himself independent of the duke of Savoy. Louis de Sales refused to follow Nemours in his revolt. The duke of Savoy's reaction was to send several troops to occupy Annecy on June 24. Nemours, who had been driven back into France, appeared before the walls of Annecy on July 22, 1616, with three French companies, "weapons in hand and bugles at their lips". But the people of Annecy had recovered their courage, thanks to the example of their bishop, and they refused to allow the French to pass through their city. Serene and calm, Francis assured them that they were courting no danger, that "all this would disappear with no other result than that of a good peace that came about afterward".

Reinforcements arrived from Piedmont. Nemours and the French withdrew. On August 12 the prince of Piedmont, whom the duke, his father, had sent to reestablish order in Geneva, arrived at Annecy and, "unexpected", took his lodging at the bishop's house. Francis had a long conversation with him. They were pleased with each other. "He is the most gentle, gracious, and devout prince", the bishop wrote. As for the prince, who had "a heart full of courage and justice, a head full of judgment and wit, a soul that breathed only goodness and virtue", he would become attached, like a true Theotimus, to the bishop of Geneva. Within three years Francis would be part of the embassy—led by Cardinal Maurice of Savoy—to request the hand of Mme Christine de France for the prince; he would assist at the wedding, and then the prince and his spouse would choose him as their "principal chaplain".

Lent at Grenoble

The third event was preaching the Advent sermons at Grenoble, which was followed by the Lenten sermons for 1617 and then Advent of that same year. Three long contacts with this city for Francis about which he would say: "I have never seen a more docile or more devout people than these." It is true that he added, "The women, above all, are very pious here, because—as everywhere else—the men leave the care of the household and of devotion to the women." But this was the first time—outside of the Lent at Dijon in 1604—that the duke of Savoy authorized the bishop of Geneva to preach a "station" in Advent or Lent in a large city in France, so afraid was he that Francis—under the cover of religion—might get ensnared with the French court in some clever intrigue. In fact, what did interest Francis was something totally different: among his services to the souls in his diocese, he did not forget the Protestants, and he strove to find ground for good, sincere understanding; witness this mysterious letter of April 27, 1616, and the *Note for the Conversion of the Heretics and Their Reunion with the Church.* "Here are my thoughts", he concluded. "So many heretics and heretical republics are so close to me that my spirit cannot prevent itself from thinking about this frequently, or from taking pity on such a desolation—not only in the present—but in the future" (Pl. lxxiv).

But in 1616 Dauphiné was ruled (the word is not excessive) by the marshal-duke of Lesdiguières. He was a very great soldier, at the time, and the most prominent leader of French Protestantism. In order to soften their impetuous adversary, the Catholics of Grenoble saw only one chance: to get him acquainted with Francis de Sales. With the full approval of the Bishop of Grenoble, Mgr. Jean de la Croix de Chevrières, the first president of the chamber of audits, invited the prince-bishop of Geneva to preach the Advent sermons in the royal chapel of parliament in 1616 and the Lenten course in 1617.

Among those assembled for the sermons on the appointed day were several Protestants mixed with the Catholics. The duke of Lesdiguières was one of them. On December 19, 1616, the duke had to leave to wage war against the Spanish on behalf of the duke of Savoy. Before his departure he talked with Francis de Sales, and—when leaving—was heard to say: "All that you say is good." Back with the armies, the marshal of Lesdiguières was unable to attend the Lenten sermons of 1617, but he obtained from the duke of Savoy permission for the bishop from Annecy to preach the Advent sermons again in December of 1617. He was accustomed to calling Francis "a very perfect bishop, a man truly sent from God". Lesdiguières abjured Protestantism in 1622.

At Grenoble, Francis produced in hearts the same surge of devotion that he aroused wherever he passed.

The Treatise on the Love of God *or God's Game with the Human Heart*

It was in the midst of such apostolic works—the variety and riches of which we are far from exhausting—that Francis finally published the *Treatise on the Love of God.* The book appeared in August in Lyons at Rigaud's publishers, who had already printed the *Introduction to the Devout Life.* Francis had been "ruminating" this book for at least twelve years. The *Love of God* was at the center of his thought, of his life, of his action. How many diverse experiences nourished his spirit since the time when he first planned to write the *Life of Holy Charity!* And, as time went on, it seemed to him, more and more, that all men's difficulties and problems had a single and unique solution: to teach men to love God with all their hearts and their neighbors as themselves for the love of God—In short, to live with sincerity their act of charity.

A word from the preface ought to be retained: this treatise is a "history": "Certainly, I have only thought of representing simply and sincerely, without art and even more without pretense, the history of the beginnings, peaks, and valleys of the operations, properties, advantages, and excellences of divine love."

It was necessary for him, in this history, to define clearly what comprised spiritual development. Francis said again in his preface: "This treatise is meant to help the soul that is already devout so that it may advance in its resolution." To help . . . that is to say, not only to stimulate it but to prevent it from taking false trails. What, then, is the sure way in this spiritual "advancement"? For Francis, as for all healthy mystical tradition, it is not the way of exceptional, extraordinary phenomena or rapture, ecstasies and visions, but on the contrary the way of simplification, of self-recollection in the essential. Progress in the spiritual life is made by a profound study of faith, hope, and charity, by the intensification of our will's belonging to God. The goal envisioned is "pure love" or "true love", love "that loves God for himself and by which the heart gives itself to God entirely". The soul is able only to tend toward this sincerity, loyalty, and purity of love without ever claiming to have attained it. Francis said, "There must be a simple but marvelously strong resolve, which I extend and stretch toward God so as to unite and join myself to his bounty to which I belong and that belongs to me." What a misconception, in my opinion, we would commit were we to see in the Theotimus of the *Treatise* a Philothea who was searching for ways loftier than devotion.[1]

---

[1] Recall that each of the two names can designate men as well as women (Pl., 341, 342).

In such a conception of the spiritual life, the complete human being is concerned, "committed": flesh and spirit, heart and feeling, imagination and sensitivity, intelligence and will. It is man wholly and entirely who must acquiesce to the grace of God. Francis de Sales was also unafraid to utilize the most lively manifestations of human love — that blind force that is imposed on our being — even to its most carnal depths and its most spiritual exigencies in order to enable us to understand what the love of God is. Nothing is more characteristic of this spirit than chapter XIV of book I of the *Treatise:* "That Charity Ought to Be Named Love". Francis boldly rejected the modesties of Origen, who feared that "the name of love might give some bad thoughts to weak spirits, as being more proper for signifying a carnal passion than a spiritual affection", and — passing beyond to "all suspicions of immodesty" — he chose for the title of his treatise the name of *love* as "representing more fervor, efficacy, and activity than that of *consuming attraction*" because charity is the "principal and most excellent of all loves".

Having said this, Francis can freely use throughout the *Treatise* the most tender, most human images and comparisons in the Bible: the mother who carries or "nurses" her infant, the fiancés, the wife and the husband, and, above all, the most affective book of the Old Testament, the *Canticle of Canticles.* Francis had heard long ago, in Paris, the spiritual commentary of Génébrard concerning this song of human love, and he never forgot it. He made of it the support of his own spiritual life, and he knew from experience the force of its fervor.

Precisely because he went straight to the essential of the gospel and to the "roots" of man, the *Treatise on the Love of God* — this "simple and sincere book" — concerns all men, and it has his universal style. It is a directory of the interior life for Christians firmly committed to the demands of their baptism, but it is also a book of conversion for "pagans" and sinners; it is a guide for the loftiest contemplatives and a breviary for men of action; it is a journal of the soul, a confidence, but it is also a poem.

There should be no question here of trying to analyze the *Treatise on the Love of God.* But since Francis himself presents it to us as a "history", an incessant search for man by God and for God by man, and since he frequently refers to the *Canticle of Canticles,* it appears permissible—even obvious—to present it, for our part, as a great game of love between the heart of God and the heart of man. A dramatic game with passionate appeals on the part of one to the other, with unforeseen rebounds, whose outcome is always uncertain.

The Protagonists of the Game: God and Man

Francis de Sales was profoundly convinced of the immensity, omnipotence, and holiness of God. But he also knew that this God who could be inaccessible is *Love,* that he has the desire to "communicate" (a very Salesian word) *himself,* and to give . . . and give even himself. Hence the creation of the earth and the planets, that profusion of visible and invisible beings that Francis admires in the artist, in the poet, and even more in the believer.

But, above all, what plunged Francis into a bewildered encomium was *man,* the final "work" of God the Creator. Francis made his own this verse from the Psalm: "You have made him a little less than a god." He was unafraid to affirm that "man is the perfection of the universe." That is because "God created man in his own image and likeness." What does this mean, if not that God made man *love* like himself? "God, having created man in his image and likeness, wishes that—as in himself—all might be ordered by love and for love."

Why did God wish that man should be so perfect? It is because he had an unheard-of project. He wished to make this human nature participate in his own divinity. "God considered that among all these ways of communicating himself there was none so excellent as to join himself to some created nature, and in such a way that the creature would be, as it were, grafted onto or inserted into the Divinity so as to make with it one single Person. Thus his infinite goodness . . . resolved and determined to effect such a union in this manner." God "would join and unite" himself to human nature in the mystery of the Incarnation. Thus Francis, following Saint Bonaventure and the great

Doctors of the Church, thought that even if "the human race" had not broken with God through sin, "the Word would have become flesh" in order that all men might participate through him, in him, with him in the divine life. Sin having occurred, God adjusted, so to speak, this "benevolent design" to the new situation: his gift would become pardon, his bounty mercy; the Incarnation would be at the same time redemption: "copious, abundant, superabundant, magnificent, and excessive redemption", and once again all the splendors and generosities of the first plan would be proposed to the free will of man.

Thus *after* as *before* the fault of man, there existed between God and man an extreme "conformity". "As soon as man thinks a little attentively about the Divinity, he feels a certain sweet emotion in his heart, which testifies that God is God of the human heart." Undoubtedly, human nature, at present, is no longer "endowed with original health and rectitude"; we are "greatly depraved by sin", but the "holy inclination to love God above all things has remained within us". The natural inclination to love God is only "lulled asleep" in the depth of the human heart. A trifle can awaken it. And Francis explains it by a familiar comparison:

> Among partridges it frequently happens that some hens steal the eggs of the others in order to hatch them—whether from the eagerness that they have to be mothers or through their stupidity, which makes them mistake their own eggs. And here is another strange thing—but nonetheless well documented: the chick that will have been hatched and nourished under the wings of a strange partridge—at the first call that it hears from its true mother, which laid the egg from which it proceeded—leaves the thief partridge, returns to its first mother, and begins to follow her through the correspondence that it has with its first origin. . . .
>
> It is the same with us, Theotimus, with our heart, because although it may be hatched, nourished, and raised among corporal, base and transitory things and—in a manner of speaking—under the wings of nature, nonetheless, at the first glance that it casts on God, at the first recognition that it receives from him, the natural and first inclination to love God—which was lulled asleep and imperceptible— awakens in an instant and appears like a spark among the ashes,

which—touching our will—gives it an impulse of the supreme love owed to the sovereign and first Principle of all things.

Such are the two players—may we be excused for speaking so anthropomorphically of God—confronting each other. Face to face? Yes, but preferably *heart to heart*. A love that does foolish things to make itself loved and a love that is free to love as it wishes. What a challenge! The game begins for every man at his birth, and it goes on from there to eternity.

The Enclosure in Which the Game of Love Is Played

It is in the most secret intimacy of each human being that the contest between God and man unfolds, in that mysterious and inalienable depth that the Bible calls *viscera* but that is a little closer to what moderns call *conscience*. It is a personal sanctuary, the reality of which is hardly doubted but which philosophers and psychologists have great difficulty discerning. Francis de Sales hesitates to name it; he multiplies expressions: the "summit of the soul", the "supreme point of our spirit", the "heart of our heart", and so on, and, each time he is forced to express a mysterious reality, he has recourse to image. Here he utilizes the Temple of Solomon:

"There were three courts for the Temple of Solomon; one was for the gentiles and strangers who, wishing to have recourse to God, came to adore him in Jerusalem; the second was for the Israelites, men and women; the third was for the priests and the levitical order; and, finally, beyond this there was the sanctuary, or sacred house, to which the high priest alone had access." In this Temple of Solomon, Francis de Sales discerned the symbol of the "mystical temple" that is ourselves.

In this mystical temple there were also three courts, which were three different degrees of reason: in the first, we discourse according to the experience of the senses; in the second, we discourse according to human knowledge; in the third, we discourse according to faith; and finally—beyond this—there is a certain preeminence and supreme point of reason and spiritual faculty that is not guided by the light of discourse or of reason but by a simple view of the understanding and a simple sentiment of the will by which the spirit acquiesces and submits to the truth and to God's will. But this extremity and summit of our soul, this extreme point of our spirit, is most simply represented by the sanctuary or the sacred house.

There God dwells, acts, and launches his appeals of love.

Man is free to acquiesce or turn away from these appeals by God; they are invitations, attractions, and inspirations that are *totally paternal* and to which man *always remains free* to answer Yes or No.

Here again the *image* makes up for abstract theory.

What are these ordinary ropes with which the Divine Providence is wont to draw hearts to his love? Such, certainly, as Providence himself marks them, describing the means that he used to draw the people of Israel from Egypt and from the desert into the Promised Land: *"I shall draw them",* God says through Hosea, *"with the bonds of humanity, with the bonds of charity* and of friendship. Undoubtedly, Theotimus, we are not drawn to God by bonds of iron, like the bulls and buffaloes, but by means of enticement, delightful attractions, and holy inspirations that are, on the whole, *the bonds of Adam and of humanity,* that is to say, proportioned and suitable to the human heart, to which freedom is natural. . . . In this way, our free will is in no way forced or necessitated by grace, but, notwithstanding the omnipotent strength of the merciful hand of God, which touches, surrounds, and binds the soul with so many inspirations, invitations, and attractions, this human will remains perfectly free and exempt from all kinds of constraint and necessity. Grace is so gentle and seizes our hearts so gently in order to attract them that it spoils nothing of the freedom of our will; it touches powerfully but nonetheless so delicately the resources of our spirit that our free will receives no forcing from it, thanks to certain powers, not for forcing but for enticing the heart. It has a holy violence—not to violate but to render our freedom loving. It acts strongly but so sensitively that it does not overwhelm us with so powerful an action. It encourages us, but it does not oppress our freedom, so that we are able, amid its forces, to consent or to resist its movements, as it pleases us.

Thus Francis de Sales nicely situates the spiritual combat in the most secret, most intimate, most inviolable point of man: his "heart".

There God calls man to love him and to love his neighbor; there man acquiesces or refuses in total freedom.

The Rule of the Game

The divine game is played in every heart, at every moment, in every situation. We experience how in our conscience the voice that pushes us to "do good" is never quiet: God unceasingly proposes to lead us according to "what honors man", what is most true, most beautiful: the best. He proposes it to us and offers us the grace to accomplish it. Because, by our nature, above all since it is "wounded by sin", we are incapable of answering the Yes of unfailing acquiescence. "But," says Francis de Sales, in a charming comparison, "it suffices that—like the 'apode birds' (namely, those birds without feet that let themselves be 'carried off or lifted up' by the wind)—we do not resist the divine breath, but we respond to this upsurge and first soaring."

Everything begins through "justice", in the biblical sense of the term, through resolute orientation of our heart toward what is true, beautiful, and good. If the soul acquiesces, God, by new inspirations, calls it to new progress in faith and love. "The good", says Francis, "grow like the dawn of day, from *splendor to splendor.*" It produces a kind of escalation: "God walks with us. His love presses him to encourage us and solicits his heart to urge and push ours to employ well the holy charity that he has given us."

And if, in the course of this contest, the soul turns away and refuses? Then God, in his mercy, begins again at zero: he petitions the sinner to conversion. If the sinner acquiesces, everything begins as before the fault.

Could we envisage that the soul might be contented with half fidelities and be established in a comfortable "decency", not fully agreeing to God's appeals but not rejecting them? Francis sees this as an illusion. "To remain in this state of inconsistency for long is impossible; whoever does not gain loses in this business; whoever does not ascend this ladder [allusion to Jacob's ladder] descends; whoever is not victorious is vanquished in this combat."

For all that, Francis de Sales does not intend that every Christian—even the faithful—will reach the highest spiritual states. Everyone has his personal vocation in the Church, and God has an original Providence for each. But toward the center of this vocation and of this Providence "everyone can grow endlessly, more and more in the love of God, as long as he is in this frail life".

The Finale of the Game of Divine Love

"Love tends to union." Francis informs us of this in the first pages of the *Treatise.* This is true of human love; it is even truer of divine love. What God seeks in this great game that we have presented is to unite us to himself, to make of us—in Jesus Christ—his "sons".

In fact, this game is never finished here on earth; it continues until death to the definitive encounter when our soul "will obtain" what it desires. *"I run",* says the Beloved. *"Ah, shall I never attain the prize for which I run, which is to be united, heart to heart, spirit to spirit, with my God, my Spouse, and my Life?"* "When shall I be able to pour my soul into his heart; when will he empty his heart into my soul, and thus—happily united—when shall we live inseparable?"

In the *Canticle of Canticles,* the sign of perfect union is the kiss. Francis returns to his account of this symbol: "The kiss being the living mark of union of hearts, the Spouse only intends, in all her pursuits, to be united with her Beloved: *'Let him kiss me',* she says, 'with a kiss from his mouth.'" But this game "in this mortal life cannot attain its perfection; we can begin our loves in this world, but we shall not consummate them until in the other." Here we must reproduce this finale of the game of love, such as Francis de Sales describes it to us; he alone could speak with such delicacy:

> *"I have found at last",* the Sulamite said, *"him whom my soul cherishes; I am holding him, and I shall not let him go until I introduce him to my mother's house and present him in the bedroom of her who begot me."* She then finds him, this Beloved, because he has made her aware of his presence by a thousand consolations; she holds him because this feeling produces strong affections, by which she hugs and embraces him. She protests that she will never leave him, oh, no! because these

affections pass into eternal resolutions, and, all the same, she does not think of kissing him with the nuptial kiss until she will be with him in *her mother's house,* which is the *heavenly Jerusalem,* as Saint Paul says. But notice, Theotimus, that this Spouse does not think of anything less than of holding her Beloved at her mercy, like a slave of love: hence she imagines that it is up to her to lead him at her pleasure and to introduce him to the blessed room of her mother.... The spirit pressed by loving passion is still given a slight advantage over the one he loves, and the Husband confesses that his Beloved *has ravished his heart*... swearing that he is her prisoner of love.

Only in heaven will the *nuptial feast of the Lamb* take place.

Here, in this frail life, the soul is truly Spouse and fiancée of the *Immaculate Lamb* but not yet married to him. Fidelity and promises are given, but the execution of the marriage is deferred; that is why there is always room for us to retract it, although we may never have any reason for it since our faithful Spouse never abandons us unless we compel him to do so by our disloyalty and perfidy. But, being in heaven, the nuptials of this divine union being celebrated, the bond of our hearts to their sovereign Principle will be eternally indissoluble.

Francis de Sales is well aware that here on earth God invites certain souls to taste something of the celestial union, and he has described in a masterly manner these privileged states in book VI of the *Treatise:* "Concerning Repose of the Soul Recollected in Her Beloved... concerning the flow or liquefaction of the soul in God ... concerning the wound of love ... concerning the loving languor of the heart wounded by love ... " "These kisses of the present life", he said, "relate all to the eternal kiss of the future life like attempts, preparations, and pledges from him.... They are rather like signs of the future union between my Beloved and myself, but they are not the union itself."

There is only one soul, in the eyes of Francis de Sales, who has fully won in this divine game: it is the Virgin Mary. Besides, only she could "die of love for her Son" because she "lived the life of her Son". Only she was the perfect *shepherdess* of the *Canticle of Canticles.*

An Astonishment to Dissipate

In thus making of the *Treatise on the Love of God* a kind of commentary of the *Canticle of Canticles* have we not revived the old quarrel: is it really addressed to all Christians and even to men of goodwill? Is it not reserved to a certain family of souls given to a too sentimental mystical expression?

In several pages of our study we have already dismissed this objection. But the knot of the debate, it seems, is located in this precise point: Is not human love, which Francis makes use of to penetrate some ray of the divine love, in fact the most dramatic foundation of man's life? Is not man's heart—in the sense that Francis understands it—the site of the most difficult combats? It is no accident that the final chapter of the *Treatise* is entitled "That Mount Calvary Is the True Academy of Love", that everything in this book converges toward Jesus Christ crucified: "To conclude," Francis wrote, "the death and the Passion of our Lord are the gentlest and the most violent forces that can animate our hearts in this mortal life.... Every love that does not take its origin from the Passion of the Savior is fragile and perilous." There you have something to satisfy the most manly virtues! It is not "in the bedroom of her mother" that the mystical shepherdess exchanges with her shepherd "the great, solemn, nuptial kiss"; it is on the Cross. For Francis de Sales there is only one "ecstasy" that "makes us come out of ourselves, and above ourselves", and that is the one that leads us to say with "the miraculous Saint Paul": "I live; it is no longer I who live; it is Jesus Christ who lives in me."

If we have devoted so many pages to the *Introduction* and to the *Treatise,* it is precisely because these two works—and let us include the *Conferences*—reveal to us what Francis de Sales used to say to souls—to the loftiest as to the humblest—in the secrecy of the confessional, in the parlor, or in familiar conversations. The friend of souls inspired the writer.

13

TO THE MERCY OF GOD
1617–October 1618

"The Little Larva Becomes a Bee"

From August 1616 until January 1617 Francis worked—as much as his pastoral obligations permitted him—at drawing up the new Constitutions of the Visitation, and his discussions with Bishop de Marquemont must be taken into account. In fact, Francis and Mother de Chantal had hardly ceased working on the document for two years (1615 and 1616). The text was dispatched to Rome for approbation. The Roman canonists again reinstated the cloister. Finally, the brief of approbation that established the Visitation in "formal religion" appeared on April 23, 1618.

Sunday, October 16, 1618, the eve of his departure for Paris, Francis set forth, in solemn procession, to communicate the pontifical document to Mother de Chantal and the Sisters: the humble Annecy institute became a religious Order. "From that day", the annals of the first monastery reported: "we observed strict enclosure." Who would be astonished that to the joy of the Sisters—at finally seeing the conclusion of a debate whose issue had been uncertain—there were mixed some tears in the eyes of Annecy's poor? Within a few years, (1629–30), at the time of the terrible plague that would devastate Annecy, Mother de Chantal would furnish proof that a cloistered Visitation can be the soul of the most heroic and creative charity amid such scourges. She found and organized help for all those famished for bread and for those desperately needing medicine. Every day the "bishop's men" would come to take "broth and other things that the sisters had continually prepared for the poor and the sick". And if the bishop, the chief magistrate, and several officials would not flee to the country, far from "this infected air", it would be because of the example and the eloquence of a Visitandine, who was careful, nonetheless, not to violate in any way the strict cloister that the Church had imposed on her. "Charity is inventive", said Saint Paul.

The Deaths of Bernard and Marie-Aimée de Sales

In the summer of 1617, a double—a triple—bereavement cruelly struck the two families of de Sales and de Chantal. On May 23 thirty-four-year-old Bernard de Sales died of a pestilential fever in Piedmont, where he had gone to fight, at the head of twelve hundred men, for the duke of Savoy: Marie-Aimée brought into the world a premature infant on the night of September 4 or 5. And on September 6, the young mother—only nineteen years old—died. This sorrowful and poignant story must be recounted so as to know the hearts of Francis and Jane de Chantal.

Bernard was seventeen years younger than Francis, and Francis was strongly attached to this young brother, about whom he wrote: "Every day he becomes more gentle and more gracious." Francis— with unparalleled joy—had blessed Bernard's marriage to the lovely Marie-Aimée de Chantal, and Marie-Aimée, under his direction, had progressed rapidly in a serious Christian life in spite of her young age. "My dear little sister," Francis wrote to Mother de Chantal, at the time in Lyons, "whom I find every day more lovable and desirous of becoming good and devout." Bernard and Marie-Aimée truly formed "a gracious household".

The drama continued. Bernard, knowing that he was dying, received "the sacraments with great religious fervor" from Dom Juste Guerin, a friend of Francis. Janus, another of Francis' brothers, was at Bernard's side. He immediately had word sent to his eldest brother. "Alas! How happy he is, it seems to me," Francis wrote to Mother de Bréchard on May 29, "but, nonetheless, it is impossible for me not to weep for him. You could not imagine how accomplished he was, how pleasing he made himself to everyone.... And with that, here he is taken away! But God is good, and he does all things in his goodness. *To him be honor, glory, and blessing.*" Marie-Aimée wept bitterly for her dear husband. But two lights shone through her grief: her ardent faith and the hope of an approaching birth.

To the Baron Amédée de Villette, Francis wrote: "My poor dear sister gave evidence, amid her tears and grief, of the most loving, constant, and religious piety of which it is possible to speak; in which she pleases us greatly for the desire that we have that she will preserve the infant who—we believe—has been left in her womb by the deceased, as some kind of solace to his brothers." Alas! things were going to turn in a way that Francis had not foreseen. The child was born prematurely during the night of September 4 or 5, 1617. Mother de Chantal herself received her grandson and only had time to baptize him before he died. Marie-Aimée survived her son by two days. On September 6, at eight o'clock in the evening, Francis was informed that the end was approaching. He hurried to the monastery where Marie-Aimée had been sheltered during the absence of her husband. He administered the sacraments of penance and the Eucharist to the dying girl. Then Marie-Aimée humbly asked the bishop and her mother to bestow the habit of the Visitation on her. After receiving extreme unction, she pronounced the three vows of religion. Two hours after midnight she expired.

In the letters he wrote the following days, Francis did not fear to say that "this death was marked by an extraordinary holiness". The most beautiful of these letters is perhaps that that he wrote to Mme de Montfort, on September 10:

> We had not yet finished our mourning for the loss that we had suffered in Piedmont when this second loss occurred, which, I assure you, is infinitely painful, for this dear soul had lived among us in such a way that she had made herself especially dear to all, but to me more particularly, since she regarded me with filial love and honor, and then the counterblow from the affliction of her worthy mother gives increase to our sadness. Yet, however, at the insistence of the dead girl, we embrace, love, and adore the will of God with a total submission of our hearts, because those were virtually her last words.

I assure you that I have never seen a death so holy as that of this girl, even though she had only five hours to achieve it (E.A., MCCCL).

So much suffering and so many bereavements had "pierced and transfixed" the heart of Mother de Chantal. She fell dangerously ill and "was at the gates of death". When Francis left Annecy, the invalid was "a little better, but still in danger". Suddenly, she was cured! On December 8, Francis, by a secret presentiment, was chanting his gratitude to the Virgin Mary: "I could not make my gratitude better known to the heavenly Physician who cured you", he wrote to Mother de Chantal on May 9, "than by the hands of my Lady, his Mother, Mary, conceived without sin, our dear and sovereign Mistress."

"The Apostle of Grenoble"

It was from Grenoble that Francis wrote in this way to Mother de Chantal. After having preached there during Advent in 1616, he preached the Lenten sermons in 1617. He would return again in 1617 to preach the Advent series and the Lenten sermons in 1618. He had become bound to this city by solid and warm friendships, and he had even discovered some vocations for the Visitation: in mid-January of 1618, three candidates left to begin their novitiate in Annecy. On March 11 he informed Mother de Chantal that everything was "concluded with our good ladies for the establishment of our Monastery. Everyone applauded this plan, and the good lady, Madame la Présidente Le Blanc de Mions, has a holy ardor for that. . . . I pray you, my very dear Mother, to gently prepare our little bees to make a journey in the first good weather and to come to work in the new beehive for which heaven has well prepared some dew." Mother de Chantal arrived at Grenoble on April 7, 1618; she brought with her a swarm of eight Sister-foundresses.

Grenoble, decidedly, was for Francis a favorable and favored place. Besides more of his Visitandines, there were numerous and fervent Philotheas, with whom he conferred in serious correspondence. It seems that even in his sermons he found the tone that won over numerous Protestants in the city. Without counting Lesdiguières—

who was proceeding gradually toward his abjuration of Protestantism—there were several conversions of well-known Protestants. And his correspondence would be enriched from then on by several recipients, such as Mme la Présidente Le Blanc de Mions, of whom Francis would declare after her death, "She was a rare woman", or again that admirable household of the Granieu family, which sheltered the bishop during Advent of 1616 and Lent of 1617. Madame de Granieu was such a "Philothea" that Francis, in order to clarify her method of meditation, would advise her to read the seventh book of the *Treatise on the Love of God:* "You will find there all that will be necessary for you to understand mental prayer (*oraison*)." But this book VII deals with the highest states of "union" and the life and death of the Virgin Mary—quite a reference!

During Easter week in 1618 Francis—in order to reach Annecy—passed by the Grande Chartreuse. He already knew the monastery, for he had been there "to bestow Holy Orders and to make several retreats". Since 1607 he had been "affiliated in the participation of the prayers and other spiritual works of the Carthusians". And Dom Bruno d'Affringues (at the time prior-general), as well as the monks, nourished an admiration and respectful affection for Francis—in spite of their concern about safeguarding their solitude—and this caused them to desire his visit. It is true that Francis felt at ease among the sons of Saint Bruno. At the time when, at the end of 1603, he was denouncing "the laxity of all the monasteries in Savoy" to Nuncio Tolosa, he excepted "that of the Carthusians". This brief Easter stay in 1618 at the Grande-Chartreuse pleased Francis: was he not already dreaming of that "retreat from affairs" that he attempted to realize two years later in the hermitage of Saint-Germain de Talloires?

Toward New Diplomatic Missions

No, the hour for repose had not sounded for the Apostle. It was not toward solitude that God was calling Francis, but toward Paris! He gave much thought, however, upon returning from Grenoble to Annecy—after Lent of 1618—to his ability to cope with his diocese. He felt fatigued: the "Turin" portrait, which an Annecy painter,

Jean-Baptiste Costaz, made of him in June 1618, shows him weary, his visage worn; he admitted himself that he felt old age approaching, and he was only fifty-two years old. But he did not belong to himself: his correspondence crushed him, he had to respond to a "world of letters", he presided at the Divine Office, he strove as best he could to satisfy all appeals. And so, at the end of August, he went off to Rumilly to bless the chapel of the Capuchins, who had been established there six years, because he "brought a particular affection to every Order of the seraphic father, Saint Francis of Assisi, no matter what the habit". In September he hurried to the abbey at Sixt, where the commandatory abbot, Jacques de Mouxy, who fifteen years earlier had challenged the bishop's authority, finally called him for a reconciliation, and Francis left to the Canons Regular of the monastery some wise Constitutions that would bear good fruits of reform.

At the end of September a "command" from the duke of Savoy was brought to Francis, enjoining him to accompany young Cardinal Maurice of Savoy, who had to go soon to Paris to solicit the hand of Christine of France, sister of King Louis XIII, for the prince Victor Amédée.

This was because the relations between the court at Paris and the court at Turin had greatly changed since Duke Charles-Emmanuel was embroiled with Spain under Philip II. The Convention of Pavia on October 9, 1617, had brought the war to an end but reversed the diplomacy. At this time Charles-Emmanuel was aspiring to an alliance with France, and—according to the custom of the time—there was no better assurance than a princely marriage! Thus the marriage of the crown prince of Savoy (thirty-one years of age) to Christine of France (fourteen years old) was projected.

Numerous obstacles lay in the way of this plan—in particular, the profound division of the French court. Ever since the assassination of Concini, on April 24, 1617, Louis XIII had taken absolute power, and Marie de Médici, the Queen Mother, had been exiled to Blois, where she was held prisoner. Richelieu had followed her there, hoping to be the architect of a reconciliation between the King and his mother, and the project of the marriage between the prince of Savoy and the young Christine was negotiated without the knowledge of Marie de Médici. The journey of Cardinal Maurice of Savoy had for its avowed goal that of thanking the King for the assistance that he had given to the duke in the recent war and to establish ways to bring the troubles in Italy to an end. The secret goal was the marriage. It was in this most pressing political imbroglio that Cardinal Maurice of Savoy had to accomplish his mission. Francis de Sales, whose diplomatic skill was appreciated by the duke and whose credit with the French court was also known to him, would be a very useful companion to this twenty-five-year-old ambassador. President Antoine Favre was also assigned to join them. Everything was arranged so that Paris would be dazzled by the prince's retinue.

At Montmelian, on October 17, 1618, Francis de Sales joined the cardinal of Savoy who, on October 6, had left Turin for Paris.

14

PARIS' TRIUMPHAL WELCOME TO THE BISHOP OF GENEVA
October 1618–October 1619

The Journey of the Prince's Retinue

Let us imagine, if we can, Francis' feelings in the midst of this procession, which the duke of Savoy had wanted to be so sumptuous that it would dazzle the French court, and especially young Christine, "Madame l'aînée", who dreamed of marrying a King and who was being offered a mere prince. Francis, at this time, was "attached", in the strict sense of the term, to the person of Cardinal Maurice. "I no longer belong to myself," he was compelled to write shortly after his departure, "nor have I any freedom except what he allows me." This was because "twice a day" the cardinal "strove to improve his knowledge of the French language, and to become initiated in the affairs of the realm". He had a good teacher at his disposal!

The entourage took the route through Grenoble and Lyons. But at Roanne the cardinal decided to take the passenger barge as far as Orléans. His Eminence wished to display his athletic prowess, but he soon discovered in the bishop if not his master, at least his equal: "Sometimes he rowed and made me row with him, thinking, at first, that I was ignorant of this skill, in which, however, he discovered that I was a past master" (E.A., XVIII, 307). A cardinal of twenty-five years of age and a bishop of fifty-two at the oars of a passenger barge—the spectacle must have hugely entertained the sailors and the entire company!

They navigated for five days. On the eve of All Saints, October 31,

1618, the barge docked at Orléans, and the cortège now took the Chartres route. On November 6, at Chartres, the Marquis de Coeuvres was awaiting the cardinal-prince and his escort with the court carriages to drive them to Paris. The capital's welcome was enthusiastic: "It is impossible to say", Doña Genevra Scaglia wrote on November 9, "with what honors His Eminence was received and how great was the crowd that came out to see him. In the memory of man no one had seen such a throng for a prince's entry." Evidently the eyes of all were turned toward the cardinal-prince, son of the duke of Savoy, but they were very quickly fastened upon the two distinguished persons whom the prince had installed in his own carriage: Francis de Sales and Antoine Favre. "There is the illustrious bishop of Geneva, the greatest theologian of our time! There is President Favre, who has published so many books. He and Francis de Sales are like brothers because of the incomparable bond of affection that unites them!"

The spectacle must have been triumphal: four years later Antoine Favre would admit that on that particular day he had tasted "the intoxication of glory"!

The court's welcome was perfect. It was the first time that Francis de Sales found himself face to face with the children of Henry IV, whom he had admired and loved so much. King Louis XIII and Queen Anne of Austria were seventeen years old; Gaston was ten; Henrietta, nine; as for "Madame l'aînée" (Christine), she had scarcely reached her fourteenth year. Francis wrote to Doña Genevra Scaglia after the interview, "Christine is accomplished; majesty and goodness are imprinted on her features; she is tall for her age and employs an incomparable grace to welcome—with singular gravity and modesty—those who approach her." Impressions that corresponded to the judgment of the princess' "preacher": "She is endowed with a rare piety," he said, "with an exquisite prudence and a remarkable goodness". And since Victor Amédée was an "accomplished prince", Francis applied even more ardor to making the project of the alliance succeed.

Diplomacy and the "Novitiate of the Court"

Apparently things moved rather quickly at first: on November 10, the cardinal-prince was received by the King in private audience. In the name of the duke, his father, he asked for the hand of Princess Christine of France for the prince of Piedmont, his brother, and the request was granted. On November 21 the cardinal officially renewed his request, and the marriage was decided, in principle; nonetheless, in order that the news be published, the assent of the King of Spain was necessary. But when it was a question of defining the articles of the marriage contract, some difficulties surfaced. Antoine Favre avowed later that he and Count de Verne, the duke of Savoy's negotiators, were discouraged and thought only about returning to Piedmont, when one morning after Mass Francis restored their courage: "Wait," he told them, "God will do all." Finally, the articles of the contract were signed on January 11, 1619. Prince Victor Amédée de Piedmont arrived in Paris on February 6, and on the tenth, Cardinal François de La Rochefoucauld, assisted by the bishop of Geneva, blessed the marriage.

In all these delicate negotiations, Cardinal Maurice of Savoy would demonstrate "how adroit he was in blending the qualities of a great prince ... with those of a very distinguished cardinal". But it is certain that he was greatly aided by Antoine Favre and Francis de Sales. The latter had contact with everyone, and his perfect detachment from the intrigues of money or ambition made him a man one could trust.

There was much to be done in order to pacify and reconcile all these courtiers, let alone appease this profound "misunderstanding" between the King and the Queen Mother. Marie de Médici, in quasi exile at Blois, was enraged not to have been consulted by her son concerning the marriage of her daughter Christine. She had been informed only about the engagement. She was not invited to the signing of the contract (January 11, 1619) or to the wedding (February 10). She found this so intolerable that on the night of February 23 she escaped from Blois and found refuge at Angoulême! Luynes, Louis XIII's new favorite, then made several gestures of appeasement: he sent Cardinal de La Rochefoucauld and Bérulle to Marie de Médici. He sent Richelieu—recently exiled in Avignon—to her because he judged him to be the only one capable of "soothing her spirit". An accord was even signed between Cardinal de La Rochefoucauld and Richelieu—it was called the "Treaty of Angoulême" (April 20,

1619)—and it granted Marie the right to dispose of the revenues from her property and to reside wherever it seemed good to her, and, moreover, it gave her, in exchange for the government of Normandy, that of Anjou. Diplomatic gestures, rather than sincere reconciliation. It would require another six months before an interview between the King and his mother would be possible. This took place at Couzières, and, on September 5, the mother and son made their entry into Tours, spent fifteen days together, and then left—one for Angers, and the other for Paris (L, II, 162).

Francis was plunged into this game of intrigues, and he collaborated with Cardinal de La Rochefoucauld and with Bérulle in reconciling all these great people, even though—being a Savoyard—he was not supposed to become officially involved in these affairs, which concerned only the court of France.

Francis stayed in Paris as long as Prince Victor Amédée and Princess Christine remained there. He did not leave the capital until Friday, September 13, 1619. He rejoined the French court, which was celebrating the reconciliation of Marie de Médici and her son. The prince of Piedmont and Christine were there. Among the crowd of lords and noble ladies who pressed around their Majesties and Highnesses, Francis encountered the young bishop of Luçon, Msgr. Armand du Plessis de Richelieu. After having stayed for some time in his diocese, Richelieu became detached, little by little, from his bishopric, "the most wretched in France, the most filthy; the most disagreeable",[1] and opted for a political career. It seems, however, that his conversations with Francis had impressed him. Francis would write to Mother de Chantal shortly afterward, "The bishop of Luçon has sworn total friendship with me, and he told me that he was finally going to take my advice to think only of God and of the salvation of souls." We know what became of those good intentions!

Among the distinguished persons at the court who were present in Touraine were Cardinals de Gondi and de La Rochefoucauld, and Msgr. Jean du Perron. But the archbishop was searching for a coadjutor,

---

[1] M. Avenuel, *Collected Letters of Cardinal Richelieu* (collection of unedited documents concerning the history of France, 1853–1877), *Correspondence,* I, 24.

and his choice fell upon the bishop of Geneva; the King was perfectly in accord. We shall see later what became of this project.

Monday, September 30, 1619, Prince Victor Amédée, Princess Christine, and their retinue took the return route to Piedmont. Francis de Sales had acquired no taste for worldly ostentation after this long contact of ten months with two brilliant courts and being on holiday. In December 1618 he wrote to Mother de Chantal: "I am making my novitiate at court, but I shall never make profession there, with God's help!" Nonetheless, the "friend of souls" knew how to discover Philotheas everywhere: "It is not possible to say, however, how many examples of devotion one sees here, even in the midst of the court."

This alliance of diplomacy and mysticism is one aspect of Francis de Sales that the sagacious Sainte-Beuve perceived and revealed in a masterful way:

> From reconciling contrasts, I am led to a final *middle course,* which is characteristic of Saint Francis de Sales and which alone can succeed in giving his measure. What I mean is the alliance that was effected in him among mystical, contemplative virtue, charity in all its candor, and finesse of human judgment in all its wisdom. It would, in fact, be creating a really false image to see in this benign prelate only a lovable mystic. His entire life, all his negotiations for mission and apostolate, show very precise qualities of observation and conduct.... With this essentially mystical quality there was present another compatibility in him, namely, finesse in practical relations. This blessed man ... would have been as skillful and as expert as he might have wished, whether in worldly matters or in affairs where the spiritual was complicated by the temporal, ... and even though he avoided getting involved (in external affairs) outside his domain, whenever he was inadvertently guided there or forcibly thrust there, he brought to them a moderation, a subtlety, even a boldness; in all, a happy and facile art that was bound to succeed (*Port Royal,* Pl. I, 291).

This is precisely what happened in this strange mission of Francis to Paris in 1618 and 1619. By "this alliance between affectionate conciliation and a certain diplomatic finesse", he went on to succeed.

When a Diplomat Has a Missionary's Heart

Francis found in the milieu of diplomatic worries and constraints time and strength again to give himself to souls. Here is what happened. They asked Francis for sermons, conferences, meetings, because Paris had not forgotten its guest of 1602 and had fervently welcomed the *Introduction to the Devout Life,* and then the *Treatise on the Love of God,* and Francis did not know how to refuse anyone. To someone who reprimanded him for this, he simply replied: "I would sooner give a sermon than say no."

He had hardly arrived in Paris when the churchwarden at Saint-André-des-Arts asked him to preach during Advent and Lent. Francis promised!

The day after his arrival, on November 8, his friend Father de Bérulle, who had founded the Oratory of France seven years previously, begged him to give on the eleventh — three days later — the eulogy for Saint Martin in his church. The court and the citizenry hastened to the ceremony . . . so much so that the preacher, in order to reach the pulpit, was obliged to pass through a window with the aid of a ladder! Was he seized by panic? Did he fear for his humility? Did he want to make the Parisians understand that he had no desire to "preach in style"? Instead, our preacher contented himself with recounting soberly, without oratorical flourish, the life of the saint. The audience felt disappointed! But they were forgiving, and when Advent began on December 2, the Church of Saint André-des-Arts was full. They found again the real Francis de Sales, whose thoughts and person preached at least as much as his speech: "The others, when discoursing, fly in the air," said the duchess of Montpensier, "but this orator of holy love pounces on his prey, reaches for the heart, and seizes it."

Among the works of Francis de Sales, the sermons are the most disappointing part for the modern reader. This is because we ordinarily have only the preparatory sketch of the sermon or a text reconstituted by listeners. Above all, we are lacking what made up their charm and efficacy: the person, the timbre, the voice, the actions, the conviction, and that joy that he experienced in speaking about things of God. "I have preached this morning before the Queen and her fine people," he wrote to Mother de Chantal on December 24, 1618, "but, in truth, I did not preach with more care, more affection, or more pleasure than in my poor little Visitation." Protestants, atheists, "freethinkers" mixed with Catholics, so evangelical was this preaching, stripped of all aggressiveness in its luminous, cordial rightness. People applied to him this pretty phrase: "Our Lord did not ask Saint Peter, 'Are you learned or eloquent?' in order to tell him, 'Feed my sheep', but asked 'Do you love me?' It suffices to love well in order to speak well."

Not satisfied with just listening to the bishop's sermons, certain ladies got together occasionally in a chapel or a lodging for more informal conferences with Francis. Some sought his direction, at least in confession. Vincent de Paul was referring to this era when he testified later: "What increased my admiration even more was to see a person as great and esteemed as he—preoccupied with the most serious affairs, to which he was indispensable—lending himself, for long periods of time, to all, no matter how humble their condition, without sparing himself any trouble until he had given them complete satisfaction, so much did he value peace and tranquility of soul."

A spiritual movement was born around this time in Paris, and it was particularly interesting to Francis de Sales. He encountered some religious and priests who were yearning for a renewal of the clergy and who were searching for a way to form clerics solidly. Among these were Bérulle, André Duval, and the rugged but very zealous Adrien Bourdoise, who had just come from founding such a priestly community at Saint-Nicolas-du-Chardonnet. Francis agreed to give "some conferences to all the priests of that Church and to several others". The most important of these encounters was, undoubtedly, the one with Vincent de Paul.

Francis de Sales and Vincent de Paul

In 1618 and 1619, Vincent de Paul was thirty-eight years old. He was still only a simple priest. He was just quietly beginning to found the apostolates that would immortalize his name. At this time he was the tutor of the three children of Emmanuel de Gondi, General of the Galley Ships. Vincent was also "chaplain of the Royal Galley Ships of France". Vincent de Paul was avid for priestly holiness. Thus, as soon as he learned that Francis was to preach at Saint-André-des-Arts, he rushed over there, because in his eyes, Francis — he said — was "a living angel".

The two men met around the end of 1618; they became friends at once and from then on enjoyed frequent profound discussions. Not a single manuscript has come down to us from these discussions, but we can at least be sure that Francis was enthusiastic about Vincent de Paul's projects. Did not his Ladies of Charity, and even more, the Daughters of Charity, practice the love of the poor in the manner of Philothea, caring for them "with their own hands", preparing their meals themselves and at their own expense? Did not the "priests of the Mission" and the "Tuesday conferences" realize what Francis would have desired to accomplish in his own diocese? And would not Francis have blessed God had he been called to be "chaplain to the galley slaves"? As for Vincent de Paul, who had, he assures us, prior to 1616 "a rather cynical disposition" — just around this time he was able to control these outbursts of his nature; did his contacts with Francis have something to do with it? Between the bishop and the priest there was an extraordinary affinity of soul — to such an extent that, when Francis was going to leave Paris and was searching for a "priest who might counsel, confess, and direct his Visitandines", Francis asked Vincent to assume this task, and Vincent accepted it. He would be the confidant of the Visitandines until his death, that is to say, for more than forty years.

The Visitation in Paris

Paris had been one of the first cities to request a monastery of the Visitation. Until 1604, a Parisian foundation was not feasible: Moulins, Lyons, Grenoble, and recently Bourges (the city of Archbishop Frémyot) had attracted the persons capable of establishing new monasteries. But in 1619 Francis was no longer able to resist the Parisian pressure, inasmuch as some candidates were already presenting themselves.

To tell the truth, this foundation entailed a great difficulty, which stemmed from Cardinal de Retz (Gondi) and from Cardinal de La Rochefoucauld. Their Eminences wanted to unite the Visitation community to a Parisian congregation that was called the Haudriettes, after the name of their founder, Étienne Haudri. This project did not please Francis de Sales, but he counted on Providence to arrange things. And, in spite of these "innumerable difficulties" and the virtual lack of financial resources, he could, in March 1619, ask Mother de Chantal to come to Paris.

A new obstacle: the archbishop of Bourges was opposed to his sister's departure. He did not place his "horse and carriage" at her disposal for the trip! Jane answered him: "Obedience has good legs; we shall go very nicely on foot." In fact, she did leave in the archbishop's carriage, and at Orléans she found another carriage sent from Paris! Our travelers arrived at Paris on April 7 and lodged for several weeks in the suburb Saint-Marceau.

"This affair is undertaken solely under the Providence of God", Francis wrote to Mother de Chantal. "It is a risk, and more than that, but God requires that we do it, and it is better to rely on his Holy Providence than to be governed according to human wisdom and prudence" (E.A., XVIII, 365).

Mother de Chantal was concerned about this point. She had, rather early—by her courage, prudence, tact, and humility—managed to rule out the project of a union with the Haudriettes. Gondi was so impressed by her that he defended the Visitandines concerning a not-insignificant objection: Francis had alerted Mother de Chantal about it as early as February 1619. "My dear Mother, how admirable human prudence is! Could you believe that the great servants—male and female—of God are still telling me today that the gentleness and the devotion of our Institute are so much to the taste of the French spirit that we shall remove all the appeal of the other religious houses; that, when they have seen this Mme de Chantal, there will be no more [vocations] except for her?" (E.A., XVIII, 359).

To these difficulties another, more real, was added: poverty. Yes, as astonishing as it may appear, these Visitandines, called to Paris by its richest, best-dressed ladies, inaugurated their community life in a very evangelical poverty! Mother de Chaugy relates: "At the suburb of Saint-Marceau, the Sisters were lodged between two enclosed tennis courts and, day and night, had to endure the din of the players.... They were lacking in everything: bread, linen, wood." Francis came, however, on May 1, the feast of Saints Philip and James, to "install" the Sisters canonically: he celebrated Mass, gave them a little exhortation, and exposed the Blessed Sacrament. But the discomfort was so great that the Sisters whom Mother de Chantal had brought with her fell ill one after the other. Two months later, on July 2, they moved into another dwelling, also rather uncomfortable but less noisy, situated in the suburb Saint-Michel.

"As we were on such a beautiful path," Mother de Chaugy wrote— not without humor—"God permitted the plague to rage furiously in Paris. The court and all the important people were leaving the city, to the extent that this 'city-world' thought that it had become a little desert, and, in fact, the grass was growing very high in the streets." The few benefactors and benefactresses who were interested in the monastery had fled to the country or shut themselves up in their mansions. The sisters managed to survive, thanks to Mme la Présidente Amelot.

This dreadful situation lasted about two years, until the day when— thanks to the dowries of new recruits, and, in particular, to the fortune of Hélène-Angélique Lhuilier—they were able to acquire, to begin with, a more spacious house in the rue du Petit Musc, then the outbuildings of the Hotel Zamet, rue Saint-Antoine. They finally obtained a real "religious house" ... on September 25, 1621! But the "little Visitation" did not wait to have a beautiful lodging in order to radiate charity. It is true that Mother de Chantal was there, and that Francis de Sales came there at times when his numerous occupations left him some leisure. "The tree grew tall among the stones; the Lord blessed the fidelity of his daughters."

Mother Angélique Arnauld and Her Encounters with Francis de Sales and Mother de Chantal

Francis de Sales' relations with Mother Angélique Arnauld might have been only an episode in his trip to Paris; in fact, they permit us to grasp, in a single glance, his gift as spiritual director, his ideas about reforming monasteries, and even his "natural and supernatural temperament". It is a high point of his episcopate. Besides, those historians most celebrated for spirituality have been keenly interested in these relationships, and — as it happens in these very complex cases — they take opposite sides, not without passion. We cannot enter that debate here, because it is not yet concluded. We shall simply say, in a few words, what has appeared to us while pursuing the documentary sources and, in particular, the correspondence of the three protagonists: Francis de Sales, Mother Angélique Arnauld, and Mother de Chantal.

In order not to confuse the historical background, we must recall that it happened in an era when there was not yet a question of Jansenism or even of M. de Saint-Cyran. Mother Angélique was at this time a Cistercian abbess, famous for having successfully effected the reform of Port-Royal-des-Champs, to which she had been named abbess at the age of eleven (the papal bulls record seventeen); because of that she had just now been entrusted with the reform of another Cistercian Abbey, that of Maubuisson. In 1618 she was there struggling with "extreme difficulties". She had heard "tell of marvels" about Francis de Sales. And the fine and tenacious abbess sought the opportunity to attract to Maubuisson, by some ceremony, the bishop of Geneva. But she had in her camp the daughter of M. de Bonneuil, the royal master of ceremonies. This young novice was not yet confirmed! The bishop of Geneva was asked to come to confer the sacrament on her. The ceremony took place on April 5, 1619, the Friday of Easter week. From this first interview Mother Angélique and Francis de Sales established a profound relationship. A correspondence was exchanged between Paris and Maubuisson. "Madame," he wrote as early as April 29, 1619, "it will always be a very particular consolation for me to have the happiness of receiving your letters, because, in truth, I cherish and honor you perfectly since it has pleased our Lord to enable me to see your heart, and in the midst of it, the holy desire to love unswervingly this divine bounty."

Francis made several visits to the monastery and conferred with the abbess. He even stayed there nine days toward the end of August. He was in Paris on September 10, when the scandalous former abbess,

Angélique d'Estrées, was taken mysteriously from the abbey of
Maubuisson in a manner that was half-tragic, half-comic.

In order more easily to grasp the importance of this friendship, let
us distinguish three aspects of Mother Angélique: the reformer, the
religious, and the aspirant to the Visitation.

The reformer: courageous, bold, and tenacious, she could not fail
to please Francis de Sales, who had known and still knew so many
difficulties with decadent monasteries in his own diocese. All this does
not signify that he approved all of her reforms, because certain things,
frankly, did displease him. Madame Abbess employed her authority in
a manner that did not seem completely in accord with the Gospels.
"Let your courage be humble and your humility be courageous", he
counseled her in June 1619. Or again, on September 12, before leaving
Paris: "Tame your vivacious spirit little by little to patience, gentleness,
humility, and affability amid the feminine foolishness, childishness,
and imperfections of the Sisters who are tender with themselves and
subject to bothering the ears of the Mothers.... Keep your courage
elevated in that eternal Providence that has named you by your name
and carries you engraved upon his tender and paternal breast" (L.S.F.,
665).

Francis had diagnosed immediately the weak spot of this impetuous nature, so avid "to love God in perfection". The counsels he gave
to the nuns correspond to those given to the reformer, relating to
prayer, mortification, even to perfection. Humility is the master word
in the letters that Francis addressed to her: "Do not burden yourself too much with vigils and austeries (and, believe me, my dear
daughter, I fully understand what I am saying about this) but go to
the Port-Royal of the religious life by the royal road of the love of
God and of neighbor, of humility and good humor" (E.A., XVIII,
389). The whole tactic of the director consisted in not extinguishing
this fire but in not letting it burn and shine in the pride of being
perfect.

But this spiritual problem was suddenly going to take a very
concrete form. Mother Angélique became so attached to the spirit of
Francis de Sales that she formed the project of leaving the charge of
abbess and the Cistercian Order in order to enter the Visitation as a

simple nun. Francis' direction was thus going to approach genius. He did not discourage this astonishing candidature, but he clearly perceived the thorn in it: Would Mother Angélique attain—and in a lasting way—that humility without which there is neither Visitandine nor Visitation? More than ever he oriented Mother Angélique toward "beloved humility". But his counsels did not succeed in relaxing this soul of steel and restoring it to "the freedom of love". Francis did not disapprove of the project, certainly, but he would explain it on November 11, 1621, to Father Binet: "I waited as long as I could, and I testify that I showed myself not only cold but completely opposed to her proposals until—eighteen months later—a very considerable person wrote to me in such a way that I deemed it proper not to act as sovereign judge on this occasion but to leave the final decision to the way it would turn out. . . . I saw clearly that this project was extraordinary, but I also saw an extraordinary heart."

The "very considerable person" was none other than Mother de Chantal herself! Here is what happened. Mother Angélique and Mother de Chantal met for the first time when Mother Angélique was returning from Maubuisson to Port-Royal in order to install her sister, Marie-Agnes, as coadjutrix in the early part of September 1620. The two women understood each other at once and got along very well. Around September 10, while returning to Maubuisson, Mother Angélique made a stop again at the Visitation. While Mother Angélique was writing to Mother de Chantal, on September 12, "I am your true child who puts everything, everything, completely in your hands", Mother de Chantal wrote to the bishop, "This dear daughter of Port-Royal tells me that she feels that God is calling her to the Visitation. I have this same feeling." But a perceptive Francis, before he would believe in the validity of this vocation, requested of Mother de Chantal that "this daughter be helped and tamed somewhat by your very affectionate love." It would indeed take a Mother de Chantal to form such a novice in humility!

Mother Angélique's plan, not surprisingly, became known to her associates, her relatives, and her friends. They and her spiritual advisers were divided about it. An assembly of "six or seven" theologians was set up to examine the case, among them Asseline, Father

Binet, and Father Duval, pastor of Saint-Merry. This assembly started deliberating a little after December 15, 1621. What were its conclusions? The record of it, unfortunately, has been lost. Francis certainly read it, but—respecting the secrecy—he has only left us some snatches too inadequate to be conclusive. Whatever it was, the assembly authorized Mother Angélique to undertake proceedings at Rome. The Roman decision would constitute that outcome that Francis wished for in order that the will of God might finally be known to him.

In the meantime, let them remain in peace. Francis feared Mother Angélique's too excitable assertiveness. Inasmuch as he was in Annecy at the time, he was too distant to parry with them from all sides. On January 23 he wrote to Mother de Chantal: "We must carefully warn this dear daughter lest she employ the vivacity of her spirit by retorting and answering, so that at least in such restraint she will follow the Institute of the Visitation." The next day, January 24, 1621, Francis dispatched this note to Mother Angélique: "But realize that you must wait for word from Rome and, when the word comes, remain in peace; and whatever it says, remain in peace; and always remain in peace to the best of your ability. The password of the daughters of Jesus Christ is *peace;* the joy of the daughters of our Lady is peace" (E.A., XX, 263).

Rome refused. Within a year Angélique Arnauld would lose him who had understood and counseled her so well; she would miss him terribly in the drama of the coming years.

Before leaving Mother Angélique, it is good to note that during his trip into Touraine, Francis, whenever possible, visited several members of the Arnauld family. This was because, as was his custom, by "loving wholeheartedly" Mother Angélique, he included all her relations in the friendship. In this year of 1619, he was bound in friendship not only with Mother Angélique and her five Sister religious of Port-Royal but also with the celebrated Antoine Arnauld, brother of the abbess, as well as with Mme Arnauld, Robert Arnauld d'Andilly, and Mme Le Maistre, sister of the abbess, whose marriage was a veritable martyrdom. In all these persons, Francis recognized souls inclined to devotion.

The Coadjutorship of Paris

It was in the course of this trip to Touraine that Francis was alerted about a promotion that he scarcely expected. He personally informed Mother de Chantal of the matter in a letter written between October 5 and October 19, 1619. "I have seen Cardinal de Retz (Henri Gondi, archbishop of Paris), who, from the first, invited me to remain in France for a proposition that, if it were managed well, would be the most suitable, to my mind, of all those that could have been made." This was a question—neither more nor less—of the cardinal's wanting to have Francis named his coadjutor and then his successor. Francis continued:

> The matter is not yet settled, nor will it be so soon, but, in the meantime, we shall wait to see how God will order it. I wish to commit everything to his great glory, without which I want to do nothing except on the condition of his grace.
>
> I informed my Lord Cardinal of this, and I replied to him a second time while at Amboise, where he spoke to me about it still more cordially, and Cardinal de La Rochefoucauld mentioned it before the prince of Piedmont, but in such a way that it was not discussed. They tell me that since then the archbishop of Sens (Jean du Perron) has spoken of it at great length to the King, who seemed pleased about it. But in the end, if God does not signify it with his will of approbation, I shall never even wish to want it, and I will never exert myself in anything except to give my consent to Divine Providence when I recognize that this will be for his service.

This should clarify for us Francis' feelings regarding this "proposition". It is also said that no one dared to insinuate to him that this charge would lead to the cardinalate, but, rather, that his friends pointed out how—being archbishop of Paris—he would be in contact with the English court and notably King James I, and that he would be able, perhaps, thus to work at the conversion of England about which he had once dreamed in the Chablais!

Without backing away, however, Francis made the observation that "he was not even strong enough to bear the yoke of the bishopric of Geneva, because he felt himself yielding to old age, and saw himself henceforth liable to many illnesses and infirmities". This was not an excuse: Francis' health was failing more and more. If he had been coadjutor of Paris, it would not have been for very long. Cardinal de Retz was to die in August 1622, four months before him.

We may judge the emotion that this news aroused in Mother de Chantal. She and Francis would barely speak of the project again for several weeks. This silence seemed to augur well! Then they learned that Canon Jean-François de Sales was promoted to the episcopate. Was this not intended to free Francis from the diocese of Geneva and to realize Cardinal de Retz's project? February 26, 1620, Francis reassured Mother de Chantal as well as he could, because the concern was not unfounded. To understand the wit of his reply, let us recall that the word "diocese" was at that time a feminine word, and that between the bishop and "his" diocese there existed a bond analogous to that which united Jesus Christ and his Church. "I am certainly greatly obliged to this great Cardinal (de Retz) for the esteem that he shows me, but I have never merited the least of the thoughts that he has had for me. I told him rather definitely at Tours that I would not want to sever the marriage bond only to be married again and particularly in the way that you write me. How could I burden myself with the spouse of another through obligation? That, as I think about it, would be impossible for me." Francis remained firm in the same dispositions until September: "I shall make no change in my plans until I see a signal opportunity for the service of God, and one worth following, all things permitting."

On October 22, 1619, the princely cortège that the duke of Savoy had greeted at Grenoble arrived at Chambéry. There Francis obtained permission to continue on to Annecy. On October 27 he wrote to Bishop Camus, "At last, here I am in my nest." He could have added these words, which he had said to Claude de Quoex: "I did not waste my time on this trip!"

15

WHEN A MISSIONARY DREAMS
OF A HERMITAGE
October 1619–1621

Resumption of Familiar Business and Worries

Francis had hardly returned to Annecy when he was again caught up in the pressure of business. It is possible, by purusing his letters, to measure the number and the importance of the activities that engrossed him. The letters! On December 16, 1619, after having informed his brother Jean-François, vicar-general of the diocese, about several administrative questions, he admitted to feeling "weary and tired from writing so much". This was because the Paris journey had increased the number of Theotimuses and Philotheas (like Mother Angélique Arnauld) and had created new relationships, in particular with the court of Turin, where Prince Victor Amédée and Princess Christine were residing. The monasteries of the Visitation had been augmented, and he had to write to the superiors and to the nuns in difficulties. But Mother de Chantal was in Paris, and so everything between them had to be dealt with by correspondence. Francis said: "I receive thousands of letters from Paris . . . " But then, Francis did not know how to refuse anyone; he preached the Advent series at Annecy in 1619, and he agreed to preach the Lenten sermons in 1620. (He took as his theme the commandments of God!) Basically, he had a need for these contacts: they stimulated his inspiration. "I am listened to marvelously," he wrote to Mother de Chantal, "but I also preach with all my heart."

"Love pressed him", like Saint Paul. This tired, exhausted man was preparing another visitation of his diocese, and as he had a deep feeling that this mission would overtax his strength, he would send before him — "from parish to parish" — some priests capable of confessing and confirming. He also dreamed of installing the Bérullian Oratory at Thonon and at Rumilly, and some Carthusians at Ripaille, and so on.

He resumed his visits and conferences with the Visitandines. He continued to form the Sisters of the "Sainte Source" to sustain their fervor, to direct and counsel. He "reviewed the Rules and Constitutions and the Formularies" (for the reception of the habit and profession): "I found some great omissions in them, as much in the printing as in the writing, which I am correcting." He corresponded with the monasteries already established outside Annecy; he carefully considered the "requests for houses" that were coming to him from all quarters. He missed Mother de Chantal very much in all this work. At the end of 1621, he would decide that the Visitation of Paris was sufficiently well founded to manage without her presence, so he recalled her. She would start back on February 22, 1622, visiting several monasteries on the way, and she would only join Francis at Lyons, when he passed through with the court of the duke of Savoy en route to Avignon.

He did not neglect, as far as it was possible, the other houses of religious life in his diocese. In Savoy, as elsewhere, the excessive "exemption" of the great interdiocesan orders — from the local bishop and the system of *"commendam"* — had ravaged the religious discipline in the abbeys and priories, "with the exception", Francis specified, "of the Carthusians and the mendicant Orders". Already, in 1607, he had obtained authority from the Pope to disperse the Canons Regular of Abondance and to replace them with some Feuillants. In 1609, he had undertaken the reform of the Benedictine priory of Talloires. Things dragged on and at certain moments turned to sedition, almost to drama. A solution of compromise was agreed upon, which, later on, would bear only "bitter fruit". The reform of the abbey of Sixte in Faucigny was less dramatic. In September 1620 some new difficulties had arisen there between the terrible commendatory prior, Jacques de Mouxy, and the claustral prior, and the community was divided. Francis resolved the conflict. He returned to Annecy, but fifteen days later a messenger came running from Sixte. In spite of the winter and the snow Francis set out, and on December 4, Jacques de Mouxy died absolved, reconciled by the one to whom he had given so much trouble. In 1621 and 1622 Francis continued with much patience and benignity to restore everything to order in the abbey. The reform was not to be achieved until after his death.

The reform of the royal abbey of Saint Catherine, situated a few miles from Annecy on the western side of Semnoz, was difficult in another way. Bishop Trochu—speaking of the downfall of this noble abbey—said it all in a sentence: "Sainte Catherine d'Annecy was the Port-Royal-des-Champs before the reform" of Mother Angélique Arnauld. As early as 1608, the abbot-general of Citeaux had asked Francis to reform his nuns. Francis sized up the problem but failed in his efforts and saw only one solution: to release from the abbey the group of young nuns desirous for reform and to transplant them to a new monastery. But such a project raised another problem: where to find lodging and subsistence for them! Patiently, arming himself with human wisdom and confidence in God, he acted. Mme de la Fléchère gave him a house in Rumilly, where the reformists were installed. Francis then decided on the transfer and personally carried the order for it to Saint Catherine on November 25, 1621. The first two reformists finally left, on August 2, 1622, for Rumilly, where they were soon rejoined by several Sisters, and on September 8, 1622, "without any fuss", the monastery began to live according to the reform.

These heavy cares took away none of the solicitude that Francis lavished on the priests of his diocese. He had resumed all his activities with them. If he was "greatly afflicted" around June 1620 by the apostasy of Denis de Granier, God granted him some consolations. On December 19, 1620, he proceeded—unfortunately, this would be the last time—to the great ordination called "de Noel": in spite of the strict regulations that Francis had established for access to the priesthood, Francis ordained a total of nearly nine hundred priests in the twenty years of his episcopate!

Jean-François de Sales, Coadjutor to the Bishop of Geneva

From early in the month of February 1620, it was no longer a secret that Princess Christine of the court of Turin was taking steps at Rome to have Canon Jean-François—who was carrying out, in lieu of his brother Francis, the functions of principal chaplain to His Highness— named bishop. Francis himself rejoiced in this all the more—he wrote to Mother de Chantal—because he had "never said or written a single word or asked for or procured any recommendation". Rome acceded to the requests of the princes, and so we had Jean-François, bishop of Chalcedon and coadjutor to the bishop of Geneva. The consecration would not take place until January 21, 1621. This nomination aroused in Francis the hope of retiring soon "from the pressure of affairs", and he declared—not without a mischievous smile (making allusion to the plans of Cardinal de Retz): "This is better than a cardinal's hat!"

During the final week of January, the new bishop returned to Annecy. Francis, despite the winter, went forth to meet his brother on the Faverges road. When the two parties met, he got down on his knees to receive the first blessing of Jean-François.

There was a difference of eleven years between the two brothers! But more than age, there were other differences: juridic and theological knowledge, spiritual and apostolic experience, and—it must be admitted—*character* separated them. The elder then applied himself to forming his junior. He liberally shared with him his knowledge, informed him of everything for the good of the administration of the diocese . . . and he strove to subdue that impatience, that irritability that had already provoked some difficulties with some of the priests and the faithful. The Salesian *fioretti* have preserved this souvenir of the dialogue that was exchanged one day by the two brothers while at dinner: Jean-François, once again, had just become impatient because his brother had left the table for a moment to receive a little servant girl. Francis kept silent while staring at his hotheaded table companion. "What were you thinking about just now?" Jean-François asked. "Well, since you ask, I'll tell you. I was thinking, brother, that somewhere there must be a very happy woman. Can you guess who she is?" Jean-François named one or other of their friends. "You are not even close", Francis replied. "This very happy woman is she whom you did not marry." "And why, may I ask?" "Because, since you are very irascible, you would have made her really suffer." It was then that Francis articulated his celebrated comparison: "You see, my dear brother, we bishops have to be like those great watering troughs where everyone has the right to draw water; where not only men but even beasts come to refresh themselves." Happily, Jean-François had greatly admired his eldest brother ever "since his childhood". If he was never "gentle and debonaire", he was at least a bishop faithful to the duties of his office and very zealous in the service of his flock. In 1629, when the plague was devastating Annecy, the officials and leisured classes, lay and ecclesiastic, took refuge in the country, "far from this infected air"; no one was astonished by their flight. Jean-François, however, remained among the plague-ridden, and he personally collaborated with his household staff, in the admirable organization of the relief that Mother de Chantal implemented. He gave proof then "of a heroic and burning charity". When he died in 1635, he wanted to be buried at the feet of his brother and predecessor.

The Dream of Repose in the Hermitage of Saint Germain de Talloires

Francis, the contemplative, had carried this dream within himself for a long time: had he not requested, at the time of the tragic visit to the abbot of Talloires—when the monks were wielding pistols—that the hermitage of Saint-Germain, situated a few thousand feet higher than the abbey, be restored? But he did not reveal his plan to his friends until the autumn of 1621, when—the repairs having been completed—the prior of Talloires invited him to come to bless the sanctuary. This was on October 28, 1621.

The ceremonies terminated, and after the new casket containing the relics of Saint Germain had been placed under the altar, Francis contemplated at length the admirable panorama of mountains capped with their first snow, of forests already gilded by autumn, and the blue lake, at the end of which one perceived the roofs of the suburbs of Annecy. He was unable, at this time, to avoid revealing his soul:

"It is decided", he said. "Since I have a coadjutor, if it can be arranged by the will of some princes, I shall come up here! This is where I must have my retreat. I shall live in this hermitage because I have chosen it. . . . O God! What a good and pleasant thing for us to be here! Yes, definitely, I must leave to our coadjutor the burden and heat of the day, while with our Rosary and our pen we shall serve God and his Church here!" Then, turning toward Dom de Quoex, he added: "Ideas will come into our head as thick and fast as the snow that falls in winter!"

This desire of Francis de Sales has been greatly romanticized. It is evident that he was not dreaming of a solitude in the manner of his Carthusian friends or of a rupture with the world or a departure into the desert. No, he knew very well that at the gates of Annecy his desert world would still be very populated. Visitors and beggars would come seeking him there. And "the thousands of letters" would devour his leisure. It was "the burden and the heat of the day" that he wished to leave to his coadjutor, the "worrying about affairs". His "retreat" would be an apostolic retreat: he would pray, but he would also write; he would go—thanks to his little books distributed by the thousands—to seek in their homes Philothea and Theotimus in order to help them advance with a "devout" and lively step "along the royal road of love of God and neighbor".

What Francis was nourishing were some prospective books still within his apostle's heart. In particular he would like to write a *Histoire Théandrique*

> in four volumes, of which the first would be a concise and popular-ized version of the four Gospels, united and connected together in the manner of a concordance, according to the sequence of the time and activity of our Lord. The second would establish and deduce the proofs of the principal Articles of Faith of the Catholic Church, debated and argued by the very words of our Lord in the Gospels. . . . The third would be an instruction about good habits and the perfection of the Christian life through the maxims of the gospel and the exhortations and teachings of Jesus Christ. . . . The last would be based upon the account of the Acts of the Apostles and would show what the face of the primitive Church at its birth

was like, as well as the order and the conduct that the Holy Spirit and the apostles established there in its very beginning.

What a spiritual *Summa!* Dom Jean de Saint-François, to whom Francis confided this project one day, warned him that such a program was beyond his strength. It was then that Francis gave him this astonishing response: "One must undertake greater tasks than one would know how to accomplish and as if one had a long time to live, but one must not worry about doing more than if one were supposed to die tomorrow."

Dom John of Saint Francis was right. The project did surpass Francis de Sales' age and strength. For a long time, the bishop "would very frequently suffer from bronchitis, from stomach pains, from fevers and other discomforts". And during the autumn he had to endure great pain in his legs, as well as open sores on them. "He always kept a serene countenance and never complained at all." He went wherever the service of souls called him. He remained—in spite of age and bodily misery—still the old missionary of the Chablais, the priest who preached so much and who heard so many confessions. "He spent and overspent himself" in the manner of Saint Paul, for the honor of God and the joy of the Church.

16

"EITHER TO LOVE OR TO DIE, TO LOVE AND TO DIE"

(Treatise on the Love of God, bK. XIII, chap. XIII)

1622

A noticeable alteration in Francis' health did not escape his friends . . . or himself. In answer to the concern of one such friend he said, "I feel something is warning me that I am not going to live long, and so I must hurry to do some good. Yet I can do nothing better than to obey." And to die while obeying!

The General Chapter of the Feuillants at Pignerol

On April 28, 1622, Francis received a commission from His Holiness commanding him to attend the Chapter of the Benedictine Fathers (Feuillants), which was to take place fifteen days later at Pignerol.

The mission was delicate: the Feuillants had separated from the Cistercian Order in 1588. Their Constitutions had been modified in 1615, but difficulties had arisen. In 1622 it was a question of naming a superior general for the entire Order, and minds were divided. Some leaned toward an Italian, others toward a Frenchman. Francis was designated to arbitrate the conflict and maintain unity.

He left around May 25, worn out from fatigue. The trip was very painful. His kidneys caused him terrible suffering. He even had to take to his bed in the course of the journey.

The chapter went on for twenty full days. Francis, in spite of his debility, attended all the meetings, morning and evening, and on Sundays and feast days he went about confirming the farm people in the neighboring parishes that had no bishop.

His "marvelous gentleness and goodness", his competence, and his art of conciliation went to the core of all difficulties. It is true that the assembly, in spite of its divisions, had great character. Francis would write to Cardinal Scipio Borghese, on June 25: "I can say that I have never seen an assembly more modest, more religious, or where peace is more striking than this."

It was a Frenchman who was finally elected, and almost unanimously. At the last moment, Rome would have preferred an Italian, but the messenger arrived after the election. The winning candidate's name was Dom John of Saint Francis: "They have chosen a general who is endowed with great learning, rare prudence, and singular piety, and this election was made with almost total unanimity on the part of the voters." The chapter was, to a great extent, indebted to Francis for this union of minds and hearts.

Before leaving the region, Francis had to pass through Turin, where the princes, and especially Princess Christine of France, insisted on his visit. They gave him a "remarkable reception". Instead of the magnificent lodging that had been prepared for him, Francis preferred a monk's cell—under the pretext of having already accepted the hospitality of the Benedictines of la Consolata. But the abbey was undergoing construction, and Francis was assigned a very inconvenient cell that was "exposed to the sun and overheated". Thus a few days after his arrival he was taken ill and had to go to bed. This illness persisted several days.

It was not until after August 17 that Francis reached Annecy. The return trip was as painful as the journey going had been. The little entourage was even obliged "to stop for the good of all" for twenty-four hours. Francis was so exhausted upon his arrival that for several days he had to depend upon his chaplain to reply to the urgent letters among his voluminous correspondence.

The Avignon Journey

Suddenly, at the end of October 1622, there arrived "an express command" from His Highness, the duke of Savoy, that Francis was to accompany Cardinal Maurice of Savoy to Avignon. The duke was to join him there in order to greet and congratulate King Louis XIII, who, after his victory over the Protestants in the South of France, had decided to return to Paris by way of the Rhône valley.

This time the bishop's circle of friends was genuinely alarmed. "There was not one among them who did not dread this journey for their holy bishop." All of them urged him to inform His Highness of "the precarious state of his health". But Francis said, "What do you expect? We must go where God calls us." He barely concealed his own presentiment that this journey would prove fatal for him: "I shall not do like the light cavalry; I shall go off without a trumpet," he told one of his close friends, "and when you hear it said that I am ill, know that I shall be dead."

He then bade farewell to his Visitandines: "My daughters," he said to them in the manner of a supreme mandate, "let your sole desire be God, your fear to lose him, your ambition to possess him forever."

A touching gesture from this bishop who had so frequently walked with Kings and dukes, great lords and noble ladies, was when he sent for Huguine, the granddaughter of Bernard Perrin (the baker in the bishop's residence). Huguine was a very devout girl, and Francis told her, "Good-bye, my daughter, we shall next see each other in Paradise", and Huguine did not live much longer after that.

On Sunday, November 6, he wrote his will, had a long visit with his brother Monseigneur de Chalcedoine, received the canons of his cathedral and his beloved clergy of Annecy. On Tuesday, November 8, in the morning, Francis celebrated Mass at the Visitation, then mounted his horse, but not without ordering that someone distribute some bushels of grain to the poor—for there was a famine in the city.

Then he set out. They reached Seyssel on November 8. "He then climbed onto a dinghy and put himself at the mercy of the Rhône during a very violent icy blast, and he was almost frozen by the extreme severity of the cold." Toward Massignieu they disembarked to find food and lodgings at Belley, where he had the consolation of again seeing his old friend Bishop Jean Pierre Camus and his Visitandines.

Thursday, November 10, Francis arrived at Lyons, where he had a meeting with Mother de Chantal, whom he had not seen for three years. But the time sped by; he besought her to go visit the monasteries of Montferrand and Saint Étienne.

As the bishop's party was preparing to board the boat that would take them to Avignon, a minor incident occurred. They had crossed the bridge (called the "Solomon") over the Saône River to talk to the sailors. The owner of the boat confronted them: "You are strangers, and I want to see your passports." No one had foreseen this emergency, and so they had to send to the home of the Marquis de Villeroy, governor of Lyons, for the missing passports. In the meantime there was general grumbling against the owner's incivility. "Well," Francis replied, "he knows his job as a boatman; we do not know ours as travelers." And when they were finally able to depart, Francis got acquainted with the quarrelsome owner: "I must become friends with this man so that I can speak to him a little about our Lord."

The boat reached Avignon on November 15. The reception by the populace was triumphal: "There is the great bishop of Geneva! There is the apostle of the Chablais!" All of which tempted Francis to "do something ridiculous so as to undeceive these good people, but one must play neither the sage nor the fool but live in Christian sincerity".

On Thursday, November 17, King Louis XIII and the duke of Savoy arrived in the City of the Popes. One festival succeeded another, during which the two sovereigns spoke of the peril that the Valteline crisis posed to their respective states. Francis attended only those festivals at which his service to his princes obliged him to be present. Otherwise he visited the churches and the religious houses, celebrated Mass, or preached.

On Wednesday, November 25, the King, the duke, and their followers embarked together to sail up the Rhône as far as Lyons. They were enthusiastically greeted at Lyons on November 29. Francis sent a messenger to ask hospitality of the Visitation Monastery at Bellecour. "Because of his love of holy poverty, he chose the hut of the monastery's gardener, under the pretext that he would be free to receive those who would come to visit him; besides, he would not be inconveniencing his companions, and he would be so much closer for the spiritual service of his dear daughters."

Soon, indeed, there was an uninterrupted procession to the little cottage "of princes and princesses, of lords and ladies", even of prelates, priests, and religious—all of whom came to consult the bishop of Geneva. "He didn't even have a quarter of an hour to himself." Added to this were his official ceremonial and preaching assignments. "My God," he wrote on December 19, 1622, "how fortunate are they who are released from the court and from the obsequiousness that reigns there. How blessed are those who live peaceably in holy solitude at the foot of the crucifix."

King Louis XIII made his triumphal entry on December 8. All Lyons was in the streets. Francis preferred to spend this feast of the Virgin Mary in the midst of his Visitandine daughters, since Mother de Chantal had just arrived. The foundress had been awaiting this meeting for three years, because she had great need of his counsel, and Francis had not answered—or answered briefly—her letters. She had complained to him: "You tell me that you have no news to write me. But, ah, have you not a few words to draw from your heart? It has been so long since you have said anything to me! Dear Jesus, what a consolation it would be to have a heart-to-heart talk. May the Divine Savior grant me that grace!" Here, at last, that day had come! It was December 12, and Francis had a respite from the pressure of other business. And here is the scene as described for us by Mother de Chaugy:

"Mother," Francis said, "we have a few hours free. Who will start by saying what we shall talk about?" Our worthy Mother, who was ardent and who was more concerned about her soul than anything else, answered promptly: "I, Father, if you please. My heart has great need of being reviewed by you."

The blessed Francis, who was close to his own total consummation, no longer wishing or desiring anything and perceiving a little anxiety— albeit spiritual—in her whom he wanted to see wholly perfect, told her softly, but with great gravity: "What! Mother, have you still eager desires and choices! I thought you were wholly angelic." And with that—although he knew that our Mother was one of those perfect souls of whom Saint Bernard speaks and who have no need of direction, God himself being their guide: "Mother," he said, "we shall speak about ourselves at Annecy; now let us carry out the affairs of our Congregation."

Without a word of reply, Mother de Chantal folded the notepaper on which she had written the concerns of her soul, and she unfolded the papers on which she had recorded the business of the Institute. The two of them conferred for fully four hours. Then Francis gave orders to Mother de Chantal to visit the monasteries in Grenoble, Valence, and Belley. He blessed her and bade her farewell.

Mother de Chantal obeyed at once. On the way she experienced "a great weight on her heart", but she made an act of self-abandonment to the Divine Will, and taking up her book of Psalms, she began to chant in her coach.

To Love or Die, to Love and Die

Francis remained two weeks longer in Lyons, at the request of the princes. He spent the entire time hearing confessions, counseling, preaching, receiving visitors, and returning visits, without taking into account that his health would require some rest. Besides, that winter was extremely cold. Thanks to some accurate accounts, we can follow Francis during the three days of life that remained for him.

On Christmas Eve he went "at the command of the Queen Mother" to bless the cross of the Recollect Fathers "placed in a garden located on rue Neyret". Francis "became ill in the course of the ceremony" and went home "with a very bad headache".

The bishop celebrated midnight Mass before his beloved daughters of the Visitation and made an exhortation to them that was full of tenderness. At dawn he went to hear the confessions of the princes of Piedmont in the Dominican church; he then celebrated Mass in their presence. At eleven o'clock he said his third Mass. After dinner he bestowed the habit of the Visitation on two novices and preached a very holy homily. Afterward, he went to the palace of the Queen Mother to bid her farewell, because she was going to leave the next day, but Francis had to remain there, at great inconvenience, until nearly nightfall.

The next day, the feast of Saint Stephen, he attended to several business matters. In the evening he held the last conference of his life with his daughters. Just as he was leaving, Mother de Blonay, the superior, asked him: "Bishop, what do you desire should remain most engraved in our hearts?" He replied: "I have already said it many times: 'Ask for nothing; refuse nothing.'"

On Tuesday, December 27, the feast of Saint John the Evangelist, upon rising Francis told Francis Favre, who was helping him dress: "I feel that my sight is failing; we must go forth and bless God, all the same, for we shall live as long as God pleases." He made his confession to the monastery chaplain, Father Brun; then, after having meditated alone, he celebrated Mass "with extraordinary devotion". It was nearly noon.

As Francis was emerging from the church en route to his little lodging, Duke de Bellegarde, governor of Burgundy, arrived unexpectedly, then Lord Halincourt, governor of Lyons. The bishop chatted with them, "remaining for a long time bareheaded despite the very cold weather and a very dense mist". Francis then went to take his leave of the duke of Nemours and of the prince of Piedmont, who was about to depart that day for Annecy.

Returning from these visits, Francis entered his lodging: "He was not at all well, and looked greatly exhausted." His valet, Germain Pilliod, asked him to put on his travel coat at once to warm himself. The bishop replied: "Let's put on the coat, since you wish it, but we shall not go far." He ate a very light dinner, after which he remained pensive for a long time, leaning on the table. After he revived his spirits a bit, he recalled that he had three letters to write . . . the third would remain unfinished.

George Rolland, seeing him so tired, said to him: "Bishop, it is already late; it seems to me that you ought to wait until tomorrow to send that." To which Francis replied: "You think, perhaps, that I am ill." With that he stood up. Suddenly he collapsed. It was two o'clock in the afternoon. His servants came running; they pulled off his shoes, and after having helped him walk a little, they put him to bed. A half hour later he "was seized by a serious stroke". The Father Rector of the neighboring Jesuit house rushed over, after being alerted by George Rolland. He had them heat some linens with which he rubbed the sick bishop's head while waiting for the physician. The latter did not arrive until four hours later; he immediately diagnosed a cerebral hemorrhage. The invalid remained completely lucid.

Francis, seeing himself stricken, requested extreme unction. Around midnight a vicar from a neighboring parish administered the sacrament to him. Francis responded to the prayers, but his vomiting prevented him from receiving Viaticum. He asked them to wrap his Rosary around his wrist.

Wednesday, December 28, there were visitors all day long, one of whom—the duke of Nemours—knelt and begged Francis for his blessing, "which the prelate gave him, although his arm was already very weak".

At five o'clock in the evening, "the doctors conferred and then decided to employ some extreme measures". Such "measures", truly extreme! Three times they applied "a red-hot poker" to his temple. Francis endured all with patience, "although the pain brought tears to his eyes, and forced him to lift his shoulders somewhat; otherwise he uttered nothing other than the sacred names of Jesus and Mary." This "surgical butchery", as Charles-Auguste de Sales called it, was a true martyrdom for the patient. Finally the sick bishop grew progressively weaker. Those around him began to recite the ritual litanies. Just as they were invoking the Holy Innocents—whose feast the Church was celebrating that day—Francis rendered his last breath.

He was a little more than fifty-five years old and had been bishop and prince of Geneva for twenty years.

The simultaneous presence of the courts of France and Savoy in Lyons during the Christmas holidays of 1622, had brought together some of Francis de Sales' most illustrious friends. They had all been able to converse with him. One such friend was the Marshal de Lesdiguières, who had abjured Protestantism the previous July 24 and had played an important role in the recent peace treaty concluded between Louis XIII and the Huguenots in the south. Another was the duke of Bellegarde, who remained worthy of the title that Francis had bestowed on him one day, "my very dear Theotimus", and he would remain so until his death in 1646. There was, however, one very important person missing during the end of December at Lyons: Mother de Chantal, en route to visit—upon Francis' order—the monasteries of Grenoble and Belley. Providentially, Father Jean Fourier was in Lyons. He was, we remember, the spiritual director with whom Francis had made his episcopal retreat at Sales, then later (1609?) at Chambéry. Father Fourier visited his saintly friend several times, helped him, and—according to certain biographers—assisted him at the moment of his death.

When Mother de Chantal arrived at Belley on January 4, the nuns had already received news of the death of Bishop de Sales, but for three days no one dared to inform Mother de Chantal, and the Sisters resolved to appear joyous so that she would suspect nothing. Finally, on the feast of the Epiphany—since she was dismayed that she had not had any letter from Francis—Michel Favre, her chaplain, summoned the courage to tell her. "I kneel," she is reported to have said, "embracing as best I can the most holy will of God, in this, my incomparable affliction."

Another great but absent friend was President Antoine Favre. When he learned that his eminent friend was ill in Lyons, he wrote a distraught letter to Bishop Jean-François de Sales: "I cannot believe, as long as I live, that the bishop can have died and that I survive him." His grief, at the news of Francis' death, was very intense. At the funeral service that the princess of Piedmont had celebrated at Chambéry in the Jesuit church, "the majority of the lords of the senate" were present. Favre, the first President, was there, and "he wept hot tears because of this death".

The emotion among the people was considerable. These good folk said: "A saint has just died, a saint who loved and protected us." When the news reached Annecy, "a heavy and ponderous astonishment seized all the inhabitants, so that a profound silence engulfed the entire city, and as the people met each other they only shrugged their shoulders and said nothing." At Lyons the whole city was grief-stricken. On December 29 the people filed past the body of Bishop de Sales. The surgeons had removed his heart and given it to the Sisters of the Visitation. The body was lightly embalmed. On December 30, a ceremony took place in the monastery church.

An incident occurred the next day that shows the populace's veneration for Bishop de Sales. On December 31 Rolland placed the corpse in its coffin to have it conveyed to Savoy, "when Jacques Ollier, administrator of justice—and at the urging of the Lyonnais, who were sorry to see themselves being deprived of so precious a treasure—commanded, by order of the King, that the body be held until he determined what had been the final will of the dead bishop". Rolland sped to Annecy. On January 11 they opened the testament: "The bishop prayed that he would be interred in the church of the Visitation of Annecy, but if he did not die in that city he left the choice of his burial to those persons in his entourage."

The coffin, "placed on a litter between two horses", left Lyons without ceremony "for fear that the people might cause further delay". All along the route crowds pressed forward, and everyone "tried to touch the litter or the drapery that covered the coffin". Several sick or infirm persons miraculously recovered their health. It took four days to reach Annecy, where the entire populace immediately surrounded the body of their bishop. It was a Sunday.

The solemn funeral ceremonies took place Tuesday morning, January 24. In the evening, at five o'clock, they brought the body of Francis de Sales to the Visitation, in the choir of the church, near the nuns' grille. Mother de Chantal was waiting for him there.

Francis de Sales: Sage and Saint, reads the title of this work. The two terms are scarcely compatible; the "man of good sense" and "the mystic" do not easily make good roommates! Did not Saint Paul go so far as to declare: "The wisdom of this world is foolishness to God"? The debate is serious: it is a matter of the spiritual life of many. Our tendency—sometimes our temptation—is to separate human wisdom and sanctity or, at least, to juxtapose them. The art of Francis de Sales was, on the contrary, "to synthesize them", to "meld" them, to "make them enter" one another, as Saint-Beuve says, "so as to make them balanced and stabilized within oneself". Francis de Sales was totally wise and totally holy. He was, in the precise sense of the term, a "man of God". He refused to separate creation and redemption: if he regarded nature—men-man—with such admiration and love, it was because the redeemed universe is only the created universe, restored to its first wonder. In this universe he breathes easily; he grows with a liberty that he calls (by slightly modifying Saint Paul's expression) "the liberty *of heart* of the sons of God". He is "the man who has best exemplified the Son of God on earth", affirmed those who knew him: Vincent de Paul, Jane de Chantal, and others. Henri Bremond qualified this spiritual attitude in a celebrated phrase: "devout humanism". Why not "human devotion" or, to use Mother de Chaugy's apt expression, *la dévotion civile?* It matters little in any case! The Church has said everything by conferring on Francis de Sales the title of "Doctor of Love".

Because he has gone straight to the essentials of the Christian life, and more especially to the essentials of religious life, Francis de Sales has breathed into spirituality fresh air from evangelical summits, which has made of him and still makes of him—apart from all the biasses or tensions among critics—an unchallenged master, an always available resource for the most critical times in the history of redemption.

Sources

We have striven, in this biography, to adhere very closely to the documentary sources and even to utilize their words and expressions. There was one inconvenience in this method: it was impossible to indicate our references every time; we have only noted them in the most important cases. In citations from the texts of Saint Francis de Sales, his quotations from Sacred Scripture are transcribed in italics.

The following is a list of the principal sources cited. Abbreviations in left-hand margin are used in in-text references to sources.

E.A.   *Oeuvres complètes de S. François de Sales* by the Visitandines of Annecy. 26 volumes and a 27th volume of analytical *Tables* by the Rev. Alphone Denis. Very valuable critical edition. Available at the Visitation Monastery in Annecy.

A.S.   *L'Année sainte* of the Visitation and other Archives of the Visitation.

Br   Bremond, Henri. *A Literary History of Religious Thought in France.* 3 volumes. London: S.P.C.K., 1928.

L   Lajeunie, Etienne M. O.P. *Saint Francis de Sales, The Man, the Thinker, His Influence.* 2 volumes. Translated by Rory O'Sullivan O.S.F.S. Bangalore, India: SFS Publications, 1986, 1987. A key work, which the author unfortunately was not able to see through publication before his death. Unfortunately, because it is the only biography (with references to the *Oeuvres* by the Visitandines in Annecy) that commands authority at present.

L.S.F. *François de Sales: Correspondence, Lettres d'amitié spirituelle.* Ed. André Ravier. Paris: Desclée de Brouwer, 1980.

Pl   St. François de Sales, *Oeuvres.* Ed. André Ravier and Roger Devos. Bibliothèque de la Pléiade. Paris: Editions Gallimard,

1969. This book contains the only critical edition of the *Conferences,* realized by Roger Devos.

SOME WORKS OF FRANCIS DE SALES IN TRANSLATION

Introduction to the Devout Life. Trans. Armind Nazareth, Antony Mookenthottam and Antony Kolencherry. Bangalore, India: SFS Publications, 1990.

——. Trans. John K. Ryan. New York: Doubleday, 1989.

——. Trans. Michael Day. "Everyman's Library". New York: Dutton, 1961.

Introduction to the Devout Life, a Popular Abridgment. Abridged by Yvonne Stephan. Trans. Joseph D. Bowler, O.S.F.S. and Lewis S. Fiorelli, O.S.F.S. Rockford, Ill: TAN Books and Publishers, 1990.

The Love of God, a Treatise. Trans. Vincent Kerns. Westminster, Md.: Newman Press, 1962.

Treatise on the Love of God. 2 vols. Trans. John K. Ryan. Rockford, Ill.: TAN Books and Publishers, 1974.

Francis de Sales, Jane de Chantal, Letters of Spiritual Direction. Trans. Péronne Marie Thibert, V.H.M., Selected and introduced by Wendy M. Wright and Joseph F. Power, O.S.F.S. Classics of Western Spirituality. New York: Paulist Press, 1988.

St. Francis de Sales. Selected Letters. Trans. Elisabeth Stopp. New York: Harper and Bros., 1960.

The Sermons of St. Francis de Sales. Trans. by Nuns of the Visitation, ed. Lewis S. Fiorelli, O.S.F.S. Rockford, Ill: TAN Books and Publishers, 1985—. Vol. 1: *On Prayer.* Vol. 2: *On Our Lady.* Vol. 3: *Lent.* Vol. 4: *Advent and Christmas.*

Francis de Sales, Finding God Wherever You Are, selected spiritual writings. Introduced and edited by Joseph F. Power, O.S.F.S. New Rochelle, NY: New City Press, 1993.

Wendy M. Wright. *Francis de Sales, Introduction to the Devout Life* and *Treatise on the Love of God.* New York: Crossroad, 1993.

WORKS ABOUT FRANCIS DE SALES
AND JANE DE CHANTAL

Bedoyere, Michael de la. *François de Sales.* New York: Harper, 1960.

Henry-Couannier, Maurice. *Saint Francis de Sales and his Friends.* Trans. Veronica Morrow. Staten Island, N.Y.: Alba House, 1964.

Muller, Michael. *St. Francis de Sales.* New York: Sheed and Ward, 1937; reprint, Bangalore, India: SFS Publications, 1984.

Ravier, André. *Saint Jeanne de Chantal: Noble Lady, Holy Woman.* Translated by Mary Emily Hamilton. San Francisco: Ignatius Press, 1989.

Wright, Wendy M. *Bond of Perfection: Jeanne de Chantal and François de Sales.* New York: Paulist Press, 1985.

INDEX

Treatise on the Love of God: see
   Francis de Sales, Saint
Trochu, Bishop Francis: 258

University of Padua: 34–36,
   118
University of Paris: 27, 43

Valentine, Saint: 121
Vaugelas, Claude de: 157, 183
Verncuil, Marquis de: 102
Vesseli, Antonio: 36
Villaroget, Seigneur de: 53
Villars, Bishop Pierre de: 141,
   168
Villeroy, Marquis de: 106,
   248

Villette, Baron Amédée de: 17,
   215
Vincent de Paul, Saint: 227–28,
   255;
   Ladies of Charity, 228
   Daughters of Charity, 228
Viret, Father Louis: 66, 77–78,
   93
Virgil: 28
Visitandines: 73, 145, 195–97, 214,
   216, 228–29, 233, 238,
   247–50, 253, 259. *See also*
   Congregation of the
   Blessed Virgin Mother of
   God of the Visitation
Visitation Monastery in
   Annecy: 258–59